Enter His Gates

Enter His Gates

A Daily Devotional

Charles Stanley

OLIVER
NELSON

THOMAS NELSON PUBLISHERS
Nashville

Published in Nashville, Tennessee, by Thomas Nelson, Inc.

Library of Congress Cataloging-in-Publication Data

Stanley, Charles F.
    Enter His gates : a daily devotional / Charles Stanley.
      p. cm.
    ISBN 0-7852-7546-0 (hc)
    1. Christian life—Meditations. 2. Devotional calendars. I. Title.
  BV4811.S815   1998
  242'.2—dc21   983345
                                                      CIP

Introduction

In Bible times, city gates had tremendous importance in the natural world as well as significant spiritual meaning:

- Because of their central location, gates were spoken of as symbols of power and authority.
- Gates were the focus of enemy attack (Judg. 5:8; 1 Sam. 23:7; Ezek. 21:15, 22).
- People gathered there to hear the reading of God's Word (Neh. 8:1, 3), and both legal and judicial transactions occurred at the city gates (Zech. 8:16).
- In Israel, words from God's law were—and still are—inscribed on or above the gates of private homes (Deut. 6:9).
- To "possess the gates" was to possess the city (Gen. 24:60), and that is why God promised Abraham that his descendants would possess the gates of their enemies (Gen. 22:17).
- Gates were vital to the defense of cities in ancient Israel because they protected against enemy invasion. In the event of attack, the city gates were closed to shut out the enemy.

The tremendous importance of these entries to the city explains why Jeremiah lamented over the desolate gates (Lam. 1:4) and Nehemiah had a burning desire to rebuild the gates of Jerusalem: "And they said to me, 'The survivors who are left from the captivity in the province are there in great distress and reproach. The wall of Jerusalem is also broken down, and its gates are burned with fire'" (Neh. 1:3).

Nehemiah 1–2 describes the condition of the gates and walls of Jerusalem at the time of Nehemiah. The gates were in ruins, destroyed by enemy invasion, and burned with fire. Without gates and walls, the city was open to invasion on every side from enemy forces.

Exactly how many gates were in the city of Jerusalem is unknown because the number probably varied from century to century, but each gate of Jerusalem mentioned in the Bible has spiritual significance and is symbolic of a spiritual "gate" in our lives. If you fail to maintain your spiritual "gates," you, too, are open to attack by the enemy. That is why this devotional guide focuses on rebuilding your spiritual gates.

In John's vision of the New Jerusalem, the Holy City had twelve gates of pearl—three on each of its four sides:

> She had a great and high wall with twelve gates, and twelve angels at the gates, and names written on them, which are the names of the twelve tribes of the children of Israel: three gates on the east, three gates on the north, three gates on the south, and three gates on the west. . . . The twelve gates were twelve pearls: each individual gate was of one pearl. And the street of the city was pure gold, like transparent glass. (Rev. 21:12–13, 21)

God has set before us twelve months of the coming year. These months are precious gateways to spiritual growth and development. Each month during this year, we will strengthen a different spiritual gate.

January devotions concern the New Gate (Jer. 36:10), which speaks of making a fresh start, setting goals, and preparing for the challenges ahead.

February's theme is the Water Gate, representing the Word of God in our lives, of which water is a symbol (Neh. 3:26). Devotions during this month focus on the Word, meditation, prayer, personal devotions, and listening to and communicating with God.

The Valley Gate—which represents adversity, suffering, and trials—is the emphasis for devotions during the month of *March* (Neh. 3:13).

April's theme is the Sheep Gate, the gate through which animal sacrifices were brought into the city of Jerusalem (Neh. 3:1). This gate represents the work of the Cross in our lives, and we reflect on the purpose, meaning, and significance of the cross of Jesus Christ.

In *May*, the focus is on the Horse Gate (Neh. 3:28), the gate through which returning warriors rode into the city. This gate is symbolic of warfare, so devotions for this month concern spiritual warfare.

The Refuse Gate is the focus of *June*. This is the gate through which garbage and waste materials were carried out of Jerusalem (Neh. 3:14). The Refuse Gate is not a very appealing name, but then carnality of the flesh is not appealing either, and that is what this gate represents. Devotions for this month center on habits, attitudes, and actions of the old, carnal nature that need to be transformed by God's power.

During the month of *July*, we emphasize the Fish Gate (Neh. 3:3), the entry through which fish were brought to market in Jerusalem. The sign of the fish represents our Christian witness, so meditations for this month concern witnessing, serving, and touching the lives of others.

The Fountain Gate (Neh. 3:15)—our theme for *August*—represents the work of the Spirit in our lives. Jesus described the Holy Spirit as a fountain springing up from the innermost being. Devotions focus on spiritual growth and the work of the Holy Spirit.

September's theme is the Prison Gate (Neh. 12:39), focusing on freedom in Christ and deliverance from spiritual bondage.

October emphasizes the importance of spiritual foundations as we strengthen the Foundation Gate (2 Chron. 23:5). Devotions center on a well-built life, being mighty in spirit, and basic issues such as faith, forgiveness, security, obedience, and so on.

November highlights the strengthening of the Gates of Praise (Isa. 60:18) as we learn the power of praise, how to give thanks in all things, and how to worship God.

The year concludes with *December*'s emphasis on the Miphkad Gate (Neh. 3:31). The word *Miphkad* means "to review," and that is what we will do during this final month as we stress self-examination and the importance of finishing well.

The psalmist declared,

> *Open to me the gates of righteousness;*
> *I will go through them,*
> *And I will praise the LORD.*
> *This is the gate of the LORD,*
> *Through which the righteous shall enter. (Ps. 118:19–20)*

Are you ready to join me in this yearlong spiritual quest?

> *Go through,*
> *Go through the gates! (Isa. 62:10)*

January

THEME: The New Gate
REPRESENTING: New beginnings
KEY VERSE: Isaiah 43:19

Behold, I will do a new thing,
Now it shall spring forth;
Shall you not know it?
I will even make a road in the wilderness
And rivers in the desert.

SCRIPTURE READING: Hebrews 12:1–10
KEY VERSE: Hebrews 12:1

Therefore we also, since we are surrounded by so great a cloud of witnesses, let us lay aside every weight, and the sin which so easily ensnares us, and let us run with endurance the race that is set before us.

The new year will be full of surprises. As diligently as you may plan, tomorrow, next week, or next month is a puzzle to all but God. Yet the Bible places the responsibility on you to plan, pray, and trust God for each day so that you may run the course that He has sovereignly designed.

Your supreme purpose then for this year is to walk in harmony with His predetermined will by employing three essential disciplines:

First, lay aside every encumbrance and sin. Willful sin or unproductive habits hinder your spiritual growth. You know several areas of your life that keep you from reaching God's potential. By His grace ask Him to help you abandon these unnecessary weights.

Second, concentrate on endurance. As events unfold in the coming year, you will need perseverance to plod through the difficult, strenuous times. Do not let disappointments or setbacks take you out of the race. Accept that they, too, are part of the course God has divinely planned.

Third, focus on Jesus. Turn away from all that distracts. Look by faith steadfastly to Him. Cast your burdens on Him. Seek His face daily through personal prayer and sustained intake of His Word.

A fixed focus of faith on Jesus Christ will lighten your load, equip you to handle the tough times, and guide you into His will for your life in this new year.

Dear Lord, give me the confidence to face the future. Help me lay aside every sin and focus on You. Give me the strength I need for difficult times. Equip me to handle the tough times that may lie ahead.

SCRIPTURE READING: Matthew 6:25–34
KEY VERSE: Matthew 6:33

Seek first the kingdom of God and His righteousness, and all these things shall be added to you.

Who knows what the coming year may bring? Prosperity or economic hardship? Marital intimacy or discord? Peace or war? New opportunities or lost ones?

Herein lies our confidence—God knows. He is carefully, wisely, and deliberately orchestrating all things according to His schedule and eternal design. We can be secure because God is in full control of what the year brings forth. Our confidence is not in our abilities, but in His omniscience, omnipotence, and omnipresence. What seems perplexing and puzzling to us is perfectly rational and plain to our all-seeing, all-caring Father. Nothing catches Him by surprise. Nothing thwarts His purposes. Nothing foils His plan.

You may find yourself in hard times. But if you boast in God and endure and trust in Him, you can learn. You may encounter unanticipated changes, but your fears and anxieties can be dispelled as you rest in His providential direction and provision.

Do not worry about tomorrow. God is already there. He will guide you through the fog, lift you above the pain, and clarify your uncertainty. Be confident in Him.

I am so thankful, Lord, that You are in control of my tomorrows. I am secure in the knowledge that nothing catches You by surprise. Guide me through the fog of my circumstances. Lift me above the pain. Clarify my uncertainties.

SCRIPTURE READING: Isaiah 43:16–19
KEY VERSE: Isaiah 43:19

Behold, I will do a new thing,
Now it shall spring forth;
Shall you not know it?
I will even make a road in the wilderness
And rivers in the desert.

Have you ever felt that your life was a dry, barren desert? In today's passage of Isaiah, Israel felt spiritually and emotionally desolate. In their disobedience, they had wandered from God, and He had allowed them to go. When they came to their senses, they cried out in evidence of the burden they bore in their hearts. They were alone and needed a fresh touch from God.

The wonderful thing about God is that He is never at a distance. He is always beside us. Because faithfulness is a part of His nature, He cannot be unfaithful and still be God. That means when we are faithless, He is still faithful. And in the case of Israel, He proved true to His nature.

God commissioned the prophet Isaiah to record and report His words to His people. In Isaiah 43:18, God told Israel: "Do not call to mind the former things, / Or ponder things of the past" (NASB). In other words, "Don't spend a great deal of time looking back over past failures. Today is today. Up ahead is where we are going, and this is what I plan to do."

God always works in the present but looks to the future. Life at its best is not lived in the past—worrying over what happened or what once was. Instead, it is lived in the here and now, aware of one thing: God is a God of love, and He is always at work in your life to do something for your good and His glory.

Thank You, Lord, that You will do new things in my life during the
coming year. Help me look forward and not back to the past. Work in
my present as I look to the future You have planned for me.

SCRIPTURE READING: Ecclesiastes 11:4–6
KEY VERSE: Proverbs 12:24

The hand of the diligent will rule,
But the lazy man will be put to forced labor.

In *Gone with the Wind* Scarlett O'Hara repeatedly uttered this now celebrated line whenever faced with calamity: "I'll think about that tomorrow." How often do we—either intentionally or not—develop the same "tomorrow" outlook? We too easily find ways to put off until tomorrow what we can do today.

A sober look at procrastination's aftereffects, however, might help us realize its subtle dangers. Procrastination can cause us to miss out on God's best for our lives. When we fail to confront an issue or a situation, we fail to develop the godly, positive character desired by God. By hesitating, we delay God's blessings.

Prompt obedience always brings eventual blessings. When you procrastinate, you are dangerously close to disobedience—along with its consequences.

You can learn to face and deal with undesirable circumstances by trusting God to supply what you lack. He will give courage, wisdom, grace, mercy, power—whatever the need.

As you confront your problems rather than avoid them, your faith is nurtured and stretched. Your confidence grows; your fears subside.

Let your motto be: "Do it now as the Lord directs and enables me." It will save a lot of heartache later.

> *Father, there may be difficult circumstances ahead during this year,*
> *but give me the courage to face them in Your sufficiency. Nurture and*
> *stretch my faith. Help me in Your strength and power to deal with*
> *issues as they occur.*

SCRIPTURE READING: Philippians 4:11–13
KEY VERSE: 1 Timothy 6:6

Godliness with contentment is great gain.

Secrets—whether a grandmother's special recipe or a company's unique product formula—are rarely revealed. In his letter to the Philippian church, the apostle Paul provided all who would read the Scriptures with the secret of contented living.

Paul announced to them and us that he was content in life whether he had scraps for dinner or a feast, whether his purse was flat or bulging. He shared his secret in Philippians 4:13: "I can do all things through Christ who strengthens me."

The Greek word for contentment is translated "self-sufficiency" or "self-satisfaction." That may surprise you. At first glance, Paul appeared to say that the secret to contentment lay in his resilient self.

But he was expressing this: "My self-sufficiency, my level of contentment, lies in the sufficiency of Christ to meet my every need. I can endure rain or shine, darkness or light, sorrow or joy, because through Him, I am equipped and sustained."

Paul's secret is yours. Despite circumstances, you can enjoy true contentment when you accept the truth that Christ is adequate for your every need—in good times and bad.

> *Help me be content despite the circumstances of my life. O God, my sufficiency is in Your ability to meet my needs. In You, I am equipped to face the challenges of this day.*

SCRIPTURE READING: Acts 16:5–10
KEY VERSE: Revelation 3:8

See, I have set before you an open door, and no one can shut it; for you have a little strength, have kept My word, and have not denied My name.

Your contract on your dream house just fell through. The promotion you were sure of fizzled at the last management meeting. The person you knew would become your spouse called off the relationship over the phone.

Slam. Slam. Slam. Doors you thought God had opened wide become curtains of steel. What is God doing? What is He up to? Why is He placing me in this box canyon?

Despite your disappointment, remember this: God is sovereignly leading your steps in a path that will bring Him the ultimate glory and you the ultimate benefit as you abandon yourself to His care.

"But the house was just perfect."

"I desperately need the money that would come from the promotion."

"I do not know of any other person I could marry."

From your limited perspective, all of these statements are true. But understand that God alone can see around the bend.

The next time your hopes are dashed and the doors of aspiration are slammed in your face, rely on the all-sufficient wisdom of God, who alone knows the end from the beginning.

> *Lord, my perspective is limited, so I need You to open the doors I am to walk through this day. Close the doors that You do not want me to enter. Help me understand that closed doors are just as important as those that are open to me.*

SCRIPTURE READING: Lamentations 3:19–26
KEY VERSE: Lamentations 3:24

"The LORD *is my portion," says my soul,*
"Therefore I hope in Him!"

In her book *Grace Grows Best in Winter,* Margaret Clarkson writes that foreboding circumstances can be "God's hedges":

> For most of His children, God's hedges do not seemingly entail suffering, but only protection. For some, however, they mean unending pain and weakness, disappointment and sorrow, varying in degree to total imprisonment.
>
> Why this must be so, we may not know; sufficient for us to know that God Himself has hedged us in, and God's hedges are always hedges of protection and blessing.
>
> And God Himself, living there both with us and in us, longs to make of our thorny wall a thing of wonder to men and angels and demons—a thing that will one day bring forth holy blossom and fruit.
>
> Fragrance and fruit from a thorny hedge—how can it be? Only by His Spirit's enabling. . . . Did not the thorniest tree of all bring forth the holy flower of redemption?
>
> If God has entrusted you with a hedge of suffering let Him teach you how to live within it so that His holy purpose and His life-giving fruit may be fully accomplished through you!

> *Father, sometimes I feel that I am hedged in by my circumstances. Let*
> *me recognize these barriers as Your protection and blessing. Let the*
> *thorny hedges in my life bring forth fragrance and fruit for Your glory.*

SCRIPTURE READING: Romans 6:1–7

KEY VERSE: Romans 6:7

He who has died has been freed from sin.

When the Holy Spirit imparts the gift of eternal life to you, far more has transpired than the mere possession of unending spiritual life. That is because the Holy Spirit brings to every Christian an entirely new quality of life that is divine, supernatural, and godlike.

Through the Holy Spirit, the born-again man or woman can enjoy a new way of living. Since the Holy Spirit allows you to share in the life of Christ, He opens up a radical new lifestyle that is conformed to God's commands and ways, not to culture.

You must remember that much of worldly behavior and methodology is based on wisdom that is flawed and tainted by sin. The Spirit of God reprograms your mind and transforms your attitude with His wisdom, dramatically altering your habits, rearranging your priorities, and establishing new standards.

At the same time, the Holy Spirit gives you a new power for living; the new lifestyle comes with the power to succeed. You are no longer limited to fighting your problems with your resources. You have God and the fullness of His Spirit to help you and deliver you.

> *Thank You, Lord, that I am living a new lifestyle. I am not bound by the culture, behavior, or methodology of this world. I do not have to conform, but I can be transformed by Your power!*

SCRIPTURE READING: 1 Samuel 19:1–12
KEY VERSE: Genesis 50:20

But as for you, you meant evil against me; but God meant it for good, in order to bring it about as it is this day, to save many people alive.

David was told that he was going to be king of Israel, but he spent most of the next ten years on the lam. Joseph had a dream in which he ruled over his brothers, but he spent the next thirteen years as a slave and a prisoner. It almost sounds as if God was perpetrating some cruel joke on a couple of trusting teenagers, doesn't it?

Although you do know the outcome in both cases, you cannot foresee your own future. Yet you can trust God to operate on the same principles.

First, God is in control. Your life is not in a tailspin, controlled by fate or circumstance. An omniscient, sovereign God is ruling over everything. There are no accidents. He is never surprised.

Second, the God who is in control is working for your good and His glory. He never promotes or fosters evil. He is always looking out for your best interests. The conflict comes because what He sees as working for your good is not what you desire. God uses adversity, dryness, temptation, and testing for your welfare.

Third, God will bless others through your wilderness. He is working not for your good only but for the benefit of all His people.

> *You are in control, Lord. Thank You that You are working all things for my good and Your glory. Help me reach out to bless others during the wilderness journeys of my life.*

SCRIPTURE READING: Luke 22:15–20
KEY VERSES: Hebrews 10:19–20

Therefore, brethren, having boldness to enter the Holiest by the blood of Jesus, by a new and living way which He consecrated for us, through the veil, that is, His flesh.

The word *testament*—as used in the biblical Old and New Testaments—originates from the Greek word for covenant. According to Bible professor Charles Ryrie, "The word *covenant* meant an arrangement made by one party which the other party involved could accept or reject but not alter."

The primary basis for the old covenant was the Mosaic Law. The sole basis for God's new arrangement in dealing with sinful human beings is the shed blood of Jesus Christ. The elements we reverently share at the Lord's Table are visual and tangible reminders that the forgiveness of God has been extended to us at a tremendous price: the spilled blood and bruised body of Jesus Christ. The blood and body of Jesus were the supreme sacrifice for sin, which was the only one that God, in His holy justice, could accept.

Since Jesus laid down His life for your sins, you now can receive God's new covenant of forgiveness. You can have peace with God because the blood of Jesus has cleansed you from all of your sin. The next time you hold the cup and bread in your hands, remember that all of the grace, love, mercy, and hope of God is now yours because of the agony experienced by Jesus on the cross.

Father, I receive the new covenant of forgiveness through Jesus Christ. I believe His blood has cleansed me from all sin. Thank You for the new covenant, which cannot be altered!

SCRIPTURE READING: Colossians 2:20–23
KEY VERSE: 1 Corinthians 10:31

Whether you eat or drink, or whatever you do, do all to the glory of God.

The Olympic Games are a masterpiece of athletes seeking to achieve enduring goals. Many accomplish their objectives, but some medal winners have been disqualified following their performances because of their illegal drug use. Their goals were reasonable, but their methods were tragically flawed—only reflecting the rationale that the end justifies the means.

That line of thinking runs against the scriptural grain in every way. God is just as interested in how you achieve a goal as He is in the goal itself.

First, you must establish the primary motivation that God desires you to use in setting your goals. The Westminster Catechism says, "Man's chief end is to glorify God and enjoy Him forever." Whatever your goal may be—financial, physical, spiritual, family—you must ask yourself this question: Is my goal's supreme purpose to glorify God?

Since that is the purpose for which you were created, it follows that your goals must reflect that basic purpose. Sift your goals through prayer, common sense, and biblical wisdom to see if your objective's chief purpose is to honor God.

Help me set goals that please You, dear Lord. In all I do—both in this
day and in the coming year—let my chief purpose be to glorify You.
Help me set my goals, then live by faith.

SCRIPTURE READING: 1 Samuel 15

KEY VERSE: 1 Samuel 15:22

Samuel said:

"Has the LORD as great delight in burnt offerings and sacrifices,

As in obeying the voice of the LORD?

Behold, to obey is better than sacrifice,

And to heed than the fat of rams."

Saul wanted to be a good king who ruled fairly and followed the ways of God. However, his motives were not pure. And for the most part, the flaw went undetected until he was faced with a tremendous decision.

God had told him to completely destroy the Amalekites in battle. They had ruthlessly pursued Israel after the Exodus, killing the weak and disabled, and God never forgot the evil they committed against His people.

Saul complied with the Lord's command and headed into battle. However, once the dust settled, he decided to spare the Amalekite king, his strongest fighting men, and the best of his sheep and oxen.

Saul tried in vain to convince Samuel that he had obeyed God by saving the best of the spoils as a sacrifice. But it was not obedience that motivated Saul; it was pride, and that cost him his throne.

Partial obedience is not obedience; it is disobedience, and there is never an excuse for it in the eyes of God. Whatever goal God has placed before you, He has a method in mind for you to follow in achieving it. Ask Him to give you His wisdom so that you may accomplish the goal perfectly, completely—and most important—obediently.

> *Total obedience—that is what I want in my life, Father. Reveal Your purposes to me, then give me the wisdom to accomplish Your plans perfectly, completely, and obediently.*

SCRIPTURE READING: Romans 8:28–30

KEY VERSE: 2 Corinthians 5:9

We make it our aim, whether present or absent, to be well pleasing to Him.

For a season MBO (Management By Objectives) ruled the business realm. The methodology was simple: set realistic goals, establish a plan to reach those goals, and periodically evaluate your plans.

Goals are still a large part of business and personal agendas. We want to earn a degree in this field; we seek to finish a project by this date; we strive to create a certain amount of savings each year. These are all good tools to exercise faith. God wants us to plan, not to wander aimlessly about.

But life is unpredictable. An ill father prevents us from pursuing a degree; an unexpected assignment takes us away from our task; a major repair bill makes savings impossible. What do we do once our goals are capsized by circumstances? Have we failed? Should we cease planning?

Absolutely not. We must remember that our chief objective is clear—to be conformed to the image of Jesus Christ. God will use our plans and schemes, as topsy-turvy as they may seem, to reproduce Christ's divine character in us.

Set your goals, but remember your priority—to allow God to use both success and failure to conform you to the image of Christ.

> *Dear Lord, frequently my life seems out of control. Sometimes I suc-*
> *ceed, but often I fail. Whether I reach my goals or fall short, continue*
> *to conform me to the image of Your dear Son.*

SCRIPTURE READING: James 3:13–18

KEY VERSE: 1 Peter 2:12

Having your conduct honorable among the Gentiles, that when they speak against you as evildoers, they may, by your good works which they observe, glorify God in the day of visitation.

History records lamentable incidents, such as the Inquisition and the Crusades, that had seemingly spiritual goals but completely wrong methods. That's why, once the proper motivation for your goals for this year is established, it is essential that you assess the wisdom of your methods.

Ask yourself the following questions:

Are my methods in keeping with the revealed will and principles of God as recorded in the Scriptures? For instance, a goal of becoming the company president may be set with the proper motivation for leading the business overseas so that the markets abroad can be used as distribution points for gospel literature. However, accomplishing that goal by manipulating accounting records that falsely increase sales figures and thus mislead others is thoroughly condemned by the Scriptures.

A second question is: *Are my methods in any way unjustly harming my fellow human beings?* If the individual described in the previous paragraph reaches his goal through slandering an employee who also seeks the same position, his methods are wrong.

Examine your methods by observing these standards. When you reach your goal, you can then be sure that God is honored.

> *Dear Lord, I pause this day to examine my ways before You. Please prevent me from harming my fellow human beings in any way. Let my methods be in harmony with Your will and the principles revealed in Your Word.*

SCRIPTURE READING: Hebrews 11

KEY VERSE: 1 Thessalonians 5:24

He who calls you is faithful, who also will do it.

A delayed promotion, an unreached goal, a broken relationship—some of life's inexplicable turns. Many of the saints mentioned in Hebrews 11 knew firsthand about life's unknowns.

Many others also had the opportunity to witness God's hand at work as He rolled back the waters of the Red Sea, defeated enemy armies, and proved faithful when times of trial and tribulation struck. The test of faith is not merely in trusting, but in trusting God when all hope has disappeared.

One way that God tests our faith is by allowing life's unknowns to invade our lives. Samuel anointed David as king over Israel. Yet nothing was mentioned about having to wait years before he sat on Israel's throne. Thanks to life's unknowns, David was forced to leave his family and friends and live like a common criminal on the run from a jealous and mentally impaired king.

At any point he could have proclaimed his frustration, but David went beyond bitterness and self-pity to claim the goodness of God. He realized God's ways were not the ways of people. All of life's unknowns are perfectly within God's sovereign control. If He has given you a promise, cling to it. He will do exactly what He has said He will do.

The year ahead—even the events of this day—are unknown to me, Father. I rest in the knowledge that You alone have sovereign control over every aspect of my life. You will do exactly what You said You would do.

SCRIPTURE READING: Ephesians 4:17–24
KEY VERSES: Hebrews 12:1–2

We also, since we are surrounded by so great a cloud of witnesses, let us lay aside every weight, and the sin which so easily ensnares us, and let us run with endurance the race that is set before us, looking unto Jesus, the author and finisher of our faith, who for the joy that was set before Him endured the cross, despising the shame, and has sat down at the right hand of the throne of God.

If most of us were to make topographical maps of our spiritual walks, they would probably look like a range of mountains jutting heavenward with many spiritual peaks and dropping just as sharply into spiritual valleys. That is because maintaining a consistent walk with Jesus Christ is one of the most difficult challenges we face.

Think for a moment. What is the primary culprit that disturbs your rest and confidence in God? Is it not looking and reacting to your circumstances?

One day the boss comes in and tells you that you have earned a hefty raise. Watch your spirit soar. The next day he returns to tell you that he was mistaken; instead your pay is cut. Watch your spirit sink.

We are too dependent on the external things of life, which rise and fall like the stock market, to govern our relationship with God. That is not the way God designed it. As believers we have the unchanging, steady, indwelling presence of Jesus Christ. He can handle and solve anything.

The internal control of Christ will lead you into a daily, deliberate walk with God. Whatever happens you turn over to Him, asking Him to sustain, strengthen, and guide you. Such confidence and trust in Him stabilize your journey.

Dear Lord, help me not to be so dependent on the external things of life. Let me walk confidently in the knowledge that You will sustain, strengthen, and guide me this day.

SCRIPTURE READING: Joshua 1:1–2, 10–18
KEY VERSE: Isaiah 58:11

The LORD will guide you continually,
And satisfy your soul in drought,
And strengthen your bones;
You shall be like a watered garden,
And like a spring of water,
*   whose waters do not fail.*

The company needs to know by Friday. Will you take the job in Wichita or not? The church wants an answer next week. Will you teach the Bible study this quarter or decline?

Decisions. Opportunities. Some of them come only once, and they demand a precise response. How do you know what to do?

The Israelites were presented with a grand command from the Lord of hosts: be ready in three days to cross the Jordan River and enter the land promised to your forefathers. There were obstacles—an overflowing, raging river with enemies on the other side. But the Israelites obeyed God, and the blessings followed.

When decisions are not so clear-cut, you still employ principles to seize the opportunities offered by God. Just as Joshua was commanded, you are to meditate in the Word constantly. His Word rolls back the darkness and doubt.

If you fail, if you make the wrong decision, God is still with you wherever you go. He uses even your botches to teach you. Above all, obey what you believe God has shown you. Even when you are wrong, you will still be all right.

I want to seize each opportunity this day affords, Father. Let Your
Word roll back the darkness and doubt threatening my life. I praise
You that even when I am wrong, You will make it right.

SCRIPTURE READING: John 6:65–69
KEY VERSE: John 14:6

Jesus said to him, "I am the way, the truth, and the life. No one comes to the Father except through Me."

In his classic book *The Pilgrim's Progress,* John Bunyan told of the adventures of Christian on his spiritual journey as a believer in Christ. Christian knew that the straight and narrow path—the way of Jesus—was the only road to heaven, the Celestial City. But the path was often rough and rocky; trials and temptations surrounded him.

Discouraged, Christian looked away from the road at the soft grass of By-path Meadow and took what he thought was a shortcut, another way to God. Moments later, he was thrown into a dark dungeon as a prisoner of the Giant Despair. Christian got a hard look at the hopelessness of other options and learned where they led—away from Christ.

Understanding who Jesus is will keep you from false, tempting choices. When compared to Jesus, all other options pale. Jesus said, "I am the way, and the truth, and the life; no one comes to the Father, but through Me" (John 14:6 NASB).

Nothing else will do. No other course brings true and lasting rewards. There are no substitutes, no bypass. His love and forgiveness are all-sufficient.

He gives direction and purpose to your life. The way may be arduous at times, but it is the best route to a meaningful life.

Jesus is the way. There are no other options for me! Keep me on the right path this day, even though it might be difficult. Thank You, Lord, for the direction and purpose You give my life.

SCRIPTURE READING: Psalm 40

KEY VERSE: Psalm 40:8

I delight to do Your will, O my God,
And Your law is within my heart.

The house was in poor condition due to a shifting foundation. Wallboard was cracked, the ceiling sagged, and numerous other repairs were warranted. Slowly, over time, the owners worked at restoring the damage. After a few years, the restoration was complete.

Shortly thereafter, interest rates on mortgages fell dramatically. The couple were able to refinance at a lower rate only because the house was appraised at a good value.

Preparation is a major part of discovering the will of God as well. You want to know God's will, and you want to know it now. But have you been willing to make the sacrificial preparations to know and obey His plan? Are you ready to follow when God makes it clear what He desires? What you do today in terms of Bible study, prayer, meditation, fellowship, worship, and other scriptural exercises prepares you to do God's will. They sensitize your spirit, bend your heart to holiness, and equip you to hear and discern the voice of God as He speaks through the Scriptures, godly counsel, or the providential arrangement of circumstances.

If you want to know the will of God for the future, be disciplined for godliness today. When the time is right, your spiritual senses will be alert to the good and perfect will of the Father.

> *Prepare me, Lord, to do Your will. Sensitize my spirit to discern Your voice today through the Word, godly counsel, and the providential circumstances of my life.*

SCRIPTURE READING: Proverbs 3:1–8
KEY VERSE: 2 Corinthians 5:7

We walk by faith, not by sight.

If you pick up a road map, you can readily discern the best route to reach your destination. But while the map logically arranges the maze of highways so that you can stay on course, it does not provide a total picture of what the journey holds in store. Hills, curves, stoplights, restaurants, service stations, school zones, and other details of the trip can be discovered only as the trip unfolds.

Knowing God's will operates in a similar manner. God has a plan for your life, but the specifics you want so desperately are revealed only as you are committed to the journey of devotion and discipleship.

Solomon wrote in Proverbs that God will guide your steps and unveil His plan as you trust wholeheartedly in God, refuse to rely solely on your limited wisdom, and obey Him consistently.

As you do these things, combined with prayer and the study of Scripture, the details of His personal plan—a place of work, a marriage partner, a church to attend—will follow.

God wants you to know His will. Delight yourself in Him; put aside preconceived notions, and concentrate on trust, obedience, and a personal relationship with Christ. Wait on Him, and at the right time, the answer will come.

> *Dear Lord, help me put aside preconceived notions of Your plan.*
> *Instead of relying on my limited wisdom, help me trust and obey You*
> *and wait patiently until the answer comes.*

SCRIPTURE READING: Hebrews 4:1–10
KEY VERSE: Hebrews 4:3

We who have believed do enter that rest, as He has said:
"So I swore in My wrath, 'They shall not enter My rest,'"
although the works were finished from the foundation of the world.

Does an apple tree struggle to produce apples? Does a pear tree labor to make its sweet crop?

As simple as it may appear, the liberating principle for doing God's work God's way is learning to abide in Christ. Abiding in Christ means resting in the finished work of the Cross. The cry of Jesus at Calvary was, "It is finished." He had accomplished the work of redemption, providing the way of victory over sin and Satan for all who place their faith in Him.

Your toil or effort can add nothing to what Christ has done. Your task is to receive the complete sufficiency of Christ for every situation. You do so with the same childlike faith you had at salvation: "Yes, Lord, I believe You can solve this problem, heal this relationship, take care of this anxiety because You are my adequacy. You are all I have, but You are enough."

The abiding life is the restful life spoken of in Hebrews 4. It is the place of absolute trust and confidence in the person and work of Jesus Christ. Christ is all-sufficient. His life richly flows through you in the person of the Holy Spirit. He will satisfy every need, fulfill every demand, and produce the abundant Christian life in you as you depend wholly on Him. He is able.

> *Father, I am tired of trying to produce fruit on my own. I yield my self-effort to You right now. Let Your life flow through me, making me sufficient for every situation. Let me learn the secret of the abiding life.*

SCRIPTURE READING: Matthew 11:28–29
KEY VERSE: Isaiah 30:21

Your ears shall hear a word behind you, saying,
"This is the way, walk in it,"
Whenever you turn to the right hand
Or whenever you turn to the left.

Hiking the Appalachian Trail is one of North America's most exciting adventures. The trail stretches from Maine's Mount Katahdin to Georgia's Springer Mountain and offers breathtaking views, challenging terrain, and a chance to experience the peace and solitude of nature.

Since 1984, the Appalachian Trail Conference (ATC), a group of volunteers and fellow hikers, has maintained the trail. These people work all year to keep it free of debris and dangerous obstructions. However, the ATC is not responsible for unauthorized footpaths leading to or from the trail. If you want to enjoy the trail, ATC volunteers will tell you to practice safety and purchase official Appalachian Trail maps. Following unmarked trails can be disastrous.

A sad fact is that many of us do this very thing in life. We purchase fraudulent maps and take unmarked routes that lead us far from God's plan. Instead of reaping a reward of peace and safety, we stumble into dangerous ravines.

However, it's never too late to begin again with God. If you think you have taken the wrong trail, ask God to show you the way. Commit yourself to following His map from this point on, and He will lead you along a safe, sure path.

O God, how often I have strayed spiritually into unmarked territory.
Forgive me. Show me the right way. I want to follow Your map from
this point on.

SCRIPTURE READING: John 3:1–17
KEY VERSE: John 3:16

For God so loved the world that He gave His only begotten Son, that whoever believes in Him should not perish but have everlasting life.

She turned toward the window and stared out at the falling rain. The sound of the door closing behind her continued to echo through her mind. Gathering her courage and strength, she whispered, "I have made it on my own before, and I will do it again."

Her husband was gone, and the finality of his departure was agonizing. She was determined not to think about his leaving—perhaps in a few days, but not now.

However, thoughts of hopelessness immediately embattled her mind. How would she live? Where would she go? How could she start over? She prayed, "Dear God, I can't make it through this alone. If You are there, please come into my life and help me start over."

Most of the people who came to Jesus were searching for new beginnings. The man born blind, the woman of Samaria, Mary Magdalene, John and Andrew, and even Nicodemus sought a solution to life's most difficult questions. Each had a need only Christ could fill—love, acceptance, freedom from bondage, and eternal life.

Only the Son of God can take your brokenness and heartache and turn them into something of wonder and grace. You can trust Him to give you a new beginning, no matter what your circumstances may be.

Thank You, Lord, that You take the heartaches of yesterday and transform them into something good. I am so glad that each day with You marks a new beginning. I start all over again this day.

SCRIPTURE READING: John 8:1–7
KEY VERSE: John 8:11

Jesus said to her, "Neither do I condemn you; go and sin no more."

While scholars argue whether or not the woman caught in adultery was a setup by the Pharisees to trap Jesus going against the Law of Moses, the overarching theme is forgiveness. God's love, mercy, and grace were all present and active. Jesus did not condemn the woman but instead challenged her accusers to throw the first stone if one among them could be found without sin.

After the Pharisees departed, Jesus looked at the woman lying at His feet. That was not the first time she had committed such an act, but it was the first time she had appeared before Jesus. There was no doubt in her mind that He was a man of God. How exposed and embarrassed she must have felt, that is, until the Savior revealed His word of forgiveness and hope to her heart.

Perhaps there is something in your life you wish you could erase. Just the thought of it brings feelings of condemnation and sorrow. Adultery was an act that the law declared punishable by stoning. Yet Jesus set the woman free.

He gave her a second chance, and that is what He gives you. If there is something you have done, know that when you bring it to God in prayer seeking His forgiveness, it is forgiven. God will never bring the matter up again. His Son's death at Calvary was sufficient payment for all your sins. Only almighty God can love you so much.

> *You are the God of the second chance, and for that I thank You, Lord.*
> *Your love and mercy cover my yesterdays and give me the opportunity*
> *to begin again. Only You can love me so much!*

SCRIPTURE READING: John 8:8–11

KEY VERSE: Romans 5:15

The free gift is not like the offense. For if by the one man's offense many died, much more the grace of God and the gift by the grace of the one Man, Jesus Christ, abounded to many.

No one knows what Jesus wrote in the dirt the morning the woman caught in adultery was brought to Him. Some say He wrote the Ten Commandments. Others think He wrote the word *forgiven*. Regardless of the written message, the principle was clear—grace would abound.

We cannot earn God's grace. It is a gift He gives to all who come to Him. Lying at the Savior's feet, the woman probably thought her fate was sealed. The punishment for adultery was stoning.

Yet suddenly and unpredictably, Jesus offered her a second chance. Warren Wiersbe writes, "For Jesus to forgive this woman meant that He had to one day die for her sins. Forgiveness is free but it is not cheap."

Jesus was not soft on sin. "Nor is Christ's gracious forgiveness an excuse to sin," continues Wiersbe. "'Go and sin no more!' was our Lord's counsel. . . . Certainly the experience of gracious forgiveness would motivate the penitent sinner to live a holy and obedient life to the glory of God." Grace is given so that we may know and accept what Jesus Christ did for us at Calvary.

Forgiven and blessed by His matchless grace are those who call Him Savior.

I am forgiven! I rejoice in this fact, dear Lord. Let me walk worthy of Your grace as I live a holy and obedient life for Your glory today.

SCRIPTURE READING: Romans 5:1–8

KEY VERSE: Romans 5:8

God demonstrates His own love toward us, in that while we were still sinners, Christ died for us.

Each of us wants to know there is hope for a second chance when we fail to reach a goal, yield to sin, or fall short of what we've been instructed to do. Second chances are particularly important when sin is involved and feelings of guilt mount. How many of us have not longed for God's cleansing touch when convicted of wrongful actions?

W. E. Vine defines *sin* as "a missing of the mark." Think of it as shooting an arrow at a target and missing it completely. Sin always falls short of God's best for your life.

Even before you knew Christ, He knew you and loved you so much that He came to earth to give you a second chance at life: "God demonstrates His own love toward us, in that while we were still sinners, Christ died for us."

Jesus' life, death, and resurrection were God's supreme brush stroke of grace across the canvas of creation. He is the embodiment of all hope and grace. If you have accepted Him as your Savior, His life is alive within you, and His grace is sufficient to meet and remove every hint of sin's stain. Praise Him, for He is worthy of all your love and praise.

> *Dear Lord, I have missed the mark. I have fallen short of Your best for my life. Forgive me. Let the supreme brush stroke of Your grace blot out my yesterdays.*

SCRIPTURE READING: Psalm 42
KEY VERSE: Psalm 42:5

Why are you cast down, O my soul?
And why are you disquieted within me?
Hope in God, for I shall yet praise Him
For the help of His countenance.

Hope brings an anticipation of blessing. We live in hope of a wedding day or the birth of a child or grandchild. We have hope over graduation from college or the day we can finally place "Dr." in front of our names. There are as many reasons to hope as there are people who live each day.

To know hope, you must endure times of hopelessness. Hope represents an end to desperate longing—a need that begs to be satisfied and in the end is fulfilled. When hope burns within your heart, it cries out to be heard.

The psalmist wrote,

As the deer pants for the water brooks,
So my soul pants for Thee, O God. . . .
My tears have been my food day and night,
While they say to me all day long,
"Where is your God?" (Ps. 42:1–3 NASB)

What is your hope, your dream, the cry of your heart? Take a moment and go to Jesus with your deepest, most earnest pleas.

Realize that whatever is important to you is even more important to the Lord. Let Him be your Source of hope today.

O Lord, my heart cries out to You today. Like the psalmist, I long for
You as a deer desires the cool, refreshing water. Rekindle the dying
embers of my hope.

SCRIPTURE READING: Psalm 138:7–8
KEY VERSE: Psalm 18:35

You have also given me the shield of Your salvation;
Your right hand has held me up,
Your gentleness has made me great.

There are many references to hands in the Bible. Men shook or struck hands as a sign of commitment or pledge. In the United States and many other countries, people shake hands as a way of greeting. In the Bible, raised hands symbolize praise and thanksgiving (Ps. 63:4). The right hand, especially when used in connection with God, is a symbol of might and power (Ps. 44:3). The very touch of another's hand can communicate blessing and love.

Hands and the way you use them often reflect the inner self. A doctor uses her hands as instruments of healing. Before starting His ministry, Jesus was a carpenter, no doubt with hands of a skilled laborer. More than likely, He had to cut His own wood and transport it back to the carpentry shop. There He would size and shape it to be used for whatever He was building.

The laying on of hands by the apostles in the New Testament separated men for God's service. It was a physical display of God's anointing (Acts 13:3). As children, we sang the song "He Has the Whole World in His Hands." This is the way God likes for us to view His awesome ability. Your entire life is kept safe in the palm of God's loving hand. There under His watch of safety are tremendous peace and security.

Father, I rest confidently in the fact that my life is in Your hands.
Underneath are Your everlasting arms. Hold me secure as I face the
challenges of this day.

SCRIPTURE READING: Colossians 2:16–23
KEY VERSE: Galatians 3:3

Are you so foolish? Having begun in the Spirit, are you now being made perfect by the flesh?

The tackler could see it coming—a fullback carrying the football loosely at his side. A sudden turn and the tackler lunged after the ball. It popped loose and spiraled toward the ground.

He started to dive on the ball, but it bounded just high enough for him to pick it up and run. Breaking free from the other players, he started running down the football field as fast as he could run.

The crowd was shouting wildly as he crossed the goal line and pounded the ball proudly in the dirt. It was the first touchdown of his high school career—and perhaps his last—he had run into the wrong end zone.

We often have the right goal in mind spiritually when tackling the Christian faith but wind up in the wrong end zone. The Colossian believers had a sincere desire to serve God. However, they had become entangled in legalism and were imposing unrealistic demands on young believers. They had also begun judging actions of others.

The moment you think you have it together enough to judge another person is the moment you run into the wrong end zone. Paul described legalism as bondage. Don't get caught up in it. Instead, "stand fast therefore in the liberty by which Christ has made [you] free" (Gal. 5:1).

Father, I have begun with You. Now keep me headed the right direction. I don't want to wind up in the wrong end zone.

SCRIPTURE READING: John 11:21–26
KEY VERSE: Colossians 1:13

He has delivered us from the power of darkness and conveyed us into the kingdom of the Son of His love.

Danny Buggs was an electrifying wide receiver in both the collegiate and the professional ranks. Playing for the University of West Virginia, the Washington Redskins, several World and Canadian Football League teams, and other National Football League teams, Buggs generated excitement and touchdowns galore.

But as with all athletes, Buggs's body soon wearied, and younger, sturdier men took his place. The story does not end there, however. Buggs received Christ as his Savior along the way and now works with youths from all walks of life, sharing Christ and His love with thousands of seeking adolescents. While his athletic exploits are finished, the gift of eternal life he received through Christ has only begun.

So it is with all believers. We here and now enjoy the benefits of eternal life. Christ, our Life, fills us with His purpose, joy, peace, power, and patience for life's daily struggles. We have a new, rich quality of life as heirs of God.

Death is but a doorway into the presence of God. Eternal life is yours forever, serving and living in the very presence of God. Eternal life means everything counts—here and hereafter. Nothing is meaningless; nothing is wasted; nothing is ever finished.

You are always just beginning.

Thank You, dear Lord, for purpose, power, and patience for my daily struggles. I rejoice that I am Your child, an heir to eternal life. I am just beginning!

SCRIPTURE READING: 1 Samuel 9–10
KEY VERSE: 1 Samuel 10:9

So it was, when he had turned his back to go from Samuel, that God gave him another heart; and all those signs came to pass that day.

One of the most important elements in a race is a good start. In swift competition a poor start is tantamount to losing.

For believers, that start is the decision to trust Christ as Savior. Just as essential is the character building in the ensuing months and years. When the prophet Samuel identified Saul as king, it was obvious that Saul had begun his journey with admirable qualities. After Samuel anointed him king, Saul demonstrated his patience and humility by enduring the taunts of "certain worthless men" who mocked him, saying, "How can this one deliver us?" (1 Sam. 10:27 NASB).

Perhaps your beginning hasn't been so favorable. Perhaps circumstances beyond your control have thwarted you at every turn. Perhaps you have never chosen to follow Christ. You can begin today. If you are not a believer, receive Jesus' offer of salvation by inviting Him in as your personal Savior.

If you do know Jesus but are continually frustrated, submit completely to His lordship, asking Him to take control of you and your circumstances. Trust Him to use even your problems for your welfare. He can do it if you turn to Him.

I want a heart to follow You, O God. Give me a good start and the power and endurance to cross the finish line in victory.

February

THEME: The Water Gate

REPRESENTING: The Word of God

KEY VERSES: John 4:13–14

Jesus answered and said to her, "Whoever drinks of this water will thirst again, but whoever drinks of the water that I shall give him will never thirst."

SCRIPTURE READING: Psalm 63

KEY VERSE: Mark 1:35

Now in the morning, having risen a long while before daylight, He went out
and departed to a solitary place; and there He prayed.

Intimacy with Jesus Christ is one of the most important elements of the Christian life. It involves a lifelong journey filled with joy and immense pleasure. However, learning to love God takes time and a deep desire to get to know Him. Jesus made a point of being alone with the Father. He rose early to be alone in prayer.

Even as complicated as life is, there is still a place where you can find hope and the assurance of a greater love than anything this world has to offer. God's presence is the place. It is open to you any time of the day or night.

You have known times of weakness when you would have given anything to know that everything was going to turn out all right. God waits for you. He is the One who has given you life, and He alone knows the needs of your heart.

In being alone with Him, you discover a deeper wisdom that is fit to handle even the toughest situations. How do you start, especially if you have never scheduled regular time to be alone with God?

Begin this very minute. Close your eyes and sit for a moment without saying anything. Just focus your heart on God and the fact that He loves you more than anything else. Then pray and ask Him to give you a desire to get to know Him better. He will never turn you away but waits for you with open arms.

Thank You, Lord, for the assurance that You love me and desire to fel-
lowship with me. Give me the desire to get to know You better. I am
starting right now as I wait in silence in Your presence.

SCRIPTURE READING: Isaiah 6:1–9
KEY VERSE: Psalm 23:3

He restores my soul;
He leads me in the paths of righteousness
For His name's sake.

Many times in the Psalms, David cried out to God to "restore," "revive," and "refresh" his soul. He uttered some pleas out of a sense of desperation. Others came out of his desire to know God more intimately.

David was seeking a fresh encounter with God. You, too, often need times of renewed spiritual vitality where you can mount up on fresh wings of the soul.

Although fresh encounters with God cannot be programmed or scheduled, they seldom happen apart from a lifestyle of meditation on God's Word combined with honest prayer. God can break into your life explosively and suddenly or quietly and gradually. But when He does, you sense His presence anew. You are keenly aware of the Holy Spirit's active ministry within.

You walk with a new assurance of God's help. Your problems may stay, your circumstances may remain, but you know God is in control. You are focused on His adequacy, not your inadequacy.

There is no end to the seasons of fresh encounters you may have with God. You can never exhaust His fullness. Personal encounters with God will help you see your weaknesses and magnify the awesome reality of Christ's love for you. They are encounters of the closest kind that can refresh the driest soul.

Restore me! Revive me! Renew me, O God. This is my cry today. I
need a fresh encounter with You.

SCRIPTURE READING: Hosea 6:1–3

KEY VERSES: Colossians 2:6–7

As you therefore have received Christ Jesus the Lord, so walk in Him, rooted and built up in Him and established in the faith, as you have been taught, abounding in it with thanksgiving.

No-till farming has become a standard practice in the Midwest. To prevent the loss of fertile topsoil, crop stubble is left after harvest instead of plowed under, maximizing dirt and moisture retention.

Spiritual slippage can likewise be minimized and steady growth fostered as the Holy Spirit applies these time-tested principles to the soil of your soul:

A renewed concentration on the Word of God. You become firmly rooted in Christ as the principles and power of God's Word are implanted into your mind and woven into your behavior. Regular reading, studying, and meditating upon the Scriptures add solid layers of Christlike character to your life, which act as invisible seawalls against the forces of spiritual erosion.

A heightened attention to worship and praise. The less awesome God becomes in your eyes, the easier it is to drift. Praise and adoration lead to an exalted view of God and restore your spiritual passion.

A revived focus on service to others. Ministering to the practical needs of others is a great stimulus for reversing spiritual erosion because it releases the power and love of God.

You can regain the joy, peace, and confidence you once had in your relationship with Christ. Apply at least one principle today, and watch God rebuild your life.

Father, I don't want to slip spiritually. I renew my concentration on Your Word. I refocus my attention on serving others. I praise and worship You this day, dear Lord.

SCRIPTURE READING: Ephesians 2:1–9
KEY VERSES: Ephesians 2:8–9

By grace you have been saved through faith, and that not of yourselves; it is the gift of God, not of works, lest anyone should boast.

Her mother worked for days making her a new school dress. Finally it was finished and ready to be worn. Giggling with excitement, she asked if she could wear it the next day. "Yes," was the answer, "but stay off the sliding board during playtime. You already have torn one dress. Let's keep this one nice."

However, playtime proved too tempting. Despite her mother's instruction, she climbed to the top of the slide and began a fast descent. It was then she heard a loud tearing noise. Later that evening, tears filled her mother's eyes as she studied the gaping hole. "It will take some effort, but I believe it can be fixed."

Even as a child, she was shocked at her mother's response. She expected punishment but received grace instead. While climbing into bed the next evening, she noticed the dress, mended and hanging in her closet. An attached note read: "Honey, I love you. Mom."

Maybe you have torn a gaping hole in the side of your life, and you think nothing can mend it. God can and will. He has already attached His note of love to your heart through the death of His Son. If you will listen, you will hear His voice: "*(Your name)*, I love you. Come to Me and I will mend your life and make you whole again."

Heavenly Father, through Jesus You provided the way for me to come with the torn fragments of my life. I wait before You right now. Make me whole again.

SCRIPTURE READING: Jeremiah 33:1–3
KEY VERSE: Ephesians 1:18

The eyes of your understanding being enlightened; that you may know what is the hope of His calling, what are the riches of the glory of His inheritance in the saints.

The Hebrew word used for "mighty" in God's dialogue with the prophet Jeremiah is the same word that described the fortified cities of Canaan. Is there a connection?

The Israelites' success in conquering Canaan and enjoying its fruit was linked to their ability to destroy the walled fortifications. That happened as they depended on God.

Your progress in knowing and obeying God and realizing His blessing in every detail of your life likewise hinges on receiving His wisdom and power. Prayer is the supernatural means by which Christ unveils His sovereign counsel and mind, giving you the direction and insight you need for yourself, your family, and your career.

Such treasures are discovered only through communion with God. They are not available to a prayerless person who is a walled fortress of mere intellect or good intentions.

Would you like the God of creation to show you great and mighty things? Is your life stuck in a rut, void of God's power and presence, lacking His loving, wise touch? If so, call on Him. Whether His answer is "yes," "no," or "wait," you can overcome your problem or reach your goal through His reply.

Dear Lord, help me conquer every walled fortification of the enemy in my life. Get me out of my rut. Show me great and mighty things.

SCRIPTURE READING: Hebrews 4:14–16
KEY VERSE: Hebrews 10:19

Therefore, brethren, having boldness to enter the Holiest by the blood of Jesus.

Your prayers may be weak and vague because you really doubt that God will come through. The writer of Hebrews, however, noted that your approach to God should be characterized by boldness. Your prayers should be like arrows from a steady bow. They can be if you grasp three significant truths that can revolutionize your prayer life.

First, you have complete freedom and access to a holy God through the blood of Christ. You do not have to be afraid; you can confess to Him your problem sins. You can come to the throne of grace to God the Father, who gives you not what you deserve but what His love bestows upon you through His Son.

Second, you come in agreement with God's Word. If you pray according to the Scriptures, you can be sure that God will honor your prayers. You may not understand the specifics of how He will work, but He will fulfill His promises to you in the Bible.

Third, focus and rest completely on the character of God. Is He strong enough to handle your adversities? Is He wise enough to correct your problems? Is He loving enough to care for your hurts?

Your assurance is in His faithfulness, not yours. Your prayer life can become a cornerstone of confidence as you trust God for all things.

Father, thank You for access to You through the blood of Jesus. I come in total agreement with Your Word. I focus my attention on You alone, O God. My assurance rests in Your faithfulness.

SCRIPTURE READING: Nehemiah 1

KEY VERSE: Colossians 1:3

We give thanks to the God and Father of our Lord Jesus Christ, praying always for you.

Nehemiah was a tremendous example of how God uses burden praying to unleash His power in others' lives. A prayer burden must come from God. Nehemiah wasn't out looking for a burden; God placed it on his heart after Nehemiah conversed with his fellow Jews from Jerusalem.

A good start is to ask God to burden your heart with His concerns. You may be surprised at His response. God may bring to your mind an individual or a circumstance you never would have chosen.

Such a burden is usually one that forces you into a new sense of dependence on God. Nehemiah wept, prayed, and fasted for God's intervention. You must know that only the power of God can bring a solution.

You must be willing to persist in burden praying. Four months passed before Nehemiah mentioned his burden to the king. The burden that God places on your heart for an unsaved mate, a crumbling marriage, or a bitter friend may last for years—even a lifetime.

Are you willing to pay the price for the burden that God puts on your heart? Will you persevere until God acts?

Burden my heart with Your concerns, Father, then help me persevere until victory comes. Make me willing to pay the price.

SCRIPTURE READING: Luke 18:1–8

KEY VERSE: Colossians 4:2

Continue earnestly in prayer, being vigilant in it with thanksgiving.

A ten-year-old boy was asked to take piano lessons during school. Weekly lessons continued for several months until the piano teacher sent a note home recommending that the child drop the lessons because of his disinterest. When asked by his parents to explain his indifference, the boy said the lessons interfered with his recess period.

Similarly most of us are not likely to be devoted to someone or some objective unless we are convinced of its importance. It is not surprising then that Paul's appeal in today's passage—for the Christian to be devoted to prayer—is taken so casually. We must first be persuaded of the significance of prayer before we commit ourselves to it.

Prayer is an avenue through which the supernatural power of God is released into your circumstances. Do you have a need for God's power, for God's provision today in a relationship or endeavor? Prayer is a God-ordained method through which you can have access to His unlimited resources for your problems.

Prayer is the means by which you come to experience the loving will of God. When you pray, you confess your dependence on your sovereign, mighty God to accomplish His purposes in you and through you; and His will is then done on earth as it is in heaven.

> *Father, thank You for the privilege of prayer. I confess my dependence on You. Accomplish Your purposes in and through me. Let Your will be done this day.*

SCRIPTURE READING: Ephesians 1:15–23
KEY VERSES: Ephesians 1:15–16

I also, after I heard of your faith in the Lord Jesus and your love for all the saints, do not cease to give thanks for you, making mention of you in my prayers.

Two compelling factors make prayer an exercise worth your whole-hearted devotion.

Prayer is a means by which you come to know God. Is there anyone else you would rather know intimately than the living, eternal, awesome God? Can there be any greater pursuit than knowing God?

When you pray, you come to know God in the most practical and personal way possible. You seek His mind and His will. You learn to understand His character, and you enter into the temple of the Most High. Knowing God can make a dull life exciting, a doubting life sure, a timid life bold, a wandering life purposeful.

Prayer is also a means by which you worship God. Have you ever thought how you worship God? Certainly you can exalt Him through your lips and actions; but when you pray, you truly acknowledge Him as the Source and End of all.

Prayer is an act of worship by which you confess your reverence and dependence on God. The Bible refers to the prayers of God's people as incense, symbolic of praise and worship.

Knowing God and worshiping God are two of the greatest privileges a Christian can enjoy. For these reasons, prayer is worth your complete devotion.

Have you prayed today?

I want to know You. There is no greater pursuit. I want to worship You. There is no greater privilege. Lord, I commit myself anew to prayer.

O our God, will You not judge them? For we have no power against this great multitude that is coming against us; nor do we know what to do, but our eyes are upon You.

Karl Marx, the Communist philosopher of the last century, sarcastically referred to religion as "the opium of the people." Christians obviously refute such tainted logic, but in practice we tend to treat prayer in a similar vein.

Prayer too often is seen as a last resort, a divine escape hatch if all else fails. We turn all the knobs, pull all the strings, exhaust all our resources—and then begrudgingly turn to prayer if what we do does not work.

Prayer is not a spiritual crutch. It is not begging God to help after all our efforts have failed. Instead, prayer is the most effective problem solver we can employ. It is a divine management tool that can be availed, regardless of the nature of our predicament.

Why don't we always view prayer as such? Pride. We do not want to admit our dependence on Christ. Sure, we had to call on Him to save us, but now we can handle most things just fine, thank you!

How blind we are; how twisted is our notion of prayer. God offers us His help, and we, in our human haughtiness, turn Him down.

God wants you to lean on Him. He longs to work on your behalf, to guide you and help you. Prayer is His divine provision. Should you ignore God's helping hand?

I confess my dependence on You. I can't handle the circumstances of my life alone, Father. Thank You for the divine provision of prayer to manage the affairs of my life.

SCRIPTURE READING: Matthew 6:5–15
KEY VERSE: John 6:15

When Jesus perceived that they were about to come and take Him by force to make Him king, He departed again to the mountain by Himself alone.

Although Christ's disciples saw Him work many miracles during their three-year apprenticeship, the Bible records only one instance in which they asked their Master to explain His phenomenal power. "Lord, teach us to pray," they requested after observing Christ in a concentrated time of communion with the Father (Luke 11:1). They must have grasped that somehow prayer was the invisible source of Jesus' ministry and their success depended on understanding its secrets.

What followed was a pattern for all believers. At the heart of Christ's instructions was the pivotal phrase: "Thy kingdom come. / Thy will be done, / On earth as it is in heaven" (Matt. 6:10 NASB). That is the core of genuine prayer, seeking and submitting to the will of God in every circumstance. That was Jesus' primary concern: "not as I will, but as Thou wilt" (Matt. 26:39 NASB).

Evangelist Dwight L. Moody explained, "Prayer means that I am to be raised up into feeling, into union and design with Him; that I am to enter into His counsel and carry out His purpose fully."

Whatever your circumstance today, let prayer steer you into His will.

Teach me to pray, dear Lord, even as You taught Your disciples. Let Your kingdom come. Let Your will be done.

SCRIPTURE READING: Colossians 4:2–3, 12
KEY VERSE: Philippians 1:19

I know that this will turn out for my deliverance through your prayer and the supply of the Spirit of Jesus Christ.

The model quarterback is Joe Montana or Bernie Kosar. The model evangelist is Billy Graham. The model pilot is Chuck Yeager. Each possesses the skills and attributes that younger generations seek to emulate.

For intercessors, the clear choice is Epaphras, Paul's dedicated coworker who prayed with fervor for the Colossian people. His strategy is a proven model that will work in any age. Epaphras always prayed for the Colossian church.

As an intercessor, you must persevere as you allow the Lord to pray through you His concerns for others. Prayers may be answered not within your urgent framework but according to God's timing. When you intercede for someone, you are to keep praying until you see the need met.

Epaphras labored in his intercession. Prayer for others is hard work; it does not come naturally; it can seem toilsome. But wouldn't you want someone else to labor in prayer on your behalf?

His purpose in intercession was that the Colossians "may stand perfect and fully assured in all the will of God" (Col. 4:12 NASB). The intercessor must make the will of God for others the chief pursuit.

Do you want to be used by God? Then pray for others and watch God work.

I want to be used by You, Lord. I want to faithfully intercede for others, to labor in prayer in their behalf. It doesn't come naturally, so I'm trusting in You to make me an intercessor.

SCRIPTURE READING: Matthew 26:36–44
KEY VERSE: Matthew 26:44

He left them, went away again, and prayed the third time, saying the same words.

In the black-and-white 1950s, one of the most engaging shows on television was *Father Knows Best*. Despite the perils of raising a son and two daughters, the wise father always seemed to have a solution. In the realm of prayer, this principle is at work: our heavenly Father knows best.

When your petitions are mercifully granted—healing for a sick spouse, extra income for a pressing need, a promotion at work—you worship and thank God for His goodness.

When your requests are not granted—a sick mate does not improve, the financial need remains unmet, you are passed over for that promotion—you still worship and thank God for His goodness.

In the first instance that is easy. In the second that is extremely difficult, and you may think, *Why doesn't God come through? What is He trying to do to me? Doesn't He care?*

Your view of God is fogged by the confusion over prayer's primary purpose. Prayer is trusting God to do what He knows is best for your life, not just in the short run but also in the long run.

The character of God is the anchor for prayer. He loves you. He always works for your best. You can always trust Him.

> *You know best, God. Let me rely on Your wisdom when my prayers seem to go unanswered. I know You are always working in my behalf. Teach me to trust.*

SCRIPTURE READING: 1 John 5:14–15
KEY VERSE: Ephesians 5:17

Do not be unwise, but understand what the will of the Lord is.

Charles Finney was one of the foremost evangelists of the nineteenth century. The foundation of his ministry was persevering prayer. In his *Principles of Prayer*, Finney instructed the believer:

> There are three ways in which God's will is revealed to men for their guidance in prayer.
>
> 1. By express promises or predictions in the Bible, that He will give or do certain things.
>
> 2. Sometimes God reveals His will by Providence. When He makes it clear that such and such events are about to take place, it is as much a revelation as if He had written it in His Word.
>
> 3. By His Spirit. When God's people are at a loss (about) what to pray for, (but while also being) agreeable to His will, His Spirit often instructs them.
>
> When there is no particular revelation and Providence leaves it dark and we know not what to pray for as we ought, we are expressly told that the "Spirit also helpeth our infirmities" and "the Spirit itself makes intercession for us with groanings which cannot be uttered."

The Word of God, the providence of God, and the Spirit of God—all are supernatural aids to discern the will of God in prayer.

> *Thank You for Your Word, Your providence, and Your Spirit. Teach me to use these supernatural aids to continually discern Your will, Father.*

The LORD said to Joshua: "Get up! Why do you lie thus on your face?"

The wise man Solomon wrote in Ecclesiastes 3:1: "There is an appointed time for everything" (NASB). Though not included in the list of appropriate seasons that followed, this principle rings just as true: "There is a time to wait—and a time to act."

How do you see the difference? When do you hover over a situation, and when do you launch out?

There are two conditions involved in determining the latter course. If you have done everything you know to discern God's leadership—praying diligently, gathering facts, searching the Word, obtaining good counsel, submitting totally to Jesus' lordship—and if a decision must be made now, then it is time to move forward.

If you want to please God sincerely, you must not worry about the consequences of your decisions. If it is the wrong decision, then He will forgive you and steer you rightly. But when a course must be charted, your confidence, faith, and courage are fully cast on the God who knows the future and has secured your relationship with Him.

Wait on God when you can, but act boldly in faith when you must, entrusting yourself to a faithful God.

Heavenly Father, I need wisdom to know when to wait and when to act. Give me the confidence that You will use my decisions for Your glory. I rest secure in the knowledge that You know the future.

SCRIPTURE READING: Luke 11:1–4

KEY VERSE: Hebrews 4:16

Let us therefore come boldly to the throne of grace, that we may obtain mercy and find grace to help in time of need.

In *The Believer's Guidebook,* Lawrence Richards writes this delightful synopsis on the privilege of coming before our loving Father in personal prayer:

> I've read many books on prayer. Too many of them approach prayer as if it were an obstacle course . . . prayer seems to become a tense, threatening chore.
>
> Our technique must be just right. God, the all-seeing Judge, gives points; and when we fail to clear the hurdles, He is quick to withhold the prize.
>
> What bothers me about such interpretations is that they're hardly honest to God. They distort the vision given in the Bible of a loving, welcoming God.
>
> To understand prayer, we simply need to look up at the character of God. We need to see the loving Father. We need to hear Him invite us to share every need and confess every sin.
>
> Prayer is nothing less than responding to the warm assurance of God's love and accepting His invitation to come to our Father and to share.

If you have received Christ as Savior, you can move freely into God's presence. You are His child, and He wants to talk with you and show you His love.

> *Thank You for the invitation, Lord. I accept! I come into Your presence right now to fellowship with You.*

SCRIPTURE READING: 1 Timothy 2:1–8
KEY VERSE: Philemon 4

I thank my God, making mention of you always in my prayers.

Prayer is a supernatural tool for developing genuine compassion and a burden for the needs of others. We are admonished to pray for all sorts of people—local, state, and national leaders (1 Tim. 2:2); the universal body of Christ, especially those under persecution (Eph. 6:18–20); laborers in God's harvest fields (Matt. 9:38); our personal enemies (Matt. 5:44); and all people, believers and unbelievers alike (1 Tim. 2:1).

That is quite a list, isn't it? If we are honest, most of our time spent in prayer is for our personal requirements, sprinkled in with a pinch of worship and a neighborly request or two for others for good measure.

Laboring in prayer for the welfare of those mentioned does not come naturally, does it? That is why when you begin earnestly and systematically to intercede for others, you find a strange release from your selfish bent. Less time is spent on yourself, but you spend significantly more time praying for the needs of others.

In so doing, prayer becomes the spiritual scalpel that lifts off the stifling layers of self-preoccupation. You are freed to heed Jesus' great command: "Love one another, just as I have loved you" (John 15:12 NASB).

Heavenly Father, expand my focus beyond myself and my needs.
Remove the stifling layers of self-preoccupation from my prayer life.

SCRIPTURE READING: 1 Peter 1:3–11

KEY VERSE: Romans 12:11

Not lagging in diligence, fervent in spirit, serving the Lord.

Like water cutting a channel through rock, spiritual erosion happens slowly but surely. The believer who started out with zeal in adolescence is on the verge of complacency by the mid-thirties. The heart that was once stirred by the Scriptures is now indifferent to them.

Such decline happens so subtly that you are often unaware of its deadly work. It often comes through these almost imperceptible means:

A gradual shift from devotion to performance. Christ commended the church at Ephesus for their ceaseless labor but admonished them for neglecting their "first love" (Rev. 2:4 NASB). Spiritual attrition is inevitable when your passion for Christ becomes secondary to your deeds.

A gradual change from commitment to convenience. Faithfulness in little things is the stuff disciples are made of. When your relationship with Christ is structured to fit into your tidy agenda, spiritual decline sets in. Christ demands your all—both in season and out of season. You will not move on to spiritual maturity if you keep making excuses for why you cannot press on to know God.

A gradual change from repentance to tolerance of sin. As your love for and commitment to Christ wanes, it becomes easier to condone your sins instead of repenting of them. Such sins then establish strongholds in your life and frustrate your growth.

> *Father, I pause right now to examine my life. Is my focus on devotion or performance? Am I more concerned with convenience than commitment? Am I increasingly tolerant of sin?*

SCRIPTURE READING: Ephesians 6:10–18
KEY VERSE: Matthew 14:23

When He had sent the multitudes away, He went up on the mountain by Himself to pray. Now when evening came, He was alone there.

Once you decide to be alone with God, don't be surprised if you have difficulty finding the time. In the middle of a spiritual battle the enemy will do anything to distract you from praying, reading, and studying God's Word.

Because of this, it is necessary to claim the armor of God each morning before you begin your quiet time or daily routine. Taking on the whole armor of God is something you should do on a regular basis. It spiritually prepares you for the enemy's tactics.

The apostle Paul outlined the armor and its function in Ephesians 6. You can use his words as a framework for your prayers. Claiming the armor should never become a ritual. Instead, it is a way to remind yourself that God is with you each and every moment. His covering protects you, and as you learn more about the spiritual tools He provides, you will become more aware of your position in Christ as His beloved child. Learning how to spend time alone with God opens doors of opportunity for spiritual growth.

Many times prayers may be one-way streets with you voicing your needs and never stopping to hear from the One who created you and loves you with His entire being. Getting to know God in a personal way is the most exciting part of life. The One who spoke all of creation into being waits for you. Be still, oh, my heart, and worship the Lord, your God.

Lord, I clothe myself today with Your truth and righteousness. I set my feet to walk in Your ways. I will think Your thoughts and rejoice in Your faithfulness. I will set aside time to fellowship with You.

SCRIPTURE READING: Psalm 119:23, 48, 78, 148
KEY VERSES: Colossians 3:1–3

If then you were raised with Christ, seek those things which are above, where Christ is, sitting at the right hand of God. Set your mind on things above, not on things on the earth. For you died, and your life is hidden with Christ in God.

In *Discipline: The Glad Surrender,* Elisabeth Elliot writes about the requirements of biblical meditation:

We have been discussing making an offering of the body, which is an act of worship . . . offered by mind and heart. The next thing we are to do is to let our minds be remade and our whole nature transformed.

We cannot do this by ourselves. It is the Holy Spirit who must do the work. But we must open our minds to that work, submit to His control, think on the things that matter rather than on the things that come to nothing in the end. Here again we see both the necessity of a sovereign God working in and through us and the responsibility of the disciple himself to adapt to what God wants to do. . . .

In times of prayer and meditation, do not try to think about nothing. "Set your mind," Paul says, not, "Empty your mind." Set it on Christ, not on earthly things. One phrase from God's Word can be taken and repeated quietly, asking that we may be given . . . the spiritual power of wisdom and vision, by which there comes the knowledge of Him.

Make sure the place you select for your quiet time is relatively distraction free. Avoid putting God in a spiritual box. Instead, be open to the newness and joy He brings each day as you enter His throne room with praise.

Father, I enter Your throne room with praise. I bow before You in quietness. Transform my earthly nature as I submit to Your divine control.

SCRIPTURE READING: Psalm 119:97–99

KEY VERSE: Psalm 104:34

May my meditation be sweet to Him;
I will be glad in the LORD.

He won three gold medals in the 1994 Winter Olympics. Johann Olav Koss's remarkable feat was the result of a minimum of six hours of training per day, devotion that even his competitors admired. Koss captured the gold and the hearts of his nation's people, the Norwegians, because he knew that hard work paid dividends. The innumerable hours of solitary rigors would eventually be rewarded.

Meditation is a deficient discipline in most people because they fail to see future benefits. It is viewed in a strangely passive light, though it calls for active engagement of mind and spirit.

Meditation is the training ground for wisdom and insight. The progressive intake of Scripture, combined with sensitivity to the Holy Spirit, renews the mind, priming it for godly decisions in tough matters.

Meditation sifts the heart. Problem areas, sins that perhaps you didn't even know lurked within, are surfaced through the work of the Holy Spirit. This may be painful, but when it is accompanied by true repentance, you are liberated to live a holy, pure life.

Meditation accelerates obedience. God speaks quietly to your heart so that you can obey and reap the rewards.

Listen and let God cull the chaff. Wait patiently and obey His prompting. The rewards are bountiful.

> *I wait before You, O God. Sift my life and cull the chaff. Surface the*
> *sins that I need to confront. Speak to my heart while I am still before*
> *You.*

SCRIPTURE READING: Psalm 63

KEY VERSE: 1 Timothy 4:15

Meditate on these things; give yourself entirely to them, that your progress may be evident to all.

In the clamor of home and job, relationships and tasks, losing your spiritual bearings is easy. You react to the latest and most pressing problem. Your life resembles a crazy quilt pattern, erratically pieced together.

Although it may be the last thing you think about, meditating on the Scriptures is God's way to restore balance to your hectic pace. Mark out a few hours in the evening or weekends, and find a quiet place (your yard, a room in the house, a neighborhood park). Take your Bible, a special book, and a notebook, and tell the Lord you are coming to find His guidance and help.

Make it your objective to listen to God. Be silent before Him. Read the Word slowly and carefully, letting His truth seep into your heart.

Give praise to Him. Sing familiar hymns. Thanksgiving stills the restless soul and focuses your attention on God's power instead of your circumstances. Seek God. He, not a new technique or method, is the answer.

Meditating upon the Scriptures will saturate your mind with His mind, helping you filter your circumstances through His wisdom. It will order your ways and thoughts, renew your vision, and refresh your soul.

> *Filter my circumstances through Your wisdom, O Lord. Order my thoughts and ways, renew my vision, and refresh my soul as I wait before You.*

SCRIPTURE READING: Psalm 19

KEY VERSE: Psalm 19:14

Let the words of my mouth and the meditation of my heart
Be acceptable in Your sight,
O LORD, my strength and my Redeemer.

Any farmer or gardener prefers a soft, steady rain for thirsty crops or plants. Heavy downfalls may appear favorable, but much of the water is wasted, the ground unable to absorb the deluge. However, the soil and rain are synchronized when the precipitation falls at a steady rate.

Meditation is akin to this analogy. Slowly, steadily, and productively, the Word of God is distilled and digested. It is the process of patiently listening, hearing, and waiting upon God. However, meditation can be hindered for two significant reasons:

First, quiet time versus busy time. You are harried and hurried. Your pace is fast, even on a slow day. But meditation requires time, still time where the voices of duty and responsibility are deliberately muted.

Second, quality versus quantity. Many Christians have a reading schedule that takes them from Genesis to Revelation in a year. This is a profitable exercise, but its benefits can be negated if the heart isn't set on digesting meaningful portions. Reading shorter passages of Scripture can facilitate biblical meditation, and often God will focus your attention on one verse.

Customize your schedule to find an appropriate quiet time that allows you to maximize your investment.

My heart is thirsty, O Lord. I need quality time with You today.
Slowly, steadily, and productively, let Your Word do its work.

SCRIPTURE READING: Luke 24:44–49
KEY VERSE: 2 Timothy 2:7

Consider what I say, and may the Lord give you understanding in all things.

Have you ever encountered a tense situation and surprised yourself with an out-of-character reaction? One way to prevent such inconsistency is through the biblical practice of meditation. When you diligently and regularly cultivate a lifestyle of biblical meditation, you store a wealth of God's wisdom and God's truth.

Since the Source of the Scriptures is Jehovah God, you need His help to allow the Word of God to penetrate your heart: "Then He opened their minds to understand the Scriptures" (Luke 24:45 NASB). To fully comprehend God's perspective, you must ponder and weigh the content of His Scriptures, asking God to speak to your innermost being. The Lord will give you understanding in "everything" (2 Tim. 2:7 NASB).

Then when a crisis arrives, your inner person is ready for the unexpected. The words of your mouth and the deeds of your hands will flow from your heart, which has been nourished in and guarded by God, with wisdom from the Helper, the Holy Spirit, who "will teach you all things, and bring to your remembrance all that I said to you" (John 14:26 NASB).

Open my mind to receive Your Word, Lord. Speak to my innermost being. Give me understanding in everything. Strengthen my inner person, and prepare me for the unexpected.

Only be strong and very courageous, that you may observe to do according to all the law which Moses My servant commanded you; do not turn from it to the right hand or to the left, that you may prosper wherever you go. This Book of the Law shall not depart from your mouth, but you shall meditate in it day and night, that you may observe to do according to all that is written in it. For then you will make your way prosperous, and then you will have good success.

The challenges of life come to us by many avenues—the death of a loved one, a new job, financial changes, the birth of a child. With every challenge, God is preparing us for the future.

Joshua faced a life-changing challenge when chosen to lead the nation of Israel into the promised land. Years of training had seen Joshua grow into a finely tuned warrior. But he was accustomed to the feel of a javelin in his hand, not the rod of leadership.

God told Joshua on three separate occasions how to handle the challenge placed before him. His message to Joshua is well summarized in these verses: "Be strong and very courageous. . . . This book of the law shall not depart from your mouth, but you shall meditate on it day and night, so that you may be careful to do according to all that is written in it; for then you will make your way prosperous, and then you will have success" (Josh. 1:7–8 NASB).

Was God questioning Joshua's ability? No. He knew that with every challenge comes the possibility of falling to doubts and fears. Joshua enjoyed success in the midst of the challenge by recalling the words of God, binding them to his heart, and determining to walk in the ways of God. Begin your day with God's Word. He will lead you through every challenge just as He did Joshua.

Heavenly Father, bring Your words to my remembrance as I face the challenges of this day. Help me to continually meditate upon Your promises.

SCRIPTURE READING: Hebrews 4:12–16
KEY VERSE: Hebrews 4:12

The word of God is living and powerful, and sharper than any two-edged sword, piercing even to the division of soul and spirit, and of joints and marrow, and is a discerner of the thoughts and intents of the heart.

Oscar Wilde's classic novel *The Portrait of Dorian Gray* is a chilling exploration of what happens when a person refuses to deal with sin inside the heart. In this fantasy tale, the handsome character Dorian commissions a portrait of himself that will capture his good looks. He is so captivated by this picture that he makes a wish. He wants to stay young forever and let the picture grow old in his place.

Dorian gets his wish and then uses his youth and attractiveness to fulfill his desires. His motives are self-seeking, vain, and greedy in everything he does. As the years pass, Dorian periodically checks the picture in his back room.

Not only is the face in the picture growing old; it is becoming gnarled and vicious. Dorian is so ashamed that he covers the picture and refuses to let anyone look at it. The picture has become a horrifying portrait of his soul!

Even though Oscar Wilde did not profess to be a Christian, he understood the effects of sin run rampant. Dorian's picture was his "sin revealer," even as God's Word is the instrument of conviction in your life.

When you meditate on Scripture and feel the tug of His Word on your heart, pay attention. God is urging you to confess your sin and experience the renewing power of forgiveness in Christ.

Search me, O Lord. Reveal my hidden faults and sins. Convict me, then renew me through the power of forgiveness in Jesus.

SCRIPTURE READING: Revelation 2:1–7
KEY VERSES: Luke 10:41–42

Jesus answered and said to her, "Martha, Martha, you are worried and troubled about many things. But one thing is needed, and Mary has chosen that good part, which will not be taken away from her."

A boat adrift on the high seas is in a dangerous state—vulnerable to uncertain changes in currents and winds. In a similar manner Christians who have drifted from a loyal, loving, intimate relationship with Jesus Christ are in danger of being swept into trivial pursuits. Christ saved us for Himself. He wants to draw us into His exciting fellowship and fit us into His plans.

Somehow on our journeys we lose sight of Him, focusing instead on our spiritual development. We begin to operate on scattered feelings or changing circumstances. Before long, our love affair with the Master has cooled. Our passion is diminished by unfulfilled expectations, tiresome labor, and the general weariness of life.

The secret of the burning heart is a never-wavering focus on the person of the Lord Jesus Christ. Not Christian work. Not Christian growth.

Drifting is minimized when you constantly seek to know Jesus—His ways, His love, His Word. Devotion's fires are fueled by trusting the Lord to work through you and then marveling at His guidance and enabling.

Christ is all! Set your heart ablaze and your paths straight by narrowing your focus on Jesus—His attributes, His character, His care, His plans, His sufficiency for all of life.

I don't want to drift from You, Father. Narrow my focus to Jesus alone. Renew my passion. Set my heart ablaze!

SCRIPTURE READING: Revelation 3:1–6
KEY VERSE: Revelation 3:12

*He who overcomes, I will make him a pillar in the temple of My God, and
he shall go out no more. I will write on him the name of My God and the
name of the city of My God, the New Jerusalem, which comes down out of
heaven from My God. And I will write on him My new name.*

A small sandbar off the coast of Tybee Island, Georgia, emerges during extremely low tides. Area natives love to venture out to it because it is a haven for sand dollars and small shells.

However, there is a trick in navigating the walk. The sandbar is located at the mouth of an inland river, and returning high tides can quickly overtake and strand inexperienced people. What appears to be a short journey back to shore can quickly turn into a dangerous venture.

Beachcombers often start back to shore with a certain destination in view. But with little warning, ankle-deep water soon becomes knee deep and then chest deep. Before they know it, they are drifting off course into dangerous waters.

The same thing happens to people when they are entangled in matters that hinder their devotion to God. Those who fall prey to spiritual drifting never see it coming. They think, *I'm just a little off course. I can get back.* But before they know it, they have been swept away by an invading sin or temptation.

Make it your goal to stay on course with God. Ask Him to order your daily steps and keep the devotion of your heart turned toward Him.

*Order my daily steps. Let the devotion of my heart be turned toward
You, Father. I don't want to drift into dangerous waters. Keep me on
course.*

March

THEME: The Valley Gate

REPRESENTING: Suffering, testing, and trials

KEY VERSE: Romans 8:18

I consider that the sufferings of this present time are not worthy to be compared with the glory which shall be revealed in us.

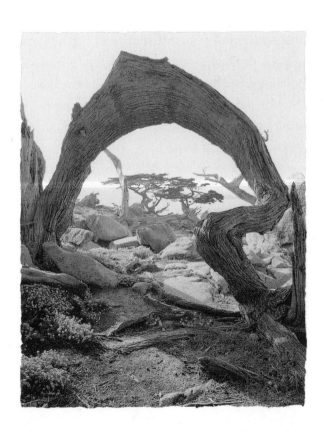

SCRIPTURE READING: Psalm 77
KEY VERSE: Isaiah 43:2

When you pass through the waters, I will be with you;
And through the rivers, they shall not overflow you.
When you walk through the fire, you shall not be burned,
Nor shall the flame scorch you.

Your spiritual moorings are tested severely when adversity's ill winds reach their zenith. It is easy to lose heart, to lose sight of God. Your raw, exposed emotions can take over, blurring your focus and weakening your endurance.

In these times you must embrace these crucial truths:

You must remember God's past deliverances. God's prior working in your life can be obscured in the storm. But in a moment of deliberate concentration, you need to remind yourself that God has delivered you before and He can do it again. David found faith to duel with Goliath by recalling how God had delivered him from the lion and the bear (1 Sam. 17:37).

You must stake your claim on God's promises. God cannot lie; His Word is certain. In adversity you can rely on the promises of Scripture to sustain you and uphold you (Num. 23:19).

You must count on God's unfailing love. God's loving-kindness—His gracious presence, power, and purpose—is constantly at work on your behalf. God will not fail you. What He has begun in your life, He will complete (Phil. 1:6).

Rely on these truths and your faith will stand firm until the storm subsides.

Father, thank You for the times You delivered me in the past. I stake
my claims upon Your promises today. I count on Your unfailing love to
see me through.

SCRIPTURE READING: Psalm 57

KEY VERSE: Matthew 27:46

About the ninth hour Jesus cried out with a loud voice, saying, "Eli, Eli, lama sabachthani?" that is, "My God, My God, why have You forsaken Me?"

"Why?" That is the universal response to adversity.

"Why did our child die?"

"Why did our business fail?"

"Why did our son reject us?"

Jesus, the all-knowing One, asked *why* as the darkness of separation from His Father reached its black climax.

David asked *why* as he sat in a wilderness exile imposed by treacherous King Saul (Ps. 57).

Moses asked *why* as millions of Hebrews clamored for food (Num. 11:11).

Jeremiah asked *why* as he mourned the destruction of Jerusalem (Lam. 5:20).

In *On Asking God Why*, Elisabeth Elliot describes the proper context in which we should echo the same probing cry when suffering buffets and baffles us:

> I seek the lessons God wants to teach me, and that means I ask why. There are those who insist that it is a very bad thing to question God. To them, "why?" is a rude question.
>
> That depends, I believe, on whether it is an honest search, in faith, for His meaning, or whether it is a challenge of unbelief and rebellion.

You may ask, but ask rightly. For God is the Potter, and you are the clay.

> *I often ask it, Lord: Why? Thank You for the times You answer and I learn from it. Help me accept the times when there seems to be no answer.*

SCRIPTURE READING: Job 42:1–6
KEY VERSE: Job 42:5

I have heard of You by the hearing of the ear,
But now my eye sees You.

Occasionally a *why* in adversity is met with a swift response from God. Periodically a *why* is discerned much later than the request.

But on most occasions, God does not directly give explanations for adversity. We live in a fallen world. We and creation suffer from the consequences of sin, initiated by human rebellion in the Garden.

To advance in your adversity, you must not dwell or linger too long on *why* but shift your focus to *who*—the person of Jesus Christ.

R. C. Sproul, in *Surprised by Suffering,* spoke of Job's situation:

Job cried out for God to answer his questions. He desperately wanted to know why he was called upon to endure so much suffering. Finally, God answered him out of the whirlwind. But the answer was not what Job expected.

God refused to grant Job a detailed explanation of His reasons for the affliction. The secret counsel of God was not disclosed to Job.

Ultimately, the only answer God gave to Job was a revelation of Himself. It was as if God said to him, "Job, I am your answer."

Real, solid growth can occur in difficult circumstances when you bow before God and entrust yourself and your problems to Him without demanding a solution.

Heavenly Father, let me shift my focus from demanding why to recognizing who. You are my Answer.

SCRIPTURE READING: 1 Peter 5:9–11

KEY VERSE: 2 Timothy 2:12

If we endure,
We shall also reign with Him.
If we deny Him,
He also will deny us.

We go out of our way to avoid suffering. We want winter homes in Florida and summer homes in Maine. We'll do all we can, humanly speaking, to keep in our comfort zone.

But if suffering is not desirable, does that also mean it cannot be profitable? Does the pain have no purpose or meaning? Since "God causes all things to work together for good" (Rom. 8:28 NASB), suffering must have some positive consequences.

For one, it drives you deeper to the heart of God. Your ultimate purpose should be not to achieve pleasure or happiness but to know Christ and become like Him. Real trouble facilitates that goal, driving you closer to Him.

For another, suffering causes You to receive more of God's marvelous, merciful grace. You think you are strong, but suffering reveals your weaknesses. That's when you discover the inexhaustible resources of God. He gives you all you need to endure. His strength replaces yours.

Still another, you develop a base of reality and compassion with which you can minister to and love others. The former or present cancer sufferer best helps another cancer patient.

Suffering is never desirable. But your sovereign, loving God can make it profitable.

I must be honest, Lord. I don't like suffering. Help me realize that trouble drives me closer to You. As my weaknesses surface, reveal to me Your inexhaustible resources.

SCRIPTURE READING: Psalm 138

KEY VERSE: John 16:32

Indeed the hour is coming, yes, has now come, that you will be scattered, each to his own, and will leave Me alone. And yet I am not alone, because the Father is with Me.

When Jesus saw that His disciples truly understood who He was, He made a startling statement. It was one they were not prepared to hear: "Behold, an hour is coming, and has already come, for you to be scattered, each to his own home, and to leave Me alone; and yet I am not alone, because the Father is with Me" (John 16:32 NASB).

God's plan for redemption did not include lifting the disciples out of their immediate surroundings. The pain and stress of facing life as children of God would never deliver them from the earthly reality of trouble. Jesus made that clear when He said, "In this world you will have trouble" (John 16:33 NIV).

Soon after He said those words, the agony of the Cross was His to bear. How did He withstand such tribulation? Christ's life was anchored in the plan of the Father, not in the things of the world. Jesus was not worried about people and their false accusations, nor was He overwhelmed by trials or earthly tribulations. He had overcome the world.

What is His personal word to you when trials come without warning? "These things I [share with] you, that in Me you may have [a] peace [that passes all human understanding]. In the world you have tribulation, but take courage; I have overcome the world" (John 16:33 AMPLIFIED).

Jesus, You overcame the world, and You live in me. I may have tribulation, but through Your power I will overcome!

SCRIPTURE READING: 2 Corinthians 1:3–7
KEY VERSE: 2 Corinthians 1:5

For as the sufferings of Christ abound in us, so our consolation also abounds through Christ.

God stooped down from the heavens to rescue you from sin, and He continues to extend His hand to you each day to soothe your damaged emotions, your frayed nerves, your broken dreams, your heartaches.

"But He seems so distant, so remote, so detached at times," you say. Although you may feel this way, it is not the truth. God said that He will not "in any way fail you nor give you up nor leave you without support. [I will] not, [I will] not, [I will] not in any degree leave you helpless, nor forsake nor let [you] down, [relax My hold on you].—Assuredly not!" (Heb. 13:5 AMPLIFIED).

What a promise! And God certainly keeps His word. He performs this divine pledge through the person of the Holy Spirit. The Holy Spirit is God inside you. He is called the *Comforter,* meaning "one called alongside to help and aid."

When you are down, the Holy Spirit knows exactly how to encourage you. When you are grieving, the Holy Spirit knows the balance between shedding tears of grief and gently wiping them from your cheeks. He is at work to comfort you through every trial and adversity.

I'm not alone, Lord. You are right here with me in the midst of my trouble. Soothe my damaged emotions. Touch my frayed nerves. Mend my broken dreams, and heal my heartaches.

SCRIPTURE READING: 1 Peter 4:12–16
KEY VERSE: John 16:33

These things I have spoken to you, that in Me you may have peace. In the world you will have tribulation; but be of good cheer, I have overcome the world.

"Surprise!"

A room full of friends have gathered to celebrate your birthday. You are caught off guard; you never expected it.

Christians easily become entrenched in daily routines. Then when trials come, we are all too often bewildered by the sudden interruption. The Scriptures tell us in today's passage that we should never be astonished at tribulation. Travail should never stagger us. We live in a hostile, sinful, decaying world. There are sun and drought, rain and floods, health and disease, food and famine.

We have an adversary, the devil, who is called "the ruler of this world" (John 12:31 NASB). At present, God allows the devil's destructive tactics to continue—aimed at humankind. Together, the power of sin and Satan warp our character and behavior, inciting all manner of evil—jealousy, murder, hatred, greed, slander.

Jesus said, "In the world you have tribulation" (John 16:33 NASB). If you are suffering, you may be confused, but don't be surprised.

Too often I am bewildered by my trials, Lord. Help me not to be surprised by suffering but to know that when it comes, You are right there with me in the midst of it.

SCRIPTURE READING: Job 1–2
KEY VERSE: Job 2:10

He said to her, "You speak as one of the foolish women speaks. Shall we indeed accept good from God, and shall we not accept adversity?" In all this Job did not sin with his lips.

The reason many of us are surprised by trials is that we have a subconsciously held notion that suffering can somehow bypass us. In *When Life Isn't Fair*, Dr. Dwight Carlson and Susan Carlson Wood relate this concept:

This assumption that if you live a good life you will be granted immunity from life's difficulties permeates our society. So many people proceed blindly until tragedy strikes, thinking they are immune from disaster because they are good.

I have often noticed that many Christians hold a non-verbalized, unconscious belief that a dedicated follower of Christ should be immune to misfortunes. . . . This unconscious belief surfaces quickly when misfortune strikes; the person becomes bitter and may even reject God. But God never promised that He would insulate you *from* misfortune. God may intervene at His sovereign choosing—but it is not our divine right to demand His intervention.

Your response to tribulation and its effects can be vastly different when you understand the character of God and His purposes.

I have not always understood when problems came, dear Lord. Help me comprehend Your character and purposes, then let me respond properly to suffering.

SCRIPTURE READING: Job 23:8–10

KEY VERSE: Psalm 66:12

You have caused men to ride over our heads;
We went through fire and through water;
But You brought us out to rich fulfillment.

You can handle adversity only when you understand several essential truths about God:

God is not the author of evil. God uses adversity to accomplish His purposes, but He does not originate evil.

God is sovereign over all adversity. He can use any pain to honor Him and benefit you because He fits all events—good and bad—into His plan for you. Margaret Clarkson writes in *Destined for Glory:* "We must recognize with absolute certainty that God is in control of His universe. He is sovereign over evil, sin, death. . . . (Satan) may hurt, but he cannot ultimately harm us."

God is trustworthy. Your pain is not outside His wisdom, love, and power; and He has promised never to fail you or forsake you (Heb. 13:5).

Understanding these truths, you must decide to trust God in your times of affliction. Margaret Clarkson writes further in *Grace Grows Best in Winter:* "We set ourselves to believe in the overruling goodness, providence, and sovereignty of God and refuse to turn aside—no matter what may come, no matter how we feel."

> *God, You are not the author of evil. You are sovereign over the enemy.*
> *You are trustworthy. I declare Your goodness and refuse to turn*
> *aside—no matter what!*

SCRIPTURE READING: Psalm 139:7–12
KEY VERSE: Proverbs 4:18

The path of the just is like the shining sun,
That shines ever brighter unto the perfect day.

The *Canadian Home* journal carried this exquisite poem on the treasures of darkness:

The shuttles of His purpose move to carry
   out His own design;
Seek not too soon to disapprove His work,
   nor yet assign;
Dark motives, when, with silent tread,
You view some somber fold;
For lo, within each darker thread
There twines a thread of gold.
Spin cheerfully,
Not tearfully,
He knows the way you plod;
Spin carefully,
Spin prayerfully,
But leave the thread with God.

God weaves the design of His purposes into your life like an intricate rug, even in times of darkness. Viewed in isolation, the stressful times appear ugly and somber. Yet intertwined with the whole of your existence, they take on new meaning and beauty.

As in all things for the believer, God uses bleak times to conform you to the image of the Lord Jesus Christ. God will work your darkness—disease, loneliness, inferiority, pain, divorce—into His masterpiece as you place your times into His skillful hands (Ps. 31:15).

Help me spin the threads of my life cheerfully, not tearfully. Help me
spin carefully and prayerfully—but leave the completed pattern to
You, dear Lord.

SCRIPTURE READING: Titus 3:3–8
KEY VERSE: Isaiah 40:31

> *But those who wait on the LORD*
> *Shall renew their strength;*
> *They shall mount up with wings like eagles,*
> *They shall run and not be weary,*
> *They shall walk and not faint.*

The story is told of an eaglet that fell from his mountain nest into a wooded valley. There he discovered a roving flock of wild turkeys, and since they appeared somewhat like him, he joined them.

He ate like the turkeys, fed like them, and eventually thought like his adopted family. Occasionally he saw a solitary eagle fly majestically overhead and felt a certain kindred spirit. But, of course, turkeys don't fly very high.

Then one memorable evening as he returned to his roost, a golden eagle landed nearby. Seeing the odd behavior of a member of his own species, the golden eagle explained to him that he, too, was a proud eagle and had no business dwelling with turkeys. The youngster decided to trust the elder eagle's advice, so he spread his wings and ascended into the heavens.

Many Christians have been deceived by Satan into acting like miserable, wretched sinners because they do not realize what their identity is in Christ. The truth is this: you are a redeemed, saved, sanctified, secure child of the Father. You are a saint, a called-out one. Believe it, act upon it, and soar above your problems into the abundant life promised by Christ to His people.

> *Thank You, dear Lord, that You are working in my life despite my*
> *problems. May Your power enable me to mount up with wings as an*
> *eagle and soar above the storm.*

DARKNESS DOES NOT HINDER GOD

SCRIPTURE READING: Psalm 143:1–12

KEY VERSE: Psalm 143:8

Cause me to hear Your lovingkindness in the morning,
For in You do I trust;
Cause me to know the way in which I should walk,
For I lift up my soul to You.

A thousand miles away from his home in the Louisiana bayous, the young hunter navigates unfamiliar terrain in the heart of the Rockies. As long as he follows his mountain-born hunting guide, he is safe. The knowledge and skill of his handpicked guide are his key to success. Just a few minutes of wandering, however, and the beautiful landscape could become his deadly adversary.

As a follower of Christ you are certain to encounter seasons of darkness and difficulty—whether it is in your home, your work, your relationships, your finances, or your emotional life. These times can be confusing: God seems distant; His will remains hidden; His voice is quiet; His presence appears dim.

You can panic; you can become frustrated; you can be disillusioned and disappointed; you can stagger and stumble. In your darkness, however, you must remember that your Guide, Christ Jesus, is the One who navigates your way.

As you cling to Him—trusting Him to guide you—and as you confess your dependence on Him, you learn to be confident in His loving care. Christ knows where you are today and where He will lead you tomorrow. The darkness cannot hinder Him.

Heavenly Father, You know where I am today. You know where You
will lead me tomorrow. Help me trust You despite the darkness.

SCRIPTURE READING: Hebrews 11:23–29

KEY VERSE: 2 Corinthians 4:17

Our light affliction, which is but for a moment, is working for us a far more exceeding and eternal weight of glory.

The sign next to a new condominium development reads: "For trouble-free living . . ." That certainly would be nice if it were true, but we all know that trials in this life are just as certain as death and taxes.

Physical, emotional, financial, or moral monsoons can strike hard at your foundation of faith in Christ. When (not if) the storms come, you do well to look to Moses' example of standing strong in the face of affliction. Moses withstood the intense pressure of both exile and leadership by a fixed focus of faith on God: "For he was looking to the reward" (Heb. 11:26 NASB).

Your troubles are guaranteed to cease in heaven. Until that time, your trials may continue on earth, but the rewards of faith, despite the circumstances, can be enjoyed in this life.

The peace that comes from knowing God is in control, the joy that flows from loving Him, and the strength that springs from His presence sustain you in your trouble: "For he endured, as seeing Him who is unseen" (Heb. 11:27 NASB). In the midst of your affliction, regardless of its nature, Christ is with you. He will never leave you or forsake you.

Spiritual monsoons are striking at my foundation, Lord, and I long to stand strong in the face of adversity. I know You are in control. Sustain me in my trouble.

SCRIPTURE READING: 2 Corinthians 1:3–11

KEY VERSE: Isaiah 51:12

I, even I, am He who comforts you.
Who are you that you should be afraid
Of a man who will die,
And of the son of a man who will be made like grass?

The God of all comfort can lovingly touch all heartache, despair, darkness, pain, evil, and desperation. Your tribulations are severe. Your path is hard. Your conditions are bleak. Your outlook is dim. But the God of all comfort—the God who Himself has suffered indescribably at the hands of people—will aid you, encourage you, strengthen you, and guide you.

Because Christ has experienced the ridicule and rejection of people and now stands as the Great High Priest, the throne of grace beckons every believer.

In the heat of the fight—the Light of Life is with you.

In the midst of the storm—the Prince of Peace is your steadfast guide.

In the bottom of the pit—the Chief Cornerstone is your rock.

If you hurt, let the healing love of Jesus Christ sustain you. He longs to comfort and encourage you with His presence, His promises, His people, and His power.

The God of all comfort will not let you go over the edge or sink beneath the mire. He will come instantly to your aid as you call on His name.

One day He will use you to personally carry His comfort to the ailing heart of another—transforming your trouble into His healing balm.

Lord, thank You that in the heat of the fight, Your Light is with me.
Thank You that in the midst of the storm, the Prince of Peace is my
guide. In the bottom of the pit, O God, the Chief Cornerstone is my
rock.

SCRIPTURE READING: 2 Corinthians 4:7–15

KEY VERSE: Isaiah 58:11

> *The LORD will guide you continually,*
> *And satisfy your soul in drought,*
> *And strengthen your bones;*
> *You shall be like a watered garden,*
> *And like a spring of water, whose waters do not fail.*

Perplexity. One dictionary defines it as a "puzzled condition; uncertainty as to what to think or do; a tangled, involved, or confused condition."

We have all been there—financial bloodbaths, emotional trauma, spiritual wrestling. The apostle Paul was familiar with perplexity. His storms were unrelenting.

The Greek word Paul used for "perplexed" in his letter to the Corinthians was *exaporeo*. *Poreo* means "a pathway." When Paul added the letter *a* (alpha) in front of the word, it became "no way." When combined with the prefix *ex*, Paul's term became "absolutely no way out."

Have you felt that way? Does it describe your current conditions?

If so, take heart. Even though it appeared to Paul as if there was no way out at times, he never despaired, never lost hope. He never walked out on his divine calling as Christ's ambassador to the Gentiles.

Why? Because he understood that Jesus Christ was his constant Companion in all of his struggles. Jesus would never fail him. Jesus would never abandon him. Jesus would never quit on him.

When you have Jesus, you have the Way to guide you although there seems to be absolutely no way out.

> *I am perplexed and I don't know what to do, Lord, but You do! My pathway seems blocked, but You are the Way. So show me!*

SCRIPTURE READING: Hebrews 13:5–9

KEY VERSE: Psalm 57:1

Be merciful to me, O God, be merciful to me!
For my soul trusts in You;
And in the shadow of Your wings I will make my refuge,
Until these calamities have passed by.

When the winds of adversity whip up swirling whitecaps of stress, you can rely on several calming biblical truths to anchor your inner person.

First, recall God's activity in the lives of His people (and yours) in the past: "Remember those who led you. . . . Imitate their faith" (Heb. 13:7 NASB). The lives of Abraham, Moses, Joshua, David, Daniel, Peter, and Paul are illustrations of God's dealing with men. Examine His methods. Investigate their response.

Second, count on God's fixed, unfluctuating character: "Jesus Christ is the same" (Heb. 13:8 NASB). God rewards your faith as He did Abraham's, your obedience as He did Joshua's, your commitment as He did Daniel's, your repentance as He did David's. You can depend on God to act consistently with the revelation of Himself through His Word.

Third, magnify the power of God's grace: "It is good for the heart to be strengthened by grace" (Heb. 13:9 NASB). Grace works every time. Grace is His supernatural provision for every need, every problem, every circumstance. Grace overwhelms every obstacle, overflows every failure, overcomes every dilemma.

> *Heavenly Father, give me the grace that overwhelms every obstacle,*
> *overflows every failure, and overcomes each dilemma. I rest in the*
> *assurance that Your grace works every time.*

SCRIPTURE READING: Psalm 18:29–33
KEY VERSE: Habakkuk 3:19

The LORD God is my strength;
He will make my feet like deer's feet,
And He will make me walk on my high hills.

The Chinese character for *crisis* and *opportunity* is identical. Literally translated, it reads, "Crisis is an opportunity riding the dangerous winds."

When crises arise, and they do so quite frequently, they appear foreboding—a pink slip at work; a somber look on the face of your physician after seeing test results; an unexpected call with the sad news of a family death.

Although you cannot diminish their gravity (the Bible never ignores or attempts to explain away pain), you can take realistic stock of your dilemma and then turn to the ultimate Realist, Jesus Christ.

The danger in facing life's crises is withdrawing into the valley of despair or seeking to surmount it with feeble self-resolve. Both tactics will end in ruin.

The opportunity is to trust God to make your feet as "deer's feet" so that through Him, you may see God at work in your problems. Faith in God and His care for you will stabilize your footing and give you a confident grip in His ability.

As God strengthens and equips you, you can ride on the divine winds of faith that help you seize the opportunity for faith in your crises and give you renewed hope in God's active presence in your life.

Dear Lord, stabilize my spiritual footing. I do not want to withdraw
to the valley of despair, and I cannot survive through self-resolve.
Enable me to ride the divine winds of faith in the midst of my storms.

SCRIPTURE READING: Psalm 46:1–3
KEY VERSE: Psalm 54:7

He has delivered me out of all trouble;
And my eye has seen its desire upon my enemies.

You have a flight from Boston to Charlotte. Inclement weather, rain, and clouds shroud the flight path. Is the flight canceled? Rarely. Today's aircraft are fully equipped to fly in harsh climatic conditions.

It is likewise important to realize that God has fitted you to navigate through turbulent times. Just as the pilot's confidence is in the instruments, so must your reliance be on God, not yourself.

Your foremost guide in rough times is God's Word. It is always a lamp unto your feet, especially when darkness is at its deepest.

If you are in tempestuous circumstances, read His Word voraciously, cling to specific promises tenaciously, and anticipate His gracious response.

You can also count on the unerring help of the Holy Spirit who lives in you. As the third person of the Trinity, He is unaffected by emotional, spiritual, financial, or psychological tumult.

He will stabilize you through His divine assistance, upright you when you fall, and constantly gird you through His unfailing strength and love.

God is the Sustainer of your soul. He will see you through when you cannot see at all.

Holy Spirit, You are unaffected by the emotional, spiritual, financial,
or psychological tumult that I may face today. See me through when I
cannot see at all.

SCRIPTURE READING: Psalm 91

KEY VERSE: Psalm 91:2

I will say of the LORD, "He is my refuge and my fortress;
My God, in Him I will trust."

"When the going gets tough, the tough get going" may be an inspiring motto on a gymnasium wall, but it is not applicable for the believer who encounters difficulty. God's promises are your strength in your weakness. If you rely on your cleverness, your inventiveness, your moral fiber, your abilities, you will never discover the amazing power of God.

The strong despise the weak, but God's strength is specifically designed for the feeble in spirit, the small in faith, the little in stamina. When you fall on His grace, exhausted and spent, you are revived. You are renewed. You ride on His wings and are borne up by His divine drafts.

God's promises are your hope as you wait on Him. Waiting on God does not mean being idle. It is active, daily obedience in the things you know to do with supreme confidence in His perfect, sovereign answer.

Waiting on God means you know that He is at work when all appears silent and frozen. In His time, in His way, He will meet your needs and bring honor to His name.

Admit your helplessness. In your weariness, cast your burdens on Him. Remember, nothing is too difficult for Him.

You are my strength, O Lord. When I am weak, You are strong. When
I am exhausted, You revive and renew me. I cast my burdens on You,
knowing nothing is too difficult for You!

SCRIPTURE READING: Philippians 1:12–18
KEY VERSE: 1 Peter 4:19

Let those who suffer according to the will of God commit their souls to Him in doing good, as to a faithful Creator.

The circumstances for a Russian inmate were bleak. Incarceration in a Soviet prison was miserable enough. The cold weather, the harsh treatment, the loneliness, and isolation made survival the chief object. Added to his woe was the ravage of cancer.

In the midst of this anguish, the prison physician, Dr. Boris Kornfield, stood in sharp relief. The doctor was a Christian who treated the inmate with kindness and shared his faith regularly. After reporting the theft of food from a patient by another prisoner, the physician was brutally killed while sleeping.

The inmate whom the doctor treated survived his bout with cancer and his prison sentence. So taken was he, however, with Dr. Kornfield's faith, that he embraced Christ as his Savior. His name is Aleksandr Solzhenitsyn, the famous Russian author whose literary works are internationally acclaimed.

Your circumstances may be as destitute as Solzenitsyn's; they may be much less severe. But the same God who worked in a Stalinist prison camp to save an indigent Russian prisoner is at work in your problems. Surrender to His care and trust Him for the outcome. He will never disappoint you.

Lord, help me realize You are at work in my problems. I surrender to Your care. I trust You for the outcome, knowing You will never disappoint me.

SCRIPTURE READING: James 5:1–11

KEY VERSE: Job 1:22

In all this Job did not sin nor charge God with wrong.

The leader of an air force tactical unit commented on the battlefield readiness of the enemy force. His commander later repudiated his remarks: "He only knows a part of what is happening. He does not see the big picture like I do."

Seeing the "big picture" is crucial if you are to live above your circumstances. Focusing on parts alone, mainly the circumstances at hand, will confuse and discourage you.

God's big picture is this: He is always at work in everything to conform you to Christ's image. God uses both blissful and dismal circumstances to accomplish that task, though you always prefer the former.

When you were saved, Christ came to indwell you so that He could live through you. As He does, you become like Him in character, thought, and deed. When your circumstances press you toward Christ, when they push you to depend on Him, the big picture is being drawn.

Never lose sight of God's sovereign purpose of molding you to Christ's image. It is what life is really about, both now and for eternity.

Ask God to help you keep your focus on Him and His purpose in your difficulty. He is quietly but firmly at work on His masterpiece—Christ formed in you.

Help me see the big picture, Father. Keep my focus on Your sovereign purpose of molding me into Christ's image. Let every circumstance press me toward You.

SCRIPTURE READING: Romans 8:26–30

KEY VERSE: Romans 8:28

We know that all things work together for good to those who love God, to those who are the called according to His purpose.

Before modernization and machines, the techniques of furniture craftsmen were simple but efficient. For example, to bend pieces of wood for chairs, they cut the wood while still green, bent the pieces around an object and tied them together, often with grapevines, or placed them in a crude mold.

There is a similar scenario in God's exercise of sovereignty, particularly as it relates to affliction. The craftsmen did not haphazardly misshape the wood. They had a purpose, a finished product, in mind.

Likewise, God never exercises His sovereignty capriciously. He is never the author of evil, but always uses the vile and the virtuous for His ultimate design—to conform men and women to the image of Jesus Christ.

This is what He died for, to redeem us from sin's curse—death—and work unceasingly in our souls to restore us to our original image—His image—stamped in the Garden and distorted by sin.

As you turn to God and cry out to Him in your affliction, the providence of God is mysteriously at work, accomplishing His intent. Absolutely nothing can thwart that purpose when your heart is bent toward Him. The pressures of life, severe as they may be, drive you only deeper into His divine mold.

> *O Master Builder, You are bending me and shaping me. You have a purpose—a finished product in mind. Help me conform to the divine mold.*

I cried to the LORD with my voice,
And He heard me from His holy hill. Selah

We like our thermostats set on seventy-two degrees and the wind always at our backs. In other words, we enjoy a level path, sustained contentment, and favorable conditions.

Adversity disrupts our controlled environment. We rise and fall on the doctor's reports, sink and soar on the response to our résumés.

Affliction barges into our ordered world, overturning our carefully tailored plans. But the intrusion of difficulty cultivates a ripe climate for spiritual growth.

When bad things happen, we cry out to God. The Psalms in particular are redundant with pleas and petitions for God's help.

Crying out to God admits our helplessness and weakness, and confesses our dependence on Him. As nothing else does, adversity causes us to realize our need for Christ.

In turning to God for help, we also learn to listen. Spiritual ears that were dull in contentment and ease become suddenly sensitized to God's Word in a crisis. The Scriptures are personalized to our individual needs.

Are you in a trial? Pour out your heart to God and listen to His encouragement. Nothing is impossible for Him.

Dear Lord, when trouble comes, let my first response be to cry out to
You. I confess my dependence on You. I need Your help!

SCRIPTURE READING: Psalm 139:1–6
KEY VERSE: Psalm 139:1

O LORD, You have searched me and known me.

Is peace possible in bad times? Can God truly give the peace that passes understanding in the cancer ward, the bankruptcy court, the funeral home?

Peace is possible only when you accept your adversity. In acceptance there is peace—genuine, deep-seated security. You can experience God's peace and accept your hardships when you realize that your problems are allowed by God to accomplish His purposes in your life.

Satan had to ask God's permission to attack and destroy Job's family and possessions. God placed a limit on Satan's activity, refusing to allow the devil to kill Job (Job 2:6).

What happens to you is not outside God's power. It is not outside His wisdom. It is not outside His love. Evil may seem to reign, but God overrules evil for His purposes.

Acceptance is not resignation. It is not denial. It is not passivity. It is conscious awareness that your pain, though not authored by God, has been filtered through His sovereignty and providence and will conform you to Christ's image.

You may never discover until eternity why He permits certain adversities. But they come with His knowledge and permission, and He knows all things perfectly.

> *Evil seems to reign right now, Lord, but I know that nothing that is happening to me is outside Your power. It is not outside Your love. It is not outside Your wisdom. All that touches my life is filtered through Your providence to conform me to Christ's image.*

Though He slay me, yet will I trust Him.
Even so, I will defend my own ways before Him.

Sometimes we sow the seeds of our afflictions. Sometimes we are the innocent victims of others' cruel actions. On other occasions God brings the thorn of adversity.

Regardless of the cause, troubles are the earthly gymnasium that exercises our heavenly faith. In the crucible of adversity, God is looking for faith in His goodness, His sovereignty, His plan, His love, His grace.

R. C. Sproul writes in *Surprised by Suffering:*

God was asking Job to exercise an implicit faith. An implicit faith is not blind faith. It is a faith with vision, a vision enlightened by a knowledge of the character of God. . . .

God deserves to be trusted. He merits our trust in Him. The more we understand of His perfections, the more we understand how trustworthy He is.

That is why the Christian pilgrimage is one that moves from faith to faith, from strength to strength, from grace to grace.

Trusting God in the dark when you doubt, when you do not understand, when you are ready to crumble at any moment, is the stamp of true faith. It rests on the faithfulness of God. You can trust Him because He is trustworthy. You can depend on Him because He is dependable.

Lord, I want to exercise faith in the gymnasium of adversity. Give me implicit faith for my workout today. Take me from strength to strength, from grace to grace.

SCRIPTURE READING: 1 Peter 1:3–9
KEY VERSE: 2 Timothy 2:1

You therefore, my son, be strong in the grace that is in Christ Jesus.

For the peach lover, there is nothing quite like the sweet scent and taste of a ripe peach. However, a peach tree requires a certain number of cold days during the winter to produce quality peaches.

You can advance through your adversities because your afflictions likewise produce spiritual growth. Genuine spiritual fruit is unlikely to fully develop unless you are put into strenuous places. In adversity you grow in grace. Grace, God's undeserved blessing, is hollow apart from suffering. Its richness, its strength, its nourishment, are released in adversity. Grace helps the weak to stand, the bruised to heal, the barren to blossom. In trouble you learn to "be strong in the grace that is in Christ Jesus" (2 Tim. 2:1).

You also grow in your knowledge of God. Paul wanted to know God above all. That intimate relationship blossomed in jail rooms, not hotel rooms. Adversity drives you into face-to-face dealings with the Father.

You grow, too, in your love for God's Word. David said, "It is good for me that I have been afflicted; that I might learn thy statutes" (Ps. 119:71 KJV). Spiritual fruit is watered by the tears of adversity.

> *Thank You for Your grace in times of trouble. When I am weak, help me stand. Where I am barren, create blossoms. When I am bruised, heal me. Let the tears of my adversity water the spiritual fruit You want to produce in my life.*

SCRIPTURE READING: Psalm 119:153–60

KEY VERSE: Job 36:15

He delivers the poor in their affliction,
And opens their ears in oppression.

Founding the Dohnavur Fellowship, Amy Carmichael ministered to the poor and oppressed children of India for fifty-five years. She encountered periodic bouts with ill health, one of which forced her to leave the mission field for almost a year. She penned the following poem, revealing her keen insight into the painful glories of suffering:

> From prayer that I may be, Sheltered from
>   winds that beat on Thee
> From fearing when I should aspire, From
>   faltering when I should climb higher,
> From silken self, Oh Captain, free Thy sol-
>   dier who would follow Thee.
> From subtle love of softening things, From
>   easy choices, weakenings,
> (Not thus are spirits fortified, not this way
>   went the Crucified)
> From all that dims Thy Calvary, oh Lamb
>   of God, deliver me.
> Give me the love that leads the way, The
>   faith that nothing can dismay,
> The hope no disappointments tire, The
>   passion that will burn like fire,
> Let me not sink to be a clod: Make me Thy
>   fuel, Flame of God.

O Lord, set me free from all that dims the vision of Calvary in my life!
Give me the love that leads the way, the faith that nothing can dismay.
Make me Thy fuel, O Flame of God!

SCRIPTURE READING: Hebrews 4:14–16
KEY VERSE: Isaiah 53:4

Surely He has borne our griefs
And carried our sorrows;
Yet we esteemed Him stricken,
Smitten by God, and afflicted.

A woman in Bangladesh holds her limp child and wails—the victim of yet another cyclone.

A son is awakened from his sleep with a call informing him of his father's sudden death. He grieves.

A Kansas wheat farmer looks numbly at his hail-flattened field and buries his weathered face in his calloused hands to hide the tears.

Jesus weeps with you as He wept at the news of Lazarus's death. In your agony He, too, is pained. He is not an automated, austere Sovereign, immune to your suffering, but a merciful High Priest who can "sympathize with [your] weaknesses" (Heb. 4:15 NASB).

"I could never myself believe in God, if it were not for the cross," writes British author Rev. John R. W. Stott. "In the real world of pain, how could one worship a God immune to it?"

Jesus came as the suffering Messiah, the slain Lamb, the tearstained and bleeding Savior. He understands and comforts your deepest sorrows.

He not only understands but actually asks you to cast your burdens and place your heartache on His shoulders so that He might sustain you in your anguish. He knows how you feel and comes tenderly to your aid.

You understand, Father, and this comforts me. You came to earth as a suffering Messiah. You tell me to cast my burdens on You, so I do that right now, dear Lord.

SCRIPTURE READING: Romans 5:1–5
KEY VERSE: Philippians 1:29

To you it has been granted on behalf of Christ, not only to believe in Him, but also to suffer for His sake.

Snoopy, the cartoon character created by Charles Schulz, reflected on the meaning of life in one humorous strip. After much contemplation, he spotted Charlie Brown coming with his supper dish and exclaimed: "Ah, meaning!"

We grin, for we all want to experience true meaning in life. It is exactly because suffering seems to have no meaning that we seek to recoil from it.

What meaning can there be in another miscarriage?

What meaning can there be in still another financial setback?

What meaning can be found for the person who has to use a wheelchair because of the intoxicated actions of another?

The meaning is this: we were placed on this planet to know and glorify God. As we suffer and turn to Christ, we accomplish both goals—to know Him intimately and to glorify Him. When our chief desire is to glorify God, suffering is but another means to achieve that end.

Others can experience and see the peace and joy of the indwelling Christ. His humility and long-suffering can shine in our darkness with radiant splendor.

You can redeem your suffering, give meaning to it, and rescue it from emptiness by realizing your pain can be used to glorify Jesus.

I may not understand my suffering, Lord, but that does not mean it is without purpose. I know You are working all things together for good. Help me redeem my suffering by realizing my pain can be used to glorify You!

SCRIPTURE READING: Genesis 50:15–20
KEY VERSE: Psalm 31:15

My times are in Your hand;
Deliver me from the hand of my enemies,
And from those who persecute me.

Joseph emerged from jail as Pharaoh's right-hand man and saved millions from starvation by administering God's wisdom over the nation's agricultural program.

David came out of the backwoods as Israel's beloved king. His psalms, many recorded during his exile, comfort and encourage believers in affliction.

Paul's jail terms were the study halls where he penned the Spirit-inspired books of Ephesians, Colossians, Philippians, and Philemon.

Adversity? Yes.	Defeat? No.
Perplexity? Yes.	Futility? No.
Discouragement? Yes.	Escapism? No.
Fear? Yes.	Resignation? No.

Each advanced through his personal adversity in different fashion, but their progress and yours in harsh times are built on the bedrock truth of the sovereignty of God.

Author and theologian Dr. J. I. Packer defines God's *sovereignty* or *providence* as "the unceasing activity of the Creator whereby, in overflowing bounty and good will, He . . . directs everything to its appointed goal."

In other words, God is in charge. Your adversity is in His hands. You are never powerless, for His power works on your behalf to accomplish His purpose.

I leave it in Your hands, God—all my suffering, all my unanswered
questions, every heartache—knowing You are at work in the midst of
my pain.

SCRIPTURE READING: Revelation 21–22
KEY VERSE: Revelation 21:4

God will wipe away every tear from their eyes; there shall be no more death, nor sorrow, nor crying. There shall be no more pain, for the former things have passed away.

Counselor and author Larry Crabb writes about the importance of eternity's perspective on suffering in his book *Inside Out:*

Modern Christianity, in dramatic reversal of its biblical form, promises to relieve the pain of living in a fallen world.

The message . . . is too often the same: The promise of bliss is now! Complete satisfaction can be ours this side of heaven. . . .

The effect of such teaching is to blunt the painful reality of what it's like to live as part of an imperfect, and sometimes evil, community.

Adversity can wreak havoc in this life. But you can advance through it as you face it with the long-term view of eternity. You can rest in the certain truth that your faithfulness and perseverance will be rewarded in eternity.

The outcome of suffering, when entrusted to God's sovereign, kind hand, is always merciful. The sufferings of this life, Paul said, cannot compare to the "glory that is to be revealed to us" (Rom. 8:18 NASB).

The light of God's countenance is upon you in your affliction. But one day you will see Him face-to-face, and that encounter will put all things into place. Sorrow and crying will flee away for all eternity.

I want to face each adversity with eternity in mind, Father. Thank You that the sufferings of this life are not worthy to be compared to the glory that is to be revealed in me!

April

THEME: The Sheep Gate

REPRESENTING: The work of the Cross

KEY VERSE: John 10:11

I am the good shepherd. The good shepherd gives His life for the sheep.

SCRIPTURE READING: Colossians 2:6–15
KEY VERSE: Acts 26:18

To open their eyes, in order to turn them from darkness to light, and from the power of Satan to God, that they may receive forgiveness of sins and an inheritance among those who are sanctified by faith in Me.

Although crosses adorn our church steeples and their likeness is printed, woven, or worn in a variety of fashions, there often is only a vague knowledge of the true meaning of the Cross.

What really happened at the cross? What does it mean for someone today? Is it all that important?

At the cross of Christ the three mortal enemies of humankind—sin, death, and the devil—were confronted and defeated by the Son of God. Jesus died for your sins, the actions that are contrary to God's character and that separate you from God's holy presence. Jesus took your sins on Himself at the cross. He bore God's judgment of death on your behalf, as your substitute. God's uncompromising wrath against sin was satisfied.

At the cross Satan and his powers were crushed. They still exist, but their fate is sealed; and the Christian has Christ's authority over the devil. You have been transferred from the kingdom of darkness to the kingdom of light, from the dominion of sin to the dominion of God.

The next time you look at a cross, wear it around your neck, or see its imprint, remember that sin was judged, death slain, and the devil conquered at Calvary.

> *Father, thank You for the Cross, which transferred me from the kingdom of darkness to the kingdom of light. Thank You that at the cross, sin was judged, death slain, and the devil defeated.*

SCRIPTURE READING: Romans 3

KEY VERSE: Romans 5:1

Therefore, having been justified by faith, we have peace with God through our Lord Jesus Christ.

The blood, agony, and torture of the cross of Christ are well known, even to unbelievers and adherents to other religions. The Cross, however, was far more than mere historic melodrama. Its significance lies not in the emotional experience of the participants but in the reality of what God accomplished through His Son's death.

At the cross of Calvary our sins were forgiven. The penalty of sin was death. Christ suffered that divinely decreed punishment on our behalf, thus enabling God to forgive us of our transgressions based on Christ's substitutionary sacrifice.

At the cross death was defeated. Since Christ tasted the bitter dregs of death at Calvary and rose again three days later, death no longer reigns over those of us who place our trust in Him. Christ triumphed over the grave, and we who come to Him for salvation share in that awesome conquest.

Perhaps you have viewed the Cross with supreme sympathy for our suffering Messiah but never understood what His death entailed. If so, realize today that on the cross Christ died for your sins and overcame death. Come to Him for forgiveness of your sins, and gain the gift of eternal life.

Thank You, Father, that through the cross of Your Son, Jesus Christ, I have forgiveness of sins and the gift of eternal life.

SCRIPTURE READING: 1 Corinthians 15:1–28
KEY VERSE: Hebrews 10:12

This Man, after He had offered one sacrifice for sins forever, sat down at the right hand of God.

The cross of Christ appears unimportant to many cultures today mainly because of the time of its occurrence: "How could the death of a Jewish carpenter on a Roman cross two thousand years ago affect my life today?" This reasoning confuses the significance of the Cross.

When Christ died is not the central issue. In God's timing He was crucified about A.D. 30, but He could have died in 100 B.C. or in 1943—had the Father so purposed. How Christ died is not the essential meaning either. He died on a cross, but had God desired, His Son could have died another way.

The timeless meaning of the Cross is that Christ, the Son of God, died there. Only God Himself was qualified to be our substitute on Calvary. It was *who* was executed that is significant. God in the flesh, Jesus the Messiah, was the single, sinless sacrifice who could bear our sins.

The death and resurrection of God's only Son made fellowship with the Father possible again. Jesus did not have to suffer, but He had to die, for death was the penalty for sin. The Cross is relevant for every man, woman, and child in every age because there the eternal God died on our behalf so that we might receive His gift of everlasting life.

You were the sinless sacrifice, Lord. You died in my place. Thank You. Through Your death and resurrection, I can have fellowship with the Father.

SCRIPTURE READING: Romans 6:1–14
KEY VERSE: Romans 6:11

Likewise you also, reckon yourselves to be dead indeed to sin, but alive to God in Christ Jesus our Lord.

The Cross is removed from a purely historical perspective when we realize that we, too, are involved in its ageless liberation. The apostle Paul informed us that by God's unfathomable working, we were included in the Lord Jesus Christ's death, burial, and resurrection.

We have been crucified, buried, and raised with Christ. Through faith in Christ Jesus, each of us has died to sin and been joined with Him to become "a new creature" (2 Cor. 5:17 NASB).

This concept is difficult to understand. Perhaps this analogy will help: Think of a book mailed to Europe. Inside the book is a three-by-five-inch photograph. Wherever the book is sent, the photograph goes also.

God placed you in Christ in His death, burial, and resurrection. What happened to Jesus also has happened in you. Daily you are told to "reckon" or "consider" yourself (count it as so) "to be dead to sin, but alive to God in Christ Jesus" (Rom. 6:11 NASB).

You can do so only because of your union with Christ. His death to sin is yours, and His life with the Father is yours. The Cross is the means to an entirely new way of living—now and forever.

I am dead to sin. I am a new creature in Christ. I am alive to You, dear God. Thank You for my new life!

SCRIPTURE READING: 1 Corinthians 1:18–25
KEY VERSE: Colossians 1:20

And by Him to reconcile all things to Himself, by Him, whether things on earth or things in heaven, having made peace through the blood of His cross.

Modern people scorn the contemporary relevance of the Cross, assailing its intellectual virtue. Despite their skepticism and ridicule, the very core of the Christian faith is the cross of the Lord Jesus Christ. A large part of the four Gospels pertains to the events leading to Christ's crucifixion.

The Cross is the central truth of both Christian doctrine and experience. In the words of Paul, the crucified Christ is both "the power of God and the wisdom of God" (1 Cor. 1:24 NASB).

The Cross is God's power and wisdom because it is the only means by which sinful human beings can be reconciled to holy God. Because God became flesh, He could die as our substitute, bearing the divinely decreed penalty of sin.

Through the Cross, the wrath of God the Father was spent on His Son. Through the Cross, the love of God is freely extended to repentant men and women who, embracing Christ and His work, may receive the gift of eternal life, that is, Jesus.

Is the cross of Christ the center of your faith? There is no other way to God except through the Cross.

Dear Lord, make the cross of Christ the center of my faith. There is no other way. I come Your way, Father.

SCRIPTURE READING: Colossians 3:1–17

KEY VERSE: Colossians 1:13

He has delivered us from the power of darkness and conveyed us into the kingdom of the Son of His love.

We are a power-conscious people. Businesspeople meet for power lunches. Politicians strive to gain ever-increasing legislative power. Individuals with common causes group together to wield more clout. The military spends billions to develop and deploy Armageddon-scale weaponry. But there has never been—and will never be—anything that rivals the awesome power of the gospel.

The gospel has the power to deliver from death. Because Christ paid the penalty of sin—which is death—and emerged from the tomb, the gospel is the only power that can liberate humankind from the horror of eternal, spiritual death. The gospel alone can transfer you from the domain of death and darkness into the kingdom of life and light (Col. 1:13).

It has the power to liberate from sin's bondage. Through the indwelling Holy Spirit, the power of the gospel transforms your behavior, unchaining you from the grip of habits and passions. You are free to obey a new Master.

The gospel also has the power to radically alter every relationship. Instead of your striving for self-dominance or self-protection, the gospel empowers you to reorient your life toward selfless giving, living, loving, and serving.

May the power of the gospel be evident in my life, Lord. Release me from the grip of sinful habits and passions. Help me give, live, love, and serve selflessly.

SCRIPTURE READING: 1 Corinthians 2
KEY VERSE: 1 Corinthians 2:2

I determined not to know anything among you except Jesus Christ and Him crucified.

The cross of Calvary—where Jesus Christ, the Son of God, died—is the extraordinary instrument of freedom where our eternal liberty was secured.

You see, our freedom cannot be purchased with a social revolution or a majority vote. The source of our oppression is spiritual, not political, economic, or cultural.

We are born sinners, separated from the life and liberty of our Creator, God. We are imprisoned by the darkness of sin, chained by its selfish grip and under the influence of the god of this world, Satan.

Our only hope is to be rescued by the One who alone has the power and right to liberate us from sin's reign and rule. That is exactly what Christ did at the cross. He bore the penalty of sin—death—making it possible for us to be reconciled to the Author of spiritual liberty, Jehovah God.

At the cross, Jesus released you from the curse of eternal death. When you receive Christ, you gain the incredible inheritance of eternal life. You still die physically, but your spirit is made alive by God. And you will be with Him forever! The Cross shattered the bonds of sin, making spiritual freedom possible for all who believe in Jesus Christ.

You rescued me, O God! I am free from the darkness of sin's reign.
Thank You for my liberty.

SCRIPTURE READING: Galatians 6:13–15
KEY VERSE: Ephesians 2:14

He Himself is our peace, who has made both one, and has broken down the
middle wall of separation.

Writing on the Persian Gulf War, a reporter for *U.S. News & World
Report* commented on the price of conflict: "Peace must be earned and
preserved. Peace is not passive. Freedom is not free."

Neither does your freedom from sin's penalty and power come cheaply.
Your symbol of true freedom—liberty from the chains of sin and self—is
a costly one. It is steeped in the blood of Jesus Christ, God's Son.

On Calvary, Christ fought and secured your deliverance from sin. He
paid the supreme price, the sacrifice of His divine life. The grace of God
is wonderful, marvelous. But it is yours only through the ransom paid by
God to God through Christ's torturous death.

Bearing the guilt of your sin, He died in your stead, turning aside the
wrath of holy God. His sacrifice satisfied God's justice and opened
heaven's doors to those who place their faith in Christ. There is nothing
passive about the Cross. There is nothing cheap about salvation. It is a
gift—a costly one.

Have you received Christ as your personal Savior? The gift of eternal
life is free if you believe, but it was secured at a most extravagant price.
Receive Christ, and treasure the invaluable gift of everlasting life.

I receive the gift of eternal life, Father. Thank You for providing it for
me, even at the extravagant price of Your Son's death. I treasure the
legacy.

SCRIPTURE READING: Luke 15:11–32
KEY VERSE: Romans 2:4

Do you despise the riches of His goodness, forbearance, and longsuffering, not knowing that the goodness of God leads you to repentance?

Repentance includes physically turning away from sin, and also includes a mental or intellectual change in the way you view sin. When you repent of a certain sin, you agree with God that what you did was wrong. Therefore, you willfully choose to step away from sin.

Repentance is not an emotional act. However, it does involve your emotional well-being. True repentance surfaces feelings of both remorse and regret over the obvious breach you have allowed to invade your life. Sin separates you from fellowship with God, while repentance restores your intimacy with Him.

Forgiveness for sin was provided once and for all by Jesus Christ at Calvary. When God views you, He acknowledges the atoning death of His Son as payment for your sins. Your acknowledgment of the same sins allows you to personally receive and enjoy His complete forgiveness.

Some Christians think they can enjoy the security of being saved by God's grace while living life with a sinful vengeance. But true salvation denotes a humble spirit and a repentant heart. There is no way to live a victorious Christian life while coveting sin. Ask God to help you come to grips with any sin in your life. His restoration is always available through repentance.

Reveal every sin in my life, dear Lord, and help me come to grips with it. I repent. Restore me to fellowship with You.

SCRIPTURE READING: 1 John 1:8–2:2

KEY VERSE: Romans 6:6

Our old man was crucified with Him, that the body of sin might be done away with, that we should no longer be slaves of sin.

As Christians, we often become discouraged when tempted by sinful habits we thought were eliminated at the point of our salvation. The truth is, we still live in a fallen world under the influence of Satan.

Because you are a child of God, the enemy no longer holds the title to your life. Spiritually you are seated in heaven with Christ (Col. 3:3). However, this does not free you from the strife of Satan's disastrous intentions. Salvation only shifts his goal for your life from one of eternal death to one of ineffectiveness.

The enemy wants to render you useless in your witness and testimony for Jesus Christ. Sin is his favorite weapon because he knows it damages your relationship with God. However, the Cross eternally broke the power of sin. You no longer have to yield to its temptation. The only way to handle sin is to put it in subjection to the Lord Jesus Christ. The key to overcoming it lies in living daily in the light of God's Word.

When temptations come, remember the enemy's power has been broken. Jesus is your strong Advocate before the Father. Confess your sins, claim His forgiveness, and continue your life in the light of His grace.

> *Jesus, You are my Advocate before the Father. I confess my sin, claim Your forgiveness, and thank You that I can continue in the light of Your grace.*

SCRIPTURE READING: Romans 5:6–11
KEY VERSE: Psalm 103:8

The LORD is merciful and gracious,
Slow to anger, and abounding in mercy.

Do you eagerly anticipate spending time alone with God, or are you fearful of His rebuke? Do you delight yourself in the Lord, or do you feel that Christianity is just another load to carry?

Christians should be the most joyful people on earth. The thrill of victory should dance on our tongues and souls since Christ has borne the agony of sin on His shoulders.

Perhaps the wonder of your relationship with Christ has been obscured by a misplaced emphasis on the character of God. Yes, He is holy; yes, He is a righteous Judge. But He always exercises these attributes within the framework of His mercy and grace.

When you were saved, God became your loving Father. You are His treasured, precious son or daughter. Nothing you do will change His steadfast, fatherly love. Run if you will; rebel against His rule; yet the Father's heart does not turn away from you.

When you were saved, Christ became your faithful Friend. He is always there for you. You can never offend Him or disappoint Him since He knew you perfectly before you were saved and still He brought you to Himself (Rom. 5:6). He wants to help you, regardless of the mess you may have made. You are free to enjoy God because He has removed all of the barriers.

Heavenly Father, I thank You that there is nothing I can do that will change Your love for me. Jesus, You are my faithful Friend. The barriers of sin are removed, and I am free to enjoy You!

SCRIPTURE READING: 1 Corinthians 6:9–11
KEY VERSE: 2 Corinthians 5:17

If anyone is in Christ, he is a new creation; old things have passed away;
behold, all things have become new.

In 1736, eleven-year-old John Newton went to sea on his father's ship, beginning a life of rebellion and immorality. He often worked on slave ships, helping to sell slaves to wealthy landowners. An ambitious young man, Newton soon owned a slave ship and was proud of his place in a bloody and cruel industry.

Only when his ship ran into a horrible storm and he feared for his life did he turn to God. In desperation he read a devotional about Christ. Newton came face-to-face for the first time with Jesus' sacrificial love, and it changed his life. He eventually renounced the evil slave trade and became a powerful and bold minister.

Years later, for his small congregation to sing, Newton penned the words to "Amazing Grace," the moving story of his conversion. Newton realized that no crime is too big, no deed is too horrible, no thought is too wicked for Christ to forgive.

Christ's amazing grace covers all sin. When you accept His payment on the cross for your sin and make Him the Lord of your life, you are cleansed completely. Past failures no longer have a hold on your life (2 Cor. 5:17). God washes old things away and makes you a new creation.

It is amazing, Lord, the grace that covers all of my sin. I am so grate-
ful that my past is gone and I am a new creature in Christ.

THE HIGH COST OF GOD'S GRACE

SCRIPTURE READING: Luke 7:36–50
KEY VERSE: Luke 7:47

I say to you, her sins, which are many, are forgiven, for she loved much. But to whom little is forgiven, the same loves little.

The evening was cool—the Capernaum sky clear and alive with the brilliance of thousands of twinkling stars. Mary knew where she could find Jesus. That night He was at the home of Simon the Pharisee.

Clutching the bottle of expensive perfume, she moved through the doorway to where Jesus and the others were seated. She realized her actions would draw their scorn. Only Jesus would understand the motive of her heart.

As she knelt and broke the seal of the fragrant oil, her eyes met His, and something passed between them. Feelings of love, yes, but not human or emotional love. It was something that was holy and pure. No matter what her past contained, the moment she bowed her heart in repentance, God's forgiveness was hers.

Mary responded in humility and repentance. His grace sufficiently covered and cleansed her sin. Many think the idea of unconditional love cheapens God's grace. But nothing can devalue such an expensive gift.

The high cost of God's grace meant Jesus had to die so that you, like this woman, could experience forgiveness and eternal life. Only Christ can save you from your sins, and only He can offer the grace you need to live confidently and securely.

It was costly, God, but Your Son paid the price so that I can experience forgiveness and eternal life. Thank You for Your unconditional love!

SCRIPTURE READING: Ephesians 2:1–10
KEY VERSE: 2 Peter 2:1

There were also false prophets among the people, even as there will be false teachers among you, who will secretly bring in destructive heresies, even denying the Lord who bought them, and bring on themselves swift destruction.

The theories of the modern world—evolution, humanism, secularism—have one basic element in common: they deal in chance, luck, and randomness. We are left, they say, to the whim and fancy of impersonal, illogical fate and circumstance, seeking at best to ride out the wildly tumultuous winds of fortune.

But the Christian faith rests on the outworking of a definitive, distinctive plan that God is relentlessly executing. His wise and perfect design, formulated in His omniscient mind, begins with salvation. This is what He unceasingly is up to in the lives of men and women who are still separated from a personal relationship with Him.

Through the death, burial, and resurrection of His Son, Jesus Christ, God seeks to save you from the penalty of sin: eternal death. He uses encounters with Christians and the Scriptures, adversity and success, creation and creatures to testify of the reality of His existence.

All that is necessary to implement His eternal plan is an admission of your sin and personal belief in Christ's forgiveness. Once you make that choice, His plan of redemption is irreversibly ignited.

I thank You, God, that Your plan of redemption is irreversibly ignited in my life. I am not left to chance, luck, or circumstance. You are implementing Your divine purposes in my life.

SCRIPTURE READING: Romans 6:15–23

KEY VERSE: 2 Corinthians 5:21

He made Him who knew no sin to be sin for us, that we might become the righteousness of God in Him.

Since we cannot remedy our sinful state or eternal destiny through any actions of our own, we must trust in God's provision for salvation: the person and work of Jesus Christ. When Jesus died on the cross, He bore our sins, paying our sin debt in full through the sacrificial offering of His body. The Father's wrath and punishment for our sin were placed squarely on His Son.

That is the biblical doctrine of justification: Jesus Christ dying on our behalf and rising again to remove our guilt and acquit us before the bar of God's holy justice. We can now be reconciled to God through Christ's substitutionary, atoning death. But we are not justified automatically. Rather, each of us must personally accept salvation by faith, receive the gift, and—not intellectually, but volitionally—trust in Christ.

When you, by grace through faith, believe in Christ as your Savior from sin, a supernatural change of condition occurs. At the moment of your salvation, the very righteousness of God—His holy, moral character—is imparted to you. Christ instantly and permanently transforms your sinful state.

It's supernatural, O God, the change in me. Your character has been imparted, and my sinful state has been permanently transformed through Your Son, Jesus Christ. I praise You!

SCRIPTURE READING: John 19:17–37
KEY VERSES: 1 Peter 1:18–19

Knowing that you were not redeemed with corruptible things, like silver or gold, from your aimless conduct received by tradition from your fathers, but with the precious blood of Christ, as of a lamb without blemish and without spot.

The sight of blood can make even the strong queasy. It is not so much the color, odor, or viscosity of blood that kindles such a reaction but the nervous awareness that life itself is at stake. The unstopped flow of blood results in death.

At Golgotha the blood of Christ oozed from His hands, feet, and head. The bright red blood of Christ stained the timber and discolored the ground, visible to all who watched the horror unfold.

But the shedding of Christ's blood is the one truth on which hangs all of Christianity—Jesus died for our sins. Christ's spilled blood eventuated in His death; and in death, the Son of God and the Son of man completed His work on earth—to die on our behalf, pay our sin debt by the sacrifice of His life, and provide the pathway to reconciliation between God and us. Jesus' death enabled God to forgive us of our iniquities by carrying out the punishment of sin—death—on His own Son.

Christ's holy blood allows the Father to declare you innocent of your sins the moment you believe and receive Jesus as Savior. Christ's bloody death is the good news that delivers you from eternal death and makes eternal life a treasured gift from God.

There is power in the blood! Thank You, Lord, that its power applies to me! The work is complete in my behalf. I am saved!

SCRIPTURE READING: Isaiah 1:18–21
KEY VERSE: Isaiah 1:18

"Come now, and let us reason together,"
Says the LORD,
"Though your sins are like scarlet,
They shall be as white as snow;
Though they are red like crimson,
They shall be as wool."

Throughout time, God has repeatedly appealed to us to step away from our sins and follow His way of righteousness. One of the strongest appeals comes in Isaiah 1:18, today's key verse.

Sin alters life by taking what God calls pure and distorting it. An iodine stain on white linen ruins the fabric's design and fiber, and nothing can remove its staining power.

Sin has the same effect on your life—it stains deeply. Yet God in His mercy has provided a way for its removal through the atoning death of Jesus Christ. Christ is your personal invitation from God to be washed clean from sin's staining power.

God's appeal for you to come and reason with Him is not a point of argument. Instead, it is a call for you to think logically of sin's ultimate purpose—to separate us from God.

Once you have accepted Jesus as your Savior, God clothes you in the righteousness of His Son. Your sins are forgiven, and you are made white as snow. His forgiveness means freedom from sin, freedom from guilt, and peace that passes all understanding. It means living forever in the vital union of fellowship with Christ.

I accept Your invitation, dear Lord. I'm coming Your way. Take away
the stains of my sin. Clothe me in the righteousness of Your Son.

SCRIPTURE READING: 1 John 1:5–2:2
KEY VERSE: Psalm 85:2

You have forgiven the iniquity of Your people;
You have covered all their sin.

We must make a critical distinction if we are to deal successfully with sin and enjoy God's provision for overcoming its deceptive and destructive power. The crucial principle is this: God dealt with sin at Calvary. That was His responsibility that could not be executed by anyone other than omnipotent God.

We, however, must deal with sins. That is a responsibility that God assigns to us as believers. At the cross, God stripped away our sin nature by crucifying it with Christ. That is why we can be new creatures in Christ. The old, corrupt, fallen nature was done away with.

There is still a potential of sin in each believer, but we are no longer under its reign. We are freed from its tyranny, for we have died to its rule. We can freely choose to obey God.

Although God dealt with our sin nature through the Cross, making us saints who occasionally sin, we must deal with sins—habits or activities that violate God's revealed truth. We do so by confessing our particular sins to God. We agree with Him that we have sinned.

You are completely forgiven. You can confess sinful acts to a Father who restores joyous fellowship. You have victory over the sin nature through Christ and cleansing from sins through confession.

Dear Lord, thank You for forgiving my sin; now please forgive my sins.
Give me victory over my sin nature today.

SCRIPTURE READING: 2 Timothy 2:24–26
KEY VERSES: Acts 26:19–20

Therefore, King Agrippa, I was not disobedient to the heavenly vision, but declared first to those in Damascus and in Jerusalem, and throughout all the region of Judea, and then to the Gentiles, that they should repent, turn to God, and do works befitting repentance.

Sometimes repentance can seem a little like commercials in that there is no end. We come before God, confess our sins, express our desire for repentance—and find ourselves in exactly the same condition the next time we approach our Father.

Biblical repentance means forsaking sin, not simply confessing it. To forsake is to leave behind, to abandon. We repent not just with our hearts but with our actions.

"Oh," you say, "I wish it were that simple. How can I quit gossiping when I seem addicted to it?"

To repent biblically, you must ask God to give you His hatred of evil, to give you repentance. God still hates sin—even in your life. Sin is not just a mistake or a shortcoming or a fault; sin is rebellion against God for which Christ died.

You possess power in the person of the Holy Spirit to conquer your sin. You can effectively repent of sin because sin's slayer, Jesus Christ, empowers you. You are not left to your own devices, your own willpower.

Is there a nagging area of disobedience in your life that you are unable to conquer? Face it as sin, count on God's unequaled power each day, and persevere as Christ frees you moment by moment from its grip.

My sin is not a mistake. It is not a shortcoming or a fault. It is rebellion. Forgive me, Lord. Liberate me from its grip.

SCRIPTURE READING: 2 Corinthians 7:9–10
KEY VERSES: Isaiah 55:6–7

Seek the LORD while He may be found,
Call upon Him while He is near.
Let the wicked forsake his way,
And the unrighteous man his thoughts;
Let him return to the LORD,
And He will have mercy on him;
And to our God,
For He will abundantly pardon.

The newspaper headline read: "Bank Robber Turns Himself in After 20 Years." The accompanying story told how a man finally had gone to a local jail and confessed to a crime he had committed twenty years earlier.

Why would he voluntarily surrender to authorities when he might not be found out, at least on earth? "I just could not live with the guilt anymore," the man said.

Guilt afflicts the entire human race. We know the inner gnawing and churning that come with having violated the moral or civil code. It drives some to depression, others to compulsive behavior, still others to suicide.

The foundation for dealing with all guilt is the cross where Christ died. Jesus, the Son of God, became a guilt offering for us. Because Christ bore God's ultimate judgment, we are free to experience the forgiveness of God.

When you receive Christ by faith, God declares you not guilty. The slate is clean—from both its penalty (which is death) and its guilt. Your conscience is cleansed, and your burdens are lifted.

The verdict is in, and I'm not guilty! I am free from sin and its penalties—both death and guilt. Thank You, Father, for a clear conscience.

SCRIPTURE READING: Romans 5:17–21
KEY VERSE: Romans 5:17

For if by the one man's offense death reigned through the one, much more those who receive abundance of grace and of the gift of righteousness will reign in life through the One, Jesus Christ.

Why is the Cross the resource for dealing with guilt? Because all men and women one day will stand before God to have their sins judged. Those who have received God's pardon by faith in Christ's atoning sacrifice will not be condemned. Those who have not had their guilt removed through the Cross will be condemned for eternity. The Cross is the basis for dealing with guilt.

The ten-year-old who steals a pen in school, the teenager who cheats on a test, the adult who cheats on income tax—all experience certain degrees of guilt.

For believers, that guilt is the work of the Holy Spirit who seeks to convict us. He does not condemn us. His conviction is to bring us back into fellowship with the Savior. That happens when we admit our wrongs, confess our sins to God, and receive His forgiveness.

Will we still endure the consequences? Yes. The ten-year-old may have to stay after class; the teenager may be suspended; the adult may pay a fine or spend time in jail.

Still, forgiveness of your sins restores your relationship with God and releases guilt's grip on your emotions. Your guilt has been atoned for by Christ, for which you can be eternally grateful.

Convict me, Holy Spirit. Forgive me, Father. Restore my fellowship with You through the blood of Jesus.

SCRIPTURE READING: John 8:1–11

KEY VERSE: Romans 8:34

Who is he who condemns? It is Christ who died, and furthermore is also risen, who is even at the right hand of God, who also makes intercession for us.

Many Christians fail to grow in their relationship with Christ, not because of indifference or sin, but because of nagging feelings of guilt and condemnation. They feel unworthy of God's blessings. They are convinced He cannot love them anymore because of what they have done or said.

This inner turmoil is the work of Satan, who seeks to destroy your fellowship with the Father. A distorted view of your performance lies at the root of this evil. You somehow think if you live righteously enough, you merit God's approval; if you falter, you must face His disapproval.

This kind of thinking is false. God has accepted you completely—based on the forgiveness provided by Christ Jesus on the cross. You are no longer under God's wrath, but you are a recipient of His grace, which is given without respect to performance. Grace came to you freely at salvation and continues to flow thereafter.

No misdeed can sever your personal relationship with God. If you have sinned, confession and repentance restore total intimacy. Sacrifice or penance in the form of good works or self-denial is useless.

If feelings of guilt have stunted your fellowship with Christ, they can be removed instantly by your humble confession. Never let your performance hinder God's grace.

> *Heavenly Father, I am so thankful that no misdeed can sever our relationship. Thank You for the grace that came to me at salvation and continues to flow today.*

SCRIPTURE READING: 2 Corinthians 3:7–18

KEY VERSE: Galatians 6:15

*In Christ Jesus neither circumcision nor uncircumcision avails anything, but
a new creation.*

English author and pastor John R. W. Stott explains the Spirit-controlled life in *Basic Christianity:*

> The more we make a habit of denying the flesh (because of our co-crucifixion) and obeying the Spirit, the more our ugly works of the flesh will disappear and the lovely fruit of the Spirit will take their place. . . . It is by the Spirit of Christ that we can be transformed into the image of Christ as we look steadfastly towards Him. We, thus, have our part to play in repentance, faith, and discipline; but. . . . holiness is the work of the Holy Spirit.

William Temple used to illustrate the point this way:

> It is not good giving me a play like *Hamlet* or *King Lear* and telling me to write a play like that. Shakespeare could do it; I can't. And it is not good showing me the life of Jesus and telling me to live a life like that. Jesus could do it; I can't.
>
> But if the genius of Shakespeare could come and live in me, then I could write plays like that. And if the Spirit of Jesus could come and live in me, then I could live a life like that. It is not that we should strive to be like Jesus, but that He by His Spirit should come and live in us.

---

*I can't do it on my own. Come and live in me, Holy Spirit. Empower
me to live the life of Christ, to become like Him.*

SCRIPTURE READING: Luke 23:26–46
KEY VERSE: Romans 11:36

For of Him and through Him and to Him are all things, to whom be glory forever. Amen.

The cross of Jesus Christ is the fulfillment of God's plan for salvation through the death, burial, and resurrection of His Son. That is why the Lord Jesus Christ cried, "It is finished!" (John 19:30) as He drew His final breath on Golgotha. Prophecy was fulfilled; redemption was accomplished.

Also the Cross is the keystone for individual destiny and deliverance. Your eternal state rests on your acceptance or rejection of God's redemptive work on Calvary. There your sins were forgiven because God's Son was sacrificed in your stead and on your behalf.

There your sin nature was judged and rendered powerless; and your archenemy, Satan, was defeated. God dealt with the old person by crucifying it with Christ so that you may enjoy a new quality of life.

You experience the transforming power of the Cross when your faith is anchored in its truth. By faith in Jesus, you are saved from eternal death and delivered from sin's domain. You overcome all obstacles, all barriers, all habits, all circumstances, by total reliance on the conquering Christ who shattered sin's penalty and power on Calvary. Christ's cross secured it all.

Hallelujah! Victory is mine through the Cross. O God, I anchor my faith in its truth. I rely on its power to overcome all obstacles, barriers, habits, and circumstances in my life.

SCRIPTURE READING: Romans 8:31–39
KEY VERSE: Exodus 14:14

The LORD will fight for you, and you shall hold your peace.

Not only is God's Spirit in you, but also God is for you. There are amazing power and freedom in knowing that almighty God is now on your side.

Have you blown your marriage due to immorality? If you are a believer, God is still for you.

Have you backed off from your commitment to God? Have you ignored His counsel, refused His direction? As staggering as it seems, God is still for you.

Here's why. When Christ died, God's judgment was fully executed on His Son. His wrath against sin was vented. God's love is steadfast for those who receive the gift of eternal life by faith in Christ Jesus. You may sin and rebel, but His love for you does not change.

Yes, He will discipline you; yes, He will chastise you if necessary. But all correction is filtered through His loyal, blessed love.

God is for you, not against you. Because of the Cross, you can abide in His presence permanently and experience His love by personal faith in Jesus Christ. Paul declared that nothing can "separate us from the love of God which is in Christ Jesus our Lord" (Rom. 8:39).

Thank You, Father, that even when my commitment to You is feeble,
You are still for me. Thank You that nothing can separate me from
Your love.

SCRIPTURE READING: Luke 10:38–42

KEY VERSE: Matthew 6:33

Seek first the kingdom of God and His righteousness, and all these things shall be added to you.

What would you list as your single greatest need today? A new house? A better job? A marriage partner? A genuine friend? An increase in income? What if that need were dramatically met before this day was over? You moved into a beautiful home, got the job you wanted, found the perfect mate, met a true friend, and came into a healthy inheritance. Would you still have a pressing need in a week or two?

You're never without needs. That's why the answer to the original question—"What would you list as your single greatest need today?"— can only be, "An intimate, steadfast, growing relationship with Jesus Christ." That is your greatest need.

When you know Christ, you can have all of your emotional needs met: "Come to Me, all who are weary and heavy-laden, and I will give you rest" (Matt. 11:28 NASB).

When you make knowing God your chief priority, your physical needs are met: "Seek first His kingdom and His righteousness; and all these things [clothing, food, drink, the necessities of life] shall be added to you" (Matt. 6:33 NASB).

To know God is to have a vital relationship with the Author, Sustainer, and End of all things. That is really the only necessary thing. Is it yours?

> *I have many needs, but my greatest need is for an intimate relationship with You, Lord. Make this the primary focus of my life. I really want to know You.*

SCRIPTURE READING: 1 John 5:10–15
KEY VERSE: Ephesians 1:13

In Him you also trusted, after you heard the word of truth, the gospel of your salvation; in whom also, having believed, you were sealed with the Holy Spirit of promise.

The most important decision you will ever make is whether to receive or refuse the offer of eternal life through Jesus Christ. Since your eternal destiny depends upon such a determination, do you think God wants you to be in continual confusion concerning the consequences of your decision?

Absolutely not. God is interested in your developing a growing, loving, secure relationship with His Son. As your Father, He wants you to be aware of your indisputable relationship as His child.

John's epistle removes any doubt about salvation being a vacillating experience—moving in and out of the presence of God, forever wandering between heaven and hell: "He who has the Son has life" (1 John 5:12). When you invite Christ in as Savior, He is there to stay. He will never leave you or forsake you (Heb. 13:5). You are sealed with the Holy Spirit. You are a child of God.

Jesus abides in you because you are forgiven of your sins through His death. The obstacle to knowing God has been removed through His sin-bearing work at Calvary.

Your acceptance of His salvation by faith is a decisive act that puts Christ in you forever. Your behavior may hinder your enjoyment of God's presence, but it can never for one second alter your oneness with Him.

Heavenly Father, clear up my confusion. Give me security in our relationship. I am Your child. We are together forever.

SCRIPTURE READING: John 3:1–21
KEY VERSE: John 3:16

For God so loved the world that He gave His only begotten Son, that whoever believes in Him should not perish but have everlasting life.

The attributes of God are many—love, mercy, grace, forgiveness, kindness, goodness. Yet none of these marvelous qualities would be known to humankind without the character trait–giving God, who by His own choice holds nothing to Himself. His love, mercy, and grace are generously bestowed upon us because He has sovereignly willed to share Himself and His bounty with us.

We have life only because He has created us by an exercise of His will. We can receive salvation only because He wills to grant it. The ultimate testimony to the Giver of all good things is, amazingly, the saints, the redeemed ones, "in order that in the ages to come He might show the surpassing riches of His grace in kindness toward us in Christ Jesus" (Eph. 2:7 NASB).

The Supreme Giver's gift to us of salvation through Christ will resound throughout eternity. Believers will be the showcase, the tangible evidence of His ever-giving heart. Thus, while we enjoy the eternal fundamental benefits of salvation, its root lies in the reality that is the preeminent Giver—God. All of the heavenly hosts will marvel without end at that truth.

You are a divine Giver, O Lord. I thankfully accept Your gifts of love, mercy, grace, forgiveness, kindness, and goodness.

SCRIPTURE READING: Acts 2:22–23
KEY VERSE: Acts 2:24

[Jesus Christ] whom God raised up, having loosed the pains of death, because it was not possible that He should be held by it.

Here is the essence of the crucified life—you can win over sin because you are joined inseparably to the Lord Jesus Christ who has conquered sin. Paul wrote that he wanted to know Christ in "the power of His resurrection" (Phil. 3:10 NASB). He desired to experience the indwelling resurrection power of Jesus Christ day by day.

For you, that possibility is a reality through your indivisible union with the risen Christ. That is precisely why the Christian life is a victorious one. You win not by undying struggle, but by submission to and reliance on the triumphant Spirit of God in you.

Jesus is Lord; His Spirit lives within you. You have been freed from the dominion of sin (not from its temptation or presence) and made a part of the kingdom of God.

Your part is determined obedience. Victory is yours when you rely on the Holy Spirit. It may not come instantly, but it will come if you walk with Christ in His power.

The Christian life can be an abundant one as you shift your focus from self-effort to the all-conquering might of Christ Jesus within whom is your hope and your victory.

Heavenly Father, please change my focus from self-effort to the powerful might of Jesus Christ. I want to live an abundant life. Help me walk in victory today.

SCRIPTURE READING: Romans 7:5–25

KEY VERSE: Romans 7:6

Now we have been delivered from the law, having died to what we were held by, so that we should serve in the newness of the Spirit and not in the oldness of the letter.

Before salvation, you were captive to the sin of envy—wanting what you could not have, desiring what others had. After salvation, you still experience the same problem, but you are all the more miserable because you realize God condemns the sin of covetousness.

The path to victory lies in the purpose and work of the Cross. Because you were crucified with Christ, you are no longer enslaved to sin. Envy has no claim on your new life lived in the power of the indwelling Holy Spirit.

You have been raised with Christ—made a partaker of His resurrection power. By faith in what God accomplished by the Cross, you can put on the new person—alive to God, filled with the Spirit, made in the image of God.

Living the crucified life is a bold act of faith. You may feel envious and be mentally assaulted by it. But now with Christ in you and you in Christ, you have a new source of power to cope with the problem. You can overcome; you can conquer; you can be content.

It is supernatural living—to be experienced, not understood—as you choose to present yourself and your affections to Christ each day as one alive from the dead.

Jealousy and envy have no place in my new life, Lord. Make me content. I want to live the crucified life.

May

THEME: The Horse Gate
REPRESENTING: The believer's warfare
KEY VERSE: 1 Timothy 6:12

Fight the good fight of faith, lay hold on eternal life, to which you were also called and have confessed the good confession in the presence of many witnesses.

SCRIPTURE READING: 1 Peter 5:8–9

KEY VERSE: Genesis 3:4

The serpent said to the woman, "You will not surely die."

One of the surest wake-up calls in the Christian life is realizing that you are in spiritual warfare. The avenues of Satan's assaults vary, but be assured that he will launch spiritual attacks against your mind, emotions, and will.

The apostle Peter warned that you should "be of sober spirit, be on the alert. Your adversary, the devil, prowls about like a roaring lion, seeking someone to devour" (1 Peter 5:8 NASB).

Before you received Christ as Savior, you were a captive of sin and Satan, whether or not you were aware of this bondage. Paul instructed Timothy not to quarrel with unbelievers but to hope that God would help them "come to their senses and escape from the snare of the devil, having been held captive by him to do his will" (2 Tim. 2:26 NASB). You lived, in Paul's words, "according to the course of this world, according to the prince of the power of the air [the devil and his evil angels]" (Eph. 2:2 NASB).

However, as a Christian, you have been delivered from "darkness to light and from the dominion of Satan to God" (Acts 26:18 NASB). You are no longer under the devil's dominion or authority. Praise God for your mighty deliverance, but be ready for conflict.

> *Lord, thank You for deliverance from darkness to light, from the dominion of Satan to You. Make me ready for the conflicts that lie ahead.*

SCRIPTURE READING: 1 John 1:5–2:2
KEY VERSE: 1 Timothy 6:12

Fight the good fight of faith, lay hold on eternal life, to which you were also called and have confessed the good confession in the presence of many witnesses.

The Gulf War was a highlight film of readiness. Each day's broadcasts usually contained a segment of how tank mechanics, flight crew, soldiers, and other military personnel took extra precautions to clean and repair their respective tools of war.

Fighting a spiritual war involves similar painstaking preparations. You cannot participate and enjoy the spoils of Christ's triumph over Satan without personal cleansing from sin. The Bible calls this repentance. It means you turn away from behavior that violates God's commands and practice what is right in His eyes.

Like abrasive desert sand, sin clogs your fellowship with the Father, disrupting your clear sense of His direction and creating static in your relationship with Him. The all-important line of communication with the Captain of your salvation is garbled, making victory more difficult.

Repentance will not happen until you are serious about sin. See it as God does. Hate it as He does. Understand its disabling effects on you.

Prepare yourself for the good fight of faith by identifying obvious sin, turning away from its practice, and in faith looking to God for His righteous help. You will be ready for the struggle with a clean and pure heart.

Lord, I want to be prepared for the good fight of faith. Eliminate anything in my life that is disrupting Your direction or creating static in my relationship with You.

SCRIPTURE READING: 2 Corinthians 2:10–11
KEY VERSE: 2 Timothy 2:26

And that they may come to their senses and escape the snare of the devil,
having been taken captive by him to do his will.

Many words are used to describe your archenemy, the devil: *evil one,*
tempter, prince of this world, the god of this age, prince of the power of the air,
and *accuser of the brethren.* He is represented as a serpent, dragon, and
angel of light. Whatever his title, you know he works craftily to deceive
both people and nations into believing his lies and doubting the truth of
God's Word.

He deceives unbelievers by blinding their minds to the truth. Such
comments as "The Bible really isn't inspired," and "How can the death of
one man thousands of years ago affect my life today?" are just two of his
distortions.

He deceives you, a Christian, by working in your mind to cause you to
doubt or ignore the truth that is God's Word. The mind is the battlefield,
and deception is his primary weapon.

Jesus resisted the devil with God's Word. When you are tempted, the
truth of the Bible is still your best defense. If you are under Satan's
assault, find the Scriptures that pertain to your battle. Memorize them,
meditate on them, and use them against the devil. The truth of God
defuses the lie of Satan every time.

Lord, teach me to use the sword of Your Spirit effectively. I praise You
that Your Word is a powerful, mighty weapon for the battles of my life
today.

SCRIPTURE READING: Ephesians 6:10–18

KEY VERSES: Ephesians 6:13–14

Take up the whole armor of God, that you may be able to withstand in the evil day, and having done all, to stand. Stand.

Proper dress is essential. If you're a football player, you put on shoulder pads. If you're a state trooper, you wear a uniform and a gun.

If you're a Christian, only one wardrobe will do: the full armor of God with which you can resist and overcome Satan. The reason you are to put on and take up this military-sounding apparel is simple: you are in a battle against an unseen foe, and you don't dress casually for warfare. The suit looks like this:

The loins of truth. This is the truth of what God's Word says about you. God accepts you unconditionally. You are His child. You belong to Him forever. This is your guard against deception.

The breastplate of righteousness. This is your standing with God. He has declared you innocent of all sin through the blood of Christ. This is your guard against guilt.

The preparation of the gospel of peace. This is your means for sharing the good news of salvation with others, bringing them the offer of peace through Christ; it is your guard against complacency and self-centeredness.

The shield of faith, helmet of salvation, and sword of the Spirit. These work together as your commitment to and reliance on the Word of God for every circumstance—refusing to yield to temptation or to falter in trials.

> *I receive Your truth, Lord. Deception will not operate in my life today.*
> *I put on Your righteousness, and I reject unrighteousness. I take the*
> *shield of faith, the helmet of salvation, and the sword of the Spirit.*
> *Now send me to share the good news with others.*

SCRIPTURE READING: 2 Corinthians 10:3–4
KEY VERSE: 2 Corinthians 10:3

For though we walk in the flesh, we do not war according to the flesh.

You don't have to be a hunter to know that you can't kill a grizzly bear with a popgun. Success in any conflict requires using weapons suitable to the task.

Second Corinthians 10:3–4 applies this principle in the spiritual realm: "For though we walk in the flesh, we do not war according to the flesh, for the weapons of our warfare are not of the flesh, but divinely powerful for the destruction of fortresses" (NASB).

The mighty arsenal described in Ephesians 6 is the only sure defense against the onslaughts of Satan and a sinful world. When you reach for other means of protection, you lose the fight and possibly make yourself even more vulnerable to attack.

In dealing with rocky relationships, do you put on the sandals of peace, or do you attempt manipulation and harmful compromise?

When you confront lies, do you use God's girdle of truth or the authority of people?

For times of temptation, are you covered by the shield of faith or by rationalization?

When emotions overpower you, do you adjust them with the breastplate of righteousness or with aggression and uncontrolled outbursts?

The choice you make in each encounter decides the outcome. Learn how to take up the arms God provides; He gives the victory every time.

> *The weapons of my warfare are powerful, Lord. Help me use them instead of fighting spiritual battles in my own strength.*

SCRIPTURE READING: Romans 8:35–39
KEY VERSE: Galatians 5:17

The flesh lusts against the Spirit, and the Spirit against the flesh; and these are contrary to one another, so that you do not do the things that you wish.

When asked who their greatest enemy is, most believers would say Satan. He is literally public enemy number one and will continue to rage and battle until Christ throws him into the everlasting lake of fire in hell (Rev. 20:10).

The devil, however, is not the only adversary on whom you must keep a watchful eye. Within the context of this overarching spiritual conflict are two less infamous, but equally notable foes.

Galatians 5:17 identifies your internal enemy: "The flesh sets its desire against the Spirit, and the Spirit against the flesh; for these are in opposition to one another, so that you may not do the things that you please" (NASB). These sinful desires cannot control you now, yet they still pack a powerful punch in your mind and emotions.

Externally your very position in Christ sets you at odds with the entire world system (1 John 2:15–17). People who don't know Him as Savior have different values, ideals, and moral codes.

Even though at times you may feel surrounded by more enemies than you can name, you are never defeated (Rom. 8:35–39). In the turbulence today and the tough times ahead, remember that you are a conqueror in Christ.

Sometimes I feel surrounded by the enemy, Lord. In tough times help me remember I am a conqueror in Christ. I am an overcomer.

SCRIPTURE READING: James 4:1–8

KEY VERSE: 1 Corinthians 16:13

Watch, stand fast in the faith, be brave, be strong.

During the Persian Gulf War, surprise was an effective tool of the Allied Forces. Both the air and the ground offensives used the element of surprise in their tactical maneuvers, catching the Iraqi military off guard on numerous occasions.

Some of our success, however, can be attributed to a lack of alertness on behalf of the Iraqi soldiers. Those soldiers, buried deep in bunkers, were mentally lulled into tactical lethargy.

Alertness to the strategy and presence of the enemy is always a fundamental part of winning a war, including the spiritual war Christians fight against the forces of the devil, the world, and sin. Alertness is dulled by pride or self-reliance.

The more confident you are in your abilities, the more complacent you are about sin and the less attentive you are to the enemy's efforts. Do you know that you wake up to a spiritual war each morning? Are you aware that the power of the evil one is set against you?

Simply stepping out into the day with a smile and a hearty breakfast may make you feel good but does not prepare you for spiritual combat. Alertness begins with awareness of the conflict and the identity of the enemy. Steeled against his schemes, you will not be caught by surprise.

Heavenly Father, remove my complacency. Let me be spiritually alert. Make me aware of the power of the evil one. Don't let his schemes catch me by surprise.

SCRIPTURE READING: Ephesians 2:1–7

KEY VERSE: Matthew 26:41

Watch and pray, lest you enter into temptation. The spirit indeed is willing, but the flesh is weak.

Once you become aware of the severe nature of your spiritual conflict, you must realize God has issued an authoritative call to arms.

"Resist him [the devil]," Peter told the suffering saints in his first epistle (1 Peter 5:9 NASB).

"Stand firm against the schemes of the devil," Paul told the Ephesian believers (Eph. 6:11 NASB).

"Resist the devil and he will flee from you," James wrote the early church (James 4:7 NASB).

God does not ask you to obey an impossible command. If it is useless to resist Satan, why would the Father insist on your defiance?

The devil was met and defeated by Christ in His life, death, and resurrection. On Calvary He dealt a mortal blow to the devil's chief weapon—death—destroying its power for those who believe in the Savior.

Although Satan conducts guerrilla warfare and still possesses deadly weapons of unbelief, doubt, and temptation, he has been confronted on the battlefield of the ages—Golgotha—and has been decisively and eternally defeated.

You can resist the devil. You can overcome his temptations and live an abundant, overcoming Christian life.

Father, thank You for the mortal blow dealt to Satan at Calvary. Because of that victory, I can stand firm and resist the devil's tactics.

SCRIPTURE READING: Psalm 25
KEY VERSE: Acts 26:18

To open their eyes, in order to turn them from darkness to light, and from the power of Satan to God, that they may receive forgiveness of sins and an inheritance among those who are sanctified by faith in Me.

How do you resist your conquered but still dangerous foe, the devil?

First, understand that you fight in God's supernatural strength, not your own. That strength is yours through the indwelling presence of the "God of all grace, who . . . will Himself perfect, confirm, strengthen and establish you" (1 Peter 5:10 NASB). Your faith in God's might is like a spiritual smart bomb that thwarts the devil's schemes.

Second, submit and draw near to God (James 4:7–8). You do not submit to your temptation; you submit to God: "Lord, You know I am strongly attracted to this person, but I am even more attracted to You. I surrender to You." When you turn and yield to God instead of your temptations, you place yourself in the "mighty hand of God" (1 Peter 5:6 NASB).

Third, persevere "with all prayer and petition" (Eph. 6:18 NASB). You are righteous in Christ, and God hears and answers the prayers of the righteous.

Prayer routs the enemy, overrunning his evil command and control system with the power and authority of Jesus Christ. Pray quickly; pray hard; pray confidently. You are already on the winning side.

Father, I fight in Your strength. I submit and draw near to You. Help me persevere in prayer until complete victory is mine.

SCRIPTURE READING: Jude 1–4

KEY VERSE: Galatians 2:4

This occurred because of false brethren secretly brought in (who came in by stealth to spy out our liberty which we have in Christ Jesus, that they might bring us into bondage).

The Christian experience is often arduous. Mingled with the peace and contentment Christ imparts are the struggle and labor of spiritual warfare. There is a fight of faith, a conflict of passions.

Realizing you are engaged in hostilities should radically alter your thinking and actions according to Peter Kreeft, a professor of philosophy at Boston College. In an article in *Christianity Today,* Kreeft writes,

When you know you are in a war, your adrenaline flows. You are passionate. You willingly make sacrifices. You don't expect or demand constant comfort, security, enjoyment, and entertainment.

Each day's tasks become a spy mission, an assignment from our Commander. The one thing life never is in battle is the very thing it is for the modern world: boring and purposeless.

When there is a "clear and present danger," life brings a great purpose and a great choice.

The whole reason for the most important event in human history, the Incarnation, was spiritual warfare: God's invasion of enemy occupied territory to redeem his children from captivity to the forces of evil.

We are at war! Help me realize this, Lord. Let me develop a wartime lifestyle that is not focused on comfort, security, enjoyment, or entertainment.

Having disarmed principalities and powers, He made a public spectacle of them, triumphing over them in it.

In occupied or totalitarian states, resistance movements commonly operate. However, they are usually small in number and vastly inferior to the dominant force. Their actions, while irritating, have little impact.

This is not the kind of opposition God asks of you when He commands you to resist the devil. You are to engage your spiritual adversary "firm in your faith" (1 Peter 5:9 NASB). The same spirit of triumph echoes from Paul, who urged you to "stand firm against the schemes of the devil" (Eph. 6:11 NASB) and "having done everything, to stand firm" (Eph. 6:13 NASB).

"But I am no match for Satan," you say. You are clearly right. Your solidity comes from your confidence in Christ who routed Satan on the cross. Though your enemy still works, his hour of doom draws near.

Martin Luther wrote in his hymn "A Mighty Fortress Is Our God":

> For still our ancient foe doth seek to work us woe—
> His craft and power are great, and armed with cruel hate, on earth is not his equal.
> Did we in our own strength confide, our striving would be losing,
> Were not the right man on our side, the man of God's own choosing.
> Dost ask who that may be? Christ Jesus, it is He.

Help me remain firm in the faith, Father. When I have done everything to stand against the enemy, then help me do just that—stand!

SCRIPTURE READING: 1 John 2:15–17, 28
KEY VERSE: John 16:33

These things I have spoken to you, that in Me you may have peace. In the world you will have tribulation; but be of good cheer, I have overcome the world.

As the *cosmocrat,* or ruler of this *cosmos* (world system), Satan has very precise schemes orchestrated to frustrate you, a believer in Christ. Recognizing and understanding his ploys can help you thwart his shrewd tactics and walk in victory.

The devil seeks to impede your spiritual progress by keeping you from prayer. He accomplishes this by propagating a defective doctrine of guilt.

When you are overloaded with guilty feelings, you withdraw from God. This is Satan's cruel hoax. Your guilt—all of it—was placed on Christ at Calvary. You are completely accepted by God. If you have sinned, sincere confession instantly restores joyful fellowship.

Satan's other primary stratagem to foil your walk with Christ is causing you to doubt God's promises. The spiritual conflict hinges upon faith. Do you really believe God will do what He says? Will He honor His Word? Can you bank on the Scriptures without reservation and expect God to fulfill His pledges?

Absolutely. God's Word was written by Himself. It is His unalterable Word to you. Reject guilt. Be of good courage and refuse doubt. Satan's chief schemes will be defused and God's truth unleashed for triumph.

I believe what You said, Lord. You will honor Your Word. You will fulfill Your promises. Your truth will bring triumph in my life today.

SCRIPTURE READING: Luke 10:18–20
KEY VERSE: Matthew 18:18

Assuredly, I say to you, whatever you bind on earth will be bound in heaven,
and whatever you loose on earth will be loosed in heaven.

In the time of rebuilding following World War II, a subtle international conflict began. Nations seeking ideological supremacy jockeyed for world position in an ongoing confrontation that has been labeled the Cold War.

Diplomacy became even more complicated, however, when leaders did not recognize that such tensions existed. Those who denied its reality formed policies that ultimately threatened their national security.

A cold war is going on right now in the spiritual realm as well. You can't see it, though; no visible shots are fired, no bombs dropped. But the war is real. First Peter 5:8 lays bare the battle plan of your number one enemy: "Be of sober spirit, be on the alert. Your adversary, the devil, prowls about like a roaring lion, seeking someone to devour" (NASB).

Ignorance is one of Satan's most potent weapons. If you dismiss him as an imaginary symbol of evil or a harmless, horned man in red tights, you have just the picture he wants you to have. You are vulnerable when your guard is down.

In Luke 10:18–20, Jesus said that His children are to expect, but not fear, Satan's schemes. Awareness is the key. God gives you insight into the invisible world so that you will be prepared for every assault.

> *Dear heavenly Father, please give me insight into the invisible world*
> *so that I will be prepared for every assault of the enemy. I want to win*
> *the spiritual cold war.*

SCRIPTURE READING: Isaiah 14:12–14
KEY VERSE: 1 John 4:1

Beloved, do not believe every spirit, but test the spirits, whether they are of God; because many false prophets have gone out into the world.

Since his prideful revolt and fall from heaven, Satan has been committed to destruction, deception, and rebellion against God. His tactics have not changed; from the first temptation in the Garden of Eden, his strategy has been the distortion of God's Word (Isa. 14:12–14).

First John 4:1 warns, "Beloved, do not believe every spirit, but test the spirits to see whether they are from God; because many false prophets have gone out into the world" (NASB). Many are led into error by those who make deceptive changes or additions to God's unerring, eternal truth.

The best line of defense against the twisting of Scripture is knowing exactly what it says. For example, you may hear this often-quoted statement: "The Bible says money is the root of all evil." But 1 Timothy 6:10 actually says, "For *the love of money* is a root of all sorts of evil" (NASB, emphasis mine). What a difference a few words make!

Whenever you hear teaching at church or receive information about the Bible, check it out yourself. Find a good concordance to help you locate pertinent passages quickly, and always compare a verse to other similar verses to verify the context.

Do you test what you hear? Ask God today for a wise and discerning spirit.

O God, help me distinguish Your truth from the spirit of error that pervades this world today. Give me a wise and discerning heart and mind.

SCRIPTURE READING: Revelation 20:7–10
KEY VERSE: Hebrews 2:14

Inasmuch then as the children have partaken of flesh and blood, He Himself likewise shared in the same, that through death He might destroy him who had the power of death, that is, the devil.

Some Christians are afraid to talk about Satan or think about spiritual warfare. While we should be careful not to underestimate his destructive arsenal (Jude 9), we should never fear the devil.

Although he is still active by God's permission, the devil has been soundly defeated. He is a rebellious angelic creature on the losing end of a cosmic struggle with Creator God. He knows his fate is the lake of fire from which he will never escape (Rev. 20:7–10).

The instrument of defeat and our guaranteed victory over his power is the cross of Christ. When Jesus died on the cross, He paid the price for our sins and conquered the power of Satan: "He Himself likewise also partook of the same, that through death He might render powerless him who had the power of death, that is, the devil" (Heb. 2:14 NASB).

At the cross, Jesus "disarmed the rulers and authorities [Satan and his demons]" and "made a public display of them, having triumphed over them through Him" (Col. 2:15 NASB).

Jesus defeated the devil at the cross by delivering you from sin's penalty, death. Satan is a vanquished foe, and he knows it. You are no longer under his dominion but under the rule and reign of Christ.

I rejoice today, dear Lord, that through the death of Your Son, I am no longer under the dominion of Satan. My victory is guaranteed through the power of the Cross.

SCRIPTURE READING: Matthew 4:1–11
KEY VERSE: Matthew 4:10

Jesus said to him, "Away with you, Satan! For it is written, 'You shall wor-ship the LORD your God, and Him only you shall serve.'"

If temptation does not come from God, what is its source? Temptation is a tool of Satan. He enticed Eve in the Garden of Eden and continues his incessant seduction.

Satan is your adversary. He desires to disable your spiritual service, dis-tract your spiritual attention, and disrupt your spiritual relationship with the Father. Since he cannot affect your eternal destiny, he seeks to disable you emotionally, short-circuiting your joy and testimony.

The world system is also a source of temptation. The world system is the prevailing philosophy of the age, devoid of God's wisdom. A quick look at the arts, entertainment, and education reveals an underlying value system ruled by ungodly appetites and reasoning, not God. The lust of the eyes and flesh and the pride of life are the key players in the world sys-tem.

Yet another source of temptation is the power of sin still abiding in each Christian. You are freed from sin's penalty by faith in Christ but must be delivered daily from its power through His sanctifying Spirit.

Whatever the source of temptation in your life, Jesus Christ can help you overcome it.

Dear Lord, I need Your help to overcome the world system and the power of sin. Deliver me from its power through Your sanctifying Holy Spirit.

SCRIPTURE READING: James 1:12–16

KEY VERSE: Proverbs 1:10

My son, if sinners entice you,
Do not consent.

A father loses his temper once more with his children. "That is the way my father treated me," he lamely reasons. "I guess I am just like him."

A teenager succumbs to another episode of intoxication. "Hey, everybody else does it," he says with a shrug. "I cannot be the only Goody Two-shoes in the crowd."

Temptation. Every believer encounters it. For some, it is an occasional struggle. For most, it is an everyday occurrence, often resulting in failure. When temptation leads to sin, we often explain our conduct by blaming others, our temperament, our environment, or any other acceptable excuse.

The Greek word for temptation is *peirazo*. It means "an enticement or inducement to evil." Although God often tests you in various ways to enlarge your faith, He never tempts you to do evil. That contradicts His absolute holiness. Tests from God are for your spiritual growth. Temptations can be for your spiritual detriment if you yield to them or to your spiritual advantage if you reject them.

Whatever temptations you face, do not accuse God. If you succumb and sin, be honest and hold yourself accountable. His forgiveness always ensures a fresh start.

Make me alert to temptation today, dear Lord. Help me meet each enticement in Your power and grow spiritually as I emerge victorious.

SCRIPTURE READING: 2 Samuel 11
KEY VERSE: John 8:44

You are of your father the devil, and the desires of your father you want to do. He was a murderer from the beginning, and does not stand in the truth, because there is no truth in him. When he speaks a lie, he speaks from his own resources, for he is a liar and the father of it.

Temptation is not sin. If that was true, then our Lord would have sinned when tempted by Satan. But Jesus was the perfect sacrifice, without sin, so that He might pay our sin debt.

Temptation is the appeal to engage in a form of unholy conduct. Dr. Henry Thiessen described the fundamental components of temptation in *Systematic Theology:* "Satan's temptation may be summed up as appealing to man in this way: it made man desire what God had forbidden, to know what God had not revealed, and to be what God had not intended for him to be."

God establishes boundaries in your personal relationship with Him. He allows you tremendous degrees of personal freedom to think, act, and speak, but His Word clearly defines when your thoughts, deeds, and words transgress His boundaries.

Temptation always entices you to transcend God's borders. It seduces you into thinking something or someone else other than God can meet your emotional, physical, or spiritual needs.

Temptation is a trap of excess and indulgence, tripped by self-gratification. It need not be sprung.

Father, I want to live within the boundaries You set. Keep me from the traps of excess and indulgence sprung by my self-gratification.

SCRIPTURE READING: Genesis 3:1–7

KEY VERSE: 2 Corinthians 11:3

I fear, lest somehow, as the serpent deceived Eve by his craftiness, so your minds may be corrupted from the simplicity that is in Christ.

Even a hungry walleye will not strike an unbaited hook. Satan, the angel of light, is the master tempter, able to conceal his evil designs through appealing camouflage.

How does he manage to deceive you, to get you to take the bait of temptation? His initial thrust works at undermining your confidence in God's goodness and provision.

God had bestowed every blessing necessary on Adam and Eve. They wanted for nothing until Satan aroused suspicion of God's faithfulness: "Indeed, has God said . . . ?" (Gen. 3:1 NASB) was and is his opening dialogue.

Has God really said you are to be faithful to your marriage partner? Has God really said you are to speak for the edification of people and not their destruction? The more you entertain doubt, the closer you move to yielding to Satan's temptation.

The next step is believing the tempter's lie: "And the serpent said to the woman, 'You surely shall not die!'" (Gen. 3:4 NASB).

"Adultery is commonplace today."

"Words never hurt anybody."

"What harm can a few pleasurable thoughts do?"

"Everybody else is in debt."

Doubts and lies. Never buy into them. The price is always exacting and never right.

You meant what You said, Lord. I accept Your word without argument or reservation. Let me never doubt what You have said!

SCRIPTURE READING: 1 Kings 11:1–4
KEY VERSE: Psalm 119:11

Your word I have hidden in my heart,
That I might not sin against You.

Temptation can storm your mind and heart with sudden fury, overwhelming you and leading you into the whirlwind of sin. Your best defense is to willfully brace yourself daily for its assaults, mindful that you are easily conquered when ill-prepared.

You must choose to spend time with the Father, fellowshipping with Him in prayer and feasting on His Word. This is more than mere exercise. It is life and breath, spiritual stamina. Your devotion is strengthened. Your awareness of Satan's subtle strategies is heightened. This is the way you build truth into your life, sensitizing yourself to error and deceit. Apart from regular, concentrated time with God, you are vulnerable to temptation.

You also prepare for temptation by maximizing the rewards of obedience while minimizing the pleasures of sin. Temptation seems sweet. But it leaves a bitter aftertaste. Resisting temptation is arduous, but the fruits of obedience are lasting and fulfilling.

Prepare now for Satan's tempting attractions. When they come, you will be ready, armed with the truth and convinced of the blessings of obedience.

Prepare me now, Lord, for the hour of temptation. Arm me with the truth. Let me be convinced of the blessings of obedience. Strengthen my devotion for tough times ahead.

The thief does not come except to steal, and to kill, and to destroy. I have come that they may have life, and that they may have it more abundantly.

Perhaps the most passionate, potent temptation of all is sexual allure. Even the strongest-willed men and women are overcome by its illicit attraction. Even the best marriages are destroyed by adulterous relationships.

One reason is the enormous emphasis our society places on sexuality. Sensuality permeates our entire culture, titillating us through television, magazines, books, and fashion.

Sexual temptation is also extremely pleasurable to contemplate. Here, more than anywhere else perhaps, Satan disguises his mischief as an angel of light, concealing its dark consequences.

But a more basic reason is the natural, God-given desire for physical relationships. Sex is God's idea but only within the bounds of marriage. Thus, Satan takes a legitimate desire for sexual fulfillment, seeking to twist and distort it, and deceives us through the illegitimate means of adultery, fornication, pornography, and other forms of sexual abuse.

The fierce struggle is to enjoy your sexuality as God intends while resisting Satan's alluring, but devastating temptation. Be thankful that God provides a way of escape.

Heavenly Father, keep me from sexual sins. You have provided a way of escape. Let me choose it. I want to conquer my sinful passions.

SCRIPTURE READING: Genesis 39

KEY VERSES: Genesis 39:9, 12

"There is no one greater in this house than I, nor has he kept back anything from me but you, because you are his wife. How then can I do this great wickedness, and sin against God?" . . . She caught him by his garment, saying, "Lie with me." But he left his garment in her hand, and fled and ran outside.

"Just say no" is a familiar echo in the war on drugs, but it has done little to reduce narcotic use. It does not work with sexual temptation either.

God warns you in the Scriptures that you cannot handle sexual temptation with mere determination or self-discipline. Rather, He provides two clear principles of defense against sensual onslaught.

The first principle is preventive: express daily devotion to Jesus Christ. You cannot simply say no. That leaves a vacuum. For the Christian, that void is always filled with an affirmative yes to Jesus Christ: "Yes, Lord, I do love You and want to follow You. I do realize my frailty and ask You to deliver me from temptation. I am committed to You." This everyday exercise takes up the shield of faith and withstands Satan's ploys.

The second principle is simple: flee temptation and avoid the source. Joseph did. You must do the same. Do not go out to lunch with your secretary. Do not meet your boss for a late night meeting. Do not visit a local hangout.

Joseph loved God too much to sin against Him (Gen. 39:9). He also fled at the peak of temptation. Both principles still work.

> *I love You, Lord. I want to follow You. I realize my frailty and ask You to deliver me from temptation. Help me avoid its source because of my love for You.*

SCRIPTURE READING: Matthew 18:6–14
KEY VERSE: Matthew 18:6

Whoever causes one of these little ones who believe in Me to sin, it would be better for him if a millstone were hung around his neck, and he were drowned in the depth of the sea.

No one likes to feel used by another person. Yet when we cause other believers to stumble in their Christian walk, we have unwittingly become tools of the tempter. When we spread gossip in the office, dress immodestly, speak coarsely, or allow questionable television programs in our homes, we can be the tempter's agents. Suppose you were asked: "Do you want to be used by Satan?" Surely your answer would be an adamant "No!"

Our wily adversary, however, has no qualms about using our sins and wayward habits to delude and deceive other Christians. While each of us is responsible for the response to temptation, we can avoid any compliance with the deceiver's tactics as we understand a crucial truth: each Christian is part of Christ's body. Our actions are never in isolation. For good or evil, our behavior affects the health and vitality of other believers.

Therefore, it is for your well-being as well as the rest of the body of Christ that you live obediently. God desires that you be a blessing to others, not a curse. Let your love for believers keep you and them from temptation.

> *Heavenly Father, as part of the body of Christ, I realize my actions are not in isolation. Let me be a blessing and not a curse to others. Don't let me lead others into temptation.*

SCRIPTURE READING: 1 Corinthians 6:12; 8:13; 10:31
KEY VERSE: 1 Corinthians 10:31

Whether you eat or drink, or whatever you do, do all to the glory of God.

Keeping a close check on your lifestyle is the most reliable means to avoid direct or indirect participation in the tempter's schemes. Jerry Bridges highlights four guidelines in his book *The Pursuit of Holiness* that will help you examine your practices for purity of motive and possibility of harm to a weaker believer in Christ:

"Everything is permissible for me"—but not everything is beneficial. (1 Corinthians 6:12)
Question 1: Is it helpful, physically, spiritually, and mentally?

"Everything is permissible for me"—but I will not be mastered by anything. (1 Corinthians 6:12)
Question 2: Does it bring me under its power?

"Therefore, if what I eat causes my brother to fall into sin, I will never eat meat again, so that I will not cause him to fall."
(1 Corinthians 8:13)
Question 3: Does it hurt others?

"So whether you eat or drink or whatever you do, do it all for the glory of God." (1 Corinthians 10:31)
Question 4: Does it glorify God?

Contemplating and applying these principles will help you deal with temptation while encouraging your brother or sister in Christ, not weakening him or her.

> *Father, I pause right now to examine my practices. Are they helpful physically, spiritually, and mentally? Is there anything I am doing that brings me under its power? Does anything I do hurt others? Does all I do glorify You?*

SCRIPTURE READING: Romans 8:1–11
KEY VERSES: Romans 12:1–2

I beseech you therefore, brethren, by the mercies of God, that you present your bodies a living sacrifice, holy, acceptable to God, which is your reasonable service. And do not be conformed to this world, but be transformed by the renewing of your mind, that you may prove what is that good and acceptable and perfect will of God.

Martin Luther was a profound reformer and premier preacher of biblical doctrine. He also had a thorough grasp of life in the practical lane and described the process of temptation with this commonsense adage: "You can't keep the birds from flying over your head; but you can keep them from building a nest in your hair." Temptation, Luther said, is inevitable. What you do with temptation is a matter of personal choice.

How do you keep temptation from leading you into sin? Promptly reject temptation's deceptive advertisements: "I recognize this thought is not from God. I refuse to entertain this uninvited and unwelcome guest."

Replace the thought with a positive promise from God's Word. Make it applicable to the nature of the temptation.

Think of someone you can help or something constructive you can do. An idle mind and idle hands are the devil's workshop where he plies his devious trade.

Pray instantly. Prayer and temptation are incompatible. Sincere prayer will magnify God's presence and leave no place for the devil's nest.

Heavenly Father, let me reject temptation as an uninvited guest. Help me resist thoughts that are not from You and replace them with applicable promises from Your Word.

SCRIPTURE READING: John 16:7–15

KEY VERSE: Matthew 6:13

And do not lead us into temptation,

But deliver us from the evil one.

For Yours is the kingdom and the power and the glory forever. Amen.

John Bunyan, the Puritan preacher and writer, said of temptations: "Temptations, when we first meet them, are as the lion that roared upon Samson; but if we overcome them, the next time we see them, we shall find a nest of honey within them."

God is faithful. God assures you that you can enjoy the sweet taste of victory over temptations, whatever their nature. When temptation presents itself, God always comes to your aid. The temptation is never more than He can handle; therefore, it is never more than you can handle, no matter how weak and helpless you feel. Knowing you can deal with the tempter in God's strength bolsters your spiritual morale.

God provides the way of escape for each temptation. The best way is by faith in the power and truth of His Word—the very tool Jesus used to overcome Satan's snare. Truth defeats error every time you obey.

God also promises that you can endure it. The temptations may not—and probably will not—vanish. But you can bear up under their load, daily casting your burdens on the Lord who will "not lead us into temptation, but deliver us from evil" (Matt. 6:13 NASB).

Thank You, dear Lord, that the temptations I face are not greater than

I can handle. You have provided a way of escape. Let me take it!

SCRIPTURE READING: Hebrews 4:11–16
KEY VERSE: Hebrews 4:14

Seeing then that we have a great High Priest who has passed through the heavens, Jesus the Son of God, let us hold fast our confession.

Temptation is universal. It tantalizes young and old, educated and unschooled, monks and mechanics. Its presence and constant pull, however, are not indictments of our spiritual condition. Indeed, when we resist them, God can use our temptations to reinforce our faith.

British author C. S. Lewis revealed in his book *Mere Christianity* how God can turn the tables on the tempter's evil desires:

A silly idea is current that good people do not know what temptation means. This is an obvious lie. Only those who try to resist temptation know how strong it is. . . .

A man who gives in to temptation after five minutes simply does not know what it would have been like an hour later. That is why bad people, in one sense, know very little about badness. They have lived a sheltered life by always giving in.

We never find out the strength of the evil impulse inside us until we try to fight it; and Christ, because He was the only man who never yielded to temptation, is also the only man who knows to the full what temptation means—the only complete realist.

Guilt should never accompany temptation. Turn it away by turning to Christ.

Lord, temptations are strong, but You are stronger! Help me turn away temptations by turning to You. Let me eliminate guilt by fighting every evil impulse.

SCRIPTURE READING: Judges 2:7–19
KEY VERSE: Judges 2:19

It came to pass, when the judge was dead, that they reverted and behaved more corruptly than their fathers, by following other gods, to serve them and bow down to them. They did not cease from their own doings nor from their stubborn way.

A young boy was assigned the chore of weeding his father's garden. At first glance, the lad appeared to have done a fine job.

To the eye, the garden was weed-free. However, after a few days and a good rain, the rows again sprouted with the unsightly greenery. The youngster had superficially achieved his assignment. He had removed the tops of the weeds but failed to uproot them.

The problem was not solved.

We tend to take the same ineffective approach concerning temptation, dealing with the surface symptoms rather than the root cause. That can explain why we frequently commit the same sin. We repeat the distasteful cycle—temptation, yielding, sin, confession—with predictable regularity.

We wrestle with drugs and alcohol without identifying the anger driving us to indulgence. We grapple with a critical spirit while ignoring the poison of bitterness that nourishes its presence.

Ask God's Spirit to illumine the root problem pertaining to a particular, persistent temptation. Depend on His grace and His power to pull down its stronghold and defuse its allure. An accurate diagnosis is the first step to healing.

Help me deal with root causes instead of surface symptoms, O Lord. Reveal the problems behind my persistent temptations, then give me the power to pull down these strongholds.

SCRIPTURE READING: Psalm 51

KEY VERSES: Psalm 51:16–17

You do not desire sacrifice, or else I would give it;
You do not delight in burnt offering.
The sacrifices of God are a broken spirit,
A broken and a contrite heart—
These, O God, You will not despise.

You failed. The tempter played his seductive tune, and you danced. For the first time, the third time, the "I don't know how many" times, you failed.

Now what? Do you cower before God, run from Him? Do you drown in your guilt, sink in your sadness, nosedive into mediocrity?

While the Father's desire is resistance to and victory over temptation, He provides a way of escape even when you capitulate. He meets and deals with your failure through forgiveness and mercy. The remedy of the Cross is still effective for a believer who drinks the poison of temptation.

Moses failed. David failed. Peter failed. On numerous occasions the people and leaders of Israel erred.

But the love and grace of God remain greater than any believer's failure. Christ's sacrificial death paid your sin debt in full, removing your guilt, and His resurrection grants you His unceasing hope and power.

Confess your sin. Acknowledge that you have grieved God. Humbly and penitently receive His forgiveness. Learn about your weakness and His provision. Cling to His stubborn love that will never forsake you. Do not give up the fight. God is with you and for you, never against you.

Your grace is greater than my failure. You are for me, and never
against me. Thank You, Lord!

SCRIPTURE READING: Revelation 3:20–22

KEY VERSE: Revelation 12:11

They overcame him by the blood of the Lamb and by the word of their tes-
timony, and they did not love their lives to the death.

Dr. A. W. Tozer stressed the need for the proper perspective on spiritual warfare in *Born After Midnight:*

The scriptural way to see things is to set the Lord always before
us, put Christ in the center of our vision, and if Satan is lurking
around, he will appear on the margin and only be seen as but a
shadow on the edge of the brightness.

It is always wrong to reverse this to set Satan in the focus of our
vision and push God out to the margin. Nothing but tragedy can
come of such inversion.

The best way to keep the enemy out is to keep Christ in. The
sheep need not be terrified by the wolf; they have but to stay close
to the shepherd. It is not the praying sheep Satan fears, but the presence of the shepherd.

The instructed Christian whose faculties have been developed by
the Word and the Spirit will not fear the devil. When necessary he
will stand against the powers of darkness and overcome them by the
blood of the Lamb and the word of his testimony.

Fill your heart and mind with the power and awe of the God who has
the keys to life and death. Fear God and you need never be terrified again
by the roar of the devilish lion, for the Lion of Judah is with you.

Satan is out, and You are in, God! Keep my focus on You instead of
the enemy. Let me rest secure in Your presence and power.

SCRIPTURE READING: Revelation 19:19–20:3

KEY VERSE: Revelation 2:7

He who has an ear, let him hear what the Spirit says to the churches. To him who overcomes I will give to eat from the tree of life, which is in the midst of the Paradise of God.

Although Jesus has conquered Satan and his hosts, they still push the battle. They are defeated but not yet confined to their final destiny—the lake of fire.

In his book *The Cross of Christ,* author John R. W. Stott explains the tension in this manner:

> For though the devil has been defeated, he has not yet conceded defeat. Although he has been overthrown, he has not yet been eliminated. In fact, he continues to wield great power.
>
> On the one hand we are alive, seated and reigning with Christ, with even the principalities and powers of evil placed by God under His (and therefore our) feet; on the other hand we are warned that these same spiritual forces have set themselves in opposition to us so that we have no hope of standing against them unless we are strong in the Lord's strength and clad in His armor.
>
> The tension is part of the Christian dilemma between the "already" and the "not yet." Already the kingdom of God has been inaugurated and is advancing; not yet has it been consummated.

The victory over the devil was won at the cross. The battle still rages, but the Victor lives in you. Place your faith in the finished work of Christ on the cross, and you will always be led in His triumph.

Victory is mine because the Victor lives in me! I place my confidence in the finished work of the Cross, Lord. Lead me in triumph!

June

THEME: The Refuse Gate

REPRESENTING: The old, carnal nature that needs to be changed by God's power

KEY VERSE: 2 Corinthians 5:17

Therefore, if anyone is in Christ, he is a new creation; old things have passed away; behold, all things have become new.

SCRIPTURE READING: Galatians 5:16–26

KEY VERSE: Galatians 5:25

If we live in the Spirit, let us also walk in the Spirit.

"Now the deeds of the flesh are evident" (Gal. 5:19 NASB).

"But the fruit of the Spirit is . . ." (Gal. 5:22 NASB).

The distinction here is so critical that it can mean the difference between an enjoyable, profitable, abundant Christian life and a mediocre, vacillating one. Here's why. Your life and journey as a Christian began through the work of the Spirit and, if they are to be successful, must continue through His work in you.

Once saved, the tendency is to revert to established behavior patterns to deal with sin. You do not understand when you fail and try harder and fail again. But resolve and grit could not save you from sin or self, and they will not free you from your problems after you are saved.

What must happen is a transforming dependence upon the power of the Holy Spirit. The victorious life is one that abides and rests in and yields to the Spirit of God.

That does not mean that you fail to pray, work, study, read, or accept responsibility. It does mean that you do these things with reliance upon the power of God to liberate you.

How does that happen? By simple faith that God will do it (just as you were saved) and a submissive, obedient heart that looks to and leans on the Spirit of God.

Give me a submissive, obedient heart, Father. Let me lean on Your Spirit instead of my flesh. The journey I've begun must continue through the work of the Spirit in me.

SCRIPTURE READING: 1 Timothy 1:12–16
KEY VERSE: Hebrews 10:17

Their sins and their lawless deeds I will remember no more.

"Be easy on others and hard on yourself" is an old saying. To a degree, that commonsense proverb rings true. But when it comes to forgiveness, it can be misapplied.

What if you are the one responsible for a divorce? What if you are the one who spread malicious gossip about another—gossip that proved false? What if you lost your temper and struck your mate?

An inability to forgive yourself can lead to a severe character disorder, plunging you ever deeper into discouragement, bitterness, and hopelessness.

If anyone had a reason to judge himself harshly, it was the apostle Paul. He was a killer, persecutor, and enemy of the church. What if Paul had allowed his past to haunt him after his dramatic conversion to Christ? Could he possibly have shared Christ so boldly and persistently?

And remember David's sin. What if he had dwelt on his sin with Bathsheba? Could he have been "a man after God's own heart"?

In each case, their refusal to forgive themselves would have damaged their lives and ministry. Being hard on yourself when it comes to forgiveness is a setup for a lifetime of self-inflicted pain.

> *Dear Lord, I have experienced much pain simply because I refused to forgive myself. I do that now, Father. I forgive myself, even as You have forgiven me.*

SCRIPTURE READING: Lamentations 3:19–26
KEY VERSE: Lamentations 3:22

Through the LORD's mercies we are not consumed,
Because His compassions fail not.

How can you forgive yourself? How can you stop the pain that comes from knowing you have injured others?

Here is the key. You can forgive yourself because Christ has forgiven you.

If Jesus Christ, the most stringent Judge, has declared your sin forgiven through His death on the cross, how can you not forgive yourself?

If you believe He can forgive even the most nightmarish sins of another, why do you feel that He cannot forgive you?

One reason is a false sense of pride. Somehow you feel more spiritual if you continually berate yourself. You feel bad if you feel good. Paul condemned that sort of self-abasement. You can no more earn God's forgiveness than you can earn your salvation. Both are a gift from God.

Another reason is an erroneous view of repentance. Repentance does mean that you say you're sorry, but its ultimate meaning lies in a change of behavior. Repentance doesn't mean that you grovel in self-pity; you deliberately trust God to transform your conduct through His Spirit.

Christ has forgiven you—He loves you as you are. Let Christ handle your past and revolutionize your today and tomorrow.

Lord, cover my past with Your forgiveness. I start fresh right now.
Revolutionize my today and change my tomorrows.

SCRIPTURE READING: Romans 8

KEY VERSE: Romans 8:1

There is therefore now no condemnation to those who are in Christ Jesus,
who do not walk according to the flesh, but according to the Spirit.

One of Satan's most potent weapons is the fraudulent use of guilt in your life. He enjoys seeing you wrestle with unnecessary guilt. He understands that if unresolved, it can lead to a miserable Christian existence, destroying joy and peace.

This doesn't have to happen to you or any believer. God has made full provision for the problem of guilt through proper understanding of His remedy and discernment of Satan's deceptive tactics.

When Jesus died on the cross, He paid the penalty of your sin and its condemning guilt. You are forgiven of all your sins—past, present, and future. Your sin debt is paid in full when you receive Christ as Savior.

When you sin after salvation, the Holy Spirit convicts you of specific transgressions. Any guilt feelings are the Spirit's loving prompting for confession and repentance. Such confession agrees with God that you have violated His truth and allows you to experience His complete forgiveness.

If you seem to be walking around in a cloud of guilt but you cannot point to a specific act of sin, then it is a lie of Satan. Reject it. Refuse it. God loves you unconditionally and never puts false guilt on you.

Thank You, Lord, that the penalty for sin is paid in full. I am free from
condemnation. I reject and refuse the guilt Satan has tried to put on
me.

SCRIPTURE READING: John 8:1–12

KEY VERSE: John 4:15

The woman said to Him, "Sir, give me this water, that I may not thirst, nor come here to draw."

Jesus' encounter with the woman at the well is a timeless marvel of divine love and forgiveness. But what would have become of His forgiveness if the woman had left without fully receiving and experiencing Christ's healing love? What if she never forgave herself as Christ did? Would she have ever known the miraculous freedom of forgiveness?

Jesus has forgiven us of all sin. He tells us to forgive others as Christ forgives us (Eph. 4:32). If Jesus forgives you and He asks you to freely extend His forgiveness to those who offend you, is there any reason why you cannot forgive yourself?

You must be able to forgive yourself if you are to truly enjoy the liberation that God's forgiveness brings. Perhaps you have done something very bad. God forgives all sins; therefore, no sin should imprison you.

All forgiveness, including forgiving self, is founded on the Cross. To deny yourself forgiveness is to try to obstruct God's holy love.

Don't wallow any longer in self-pity or guilt that unforgiveness can beget. Fully receive God's love by forgiving yourself. God has a wonderful plan for your life, and it does not include self-condemnation.

Thank You, Lord, for the wonderful plan You have for my life. I am so glad it does not include guilt and condemnation. Remove these barriers that obstruct Your love.

SCRIPTURE READING: Colossians 1:21–22
KEY VERSE: Hebrews 13:5

He Himself has said, "I will never leave you nor forsake you."

A loyal company employee is laid off after twenty years. A devoted wife is divorced suddenly by her husband of fifteen years. A once faithful friend no longer desires your fellowship.

The pain of rejection is strong. It attacks the very foundation of your personality, your concept of self-worth.

If you let the assault continue unbridled, you suffer spiritually, emotionally, and physically. You can become a prime candidate for bitterness and depression. Is there a way out? Can you recover your self-esteem when another has cast you into the ditch of rejection?

Yes, you can. It is not an easy road out. But there is a biblical path that can upright you, comfort you, and restore you to wholeness. It begins by understanding that even those closest to you are capable of rejecting you. We are imperfect people who often wrongly judge and think. We are all stained by sin. Even believers are constantly tempted to put self first.

Once you recognize this, you actually can be liberated from being hostage to others' opinions. Your self-worth is tied not to your performance or another's faulty judgment but to Christ's evaluation of you. His appraisal declares you unconditionally accepted and loved.

Father, You knew rejection, so You know how I feel. I don't want to harbor bitterness, so help me forgive those who have hurt me through their rejection. Take the pain right now.

SCRIPTURE READING: Psalm 139
KEY VERSE: Psalm 139:16

Your eyes saw my substance, being yet unformed.
And in Your book they all were written,
The days fashioned for me,
When as yet there were none of them.

The piercing arrow of rejection can be removed and the wounds healed as you understand that your intrinsic worth is forever bound to God's unchanging truth. Joseph Aldrich, author, pastor, and Bible school president, speaks to this issue in his booklet *Self-Worth:*

Here's the point: If the whole world decided you were worthless, it would not change your essential value. Why? Because as a believer you share both the image and nature of the unchanging God Himself.

Your value is tied to Him. He is the magnetic north pole of your essential worth. The Almighty Creator is the infinite reference point, the ultimate standard, the "cosmic blue book" of your value. . . . Your value was written in blood at the cross. And whatever He values is valuable.

Jesus was rejected by those He came to save. He dealt with that trauma by knowing that the Father loved Him completely. If rejection has put you into a slough of despondency, affirm God's love for you. Move forward by obediently seeking to know Him through every adversity. You can eventually put rejection behind you as you place Christ in front of you.

I put it all behind me, Lord—all the hurts caused by rejection. I change my focus from my pain to You. Help me move forward spiritually through every adversity.

SCRIPTURE READING: Psalm 46

KEY VERSE: Psalm 56:3

Whenever I am afraid,
I will trust in You.

Fear seemed to be one of the first abnormal symptoms that the man experienced following the fall from perfect union and fellowship with God: "Then the LORD God called to the man, and said to him, 'Where are you?' And he said, 'I heard the sound of Thee in the garden, and I was afraid'" (Gen. 3:9–10 NASB).

Since then every heart has known the panic and trembling that fear brings. Fear of failure. Fear of today. Fear of the future.

We live in fearful times. The only antidote for fear is trust. David, who knew the depth of fear as few people ever have, came to this conclusion as he was seized by the Philistines: "When I am afraid, / I will put my trust in Thee" (Ps. 56:3 NASB). David did not deny his fear. He did not rationalize it or try to outman it. He admitted his fear and then affirmed his trust in the Lord.

Elizabeth Cheney wrote this succinct and powerful poem:

> Faith came singing into my room
> And other guests took flight.
> Grief, anxiety, fear, and gloom
> Sped out into the night.

Identify the source of your fear. Bring it before God. Then confidently assert His ability to handle your fears and His willingness to replace your fears with His courage and peace.

Heavenly Father, I confess—I am fearful. Replace my fears with Your courage and peace. Whenever I am afraid, I will put my trust in You.

SCRIPTURE READING: James 2:20–23
KEY VERSE: Proverbs 18:24

A man who has friends must himself be friendly,
But there is a friend who sticks closer than a brother.

A pastor shared the good news of God's love in a small Russian village. He talked of Jesus as Savior, Lord, and Friend.

A young man thoughtfully responded to the message with this simple but profound truth: "Before, I had known Jesus as my Savior and Master. But I had always thought of Him as Boss. It never occurred to me that He was my Friend. This will change everything about my faith."

Christians become mired in the murky waters of loneliness for many reasons—an extended illness, a divorce, an empty nest, the death of a genuine friend. The starting place to lift loneliness's enveloping emotional fog is to build intimacy with Jesus as our Friend.

Fellowship with Jesus is sweet friendship with your most loyal Friend. It is coming to Christ with honesty and sincerity. You need not hide your feelings. He understands them and does not condemn you. You can draw as close to Christ as you desire.

Jesus stands ready now to embrace you with the love that died for you and now lives within you. He is no fair-weather Friend. He will stand with you and comfort you in your darkest hour.

Thank You for Your friendship, Jesus. I embrace Your love right now. I rejoice that You will stand with me and comfort me in my darkest hour.

SCRIPTURE READING: Psalm 27:1–10
KEY VERSE: Proverbs 27:19

As in water face reflects face,
So a man's heart reveals the man.

The ache of alienation is soothed first by building new intimacy with Christ Jesus as Friend. But it does not stop there, for Jesus knows our needs for mutual love and fellowship as well.

Elijah had Elisha. The disciples traveled in pairs. And Paul always had traveling companions. God knew each person needed the support of a friend as well as His supernatural presence.

Seek to cultivate new depths of intimacy with your family. Pray for your family. Look for creative ways to do things together.

God also understands your need for other beneficial friendships. Ask Him to provide one friend of the same sex with whom you can develop openness and sharing.

If you are single, widowed, or divorced, ask God to bring someone into your life who will brighten your day.

Don't force a futile friendship. Let Him guide you. Look for avenues of service to your neighbor, church, or community that will open the door of fellowship.

You need others, and God knows that. As your most noble Friend, He will help you build godly friendships that keep loneliness at bay and sharpen you for His good and blessed purposes.

Lord, please bring good relationships into my life. As my greatest
Friend, help me build godly friendships that will encourage me to
accomplish Your purposes.

SCRIPTURE READING: Ephesians 4:26–32
KEY VERSE: Ephesians 4:27

Nor give place to the devil.

A jarring tackle by a linebacker on a running back at midfield is perfectly acceptable behavior. On the other hand, a blow by the same linebacker on the same running back out of bounds is a rule infraction met by a penalty.

Thinking of anger in similar terms is helpful. If you keep your anger within certain acceptable bounds, it is not sin. David's anger is obvious in the Psalms. Jesus visibly vented His anger in the temple. Nowhere are these actions described as sin.

But when anger crosses certain boundaries, it becomes sinful behavior. Knowing those emotional and spiritual land lines is difficult, but here are a few helpful guidelines.

Anger is okay as long as it is not a synonym for a constant, irritable temper. If you frequently stew over matters and are quickly irritated, you are not walking in the Spirit. You need His self-control and a megadose of biblical love.

Anger is acceptable as long as it is directed at another's behavior and not the person. God does not treat you as your sins deserve; likewise, you must be careful not to attack a person's self-worth. Let your anger be directed at the problem, not the person. Don't always suppress your feelings. Express your ire, but keep it within legitimate bounds.

> *Dear Lord, help me learn how to express my anger properly. I want to exhibit better self-control in difficult times. Give me a megadose of Your love.*

SCRIPTURE READING: Colossians 3:5–15

KEY VERSE: Colossians 3:8

Now you yourselves are to put off all these: anger, wrath, malice, blasphemy, filthy language out of your mouth.

Some boundary markers on handling volatile emotions include the following:

Deal directly with the situation or responsible party who has irked you. Face conflict head-on. Refuse to spread your anger to other parties. Receive counsel only if you are unsure how to constructively deal with your anger.

Resolve your anger as quickly as possible under the leadership of the Holy Spirit. Sometimes you need a cool-down period before expressing your anger. But it is folly to let your anger brew over days, weeks, or months. That is the perfect breeding ground for bitterness and division.

Remember that the temperament and personality of other people can easily provoke you. If this is the catalyst that makes you angry, your best choice is to accept others as God accepts you—freely and unconditionally.

Make a daily choice to submit to the reign of the Holy Spirit in your emotional life. Put your focus on Christ and the peace He gives in all circumstances. The sweeter your fellowship with Jesus, the more like Him you will naturally become with the Spirit's help.

That is the lifestyle God has called you to, and anger can be handled appropriately within that context.

Father, I want to live the lifestyle You have called me to. Help me resolve my anger quickly and accept others as You accept me. I submit to the reign of the Holy Spirit in my emotional life today.

SCRIPTURE READING: Isaiah 41:10–13
KEY VERSE: Isaiah 41:10

Fear not, for I am with you;
Be not dismayed, for I am your God.
I will strengthen you,
Yes, I will help you,
I will uphold you with My righteous right hand.

A favorite story of Dr. E. V. Hill tells of a young man taking a shortcut home late one evening through a vacant lot. It was dark and the shadows from the trees loomed all around him.

Suddenly he became aware of someone following him. The faster he walked, the faster the person walked. Frightened and frustrated, he turned quickly to meet his predator; but no one was there. As he turned to continue home, he heard the noise again. That was when he realized that he heard the rubbing of his corduroy pants.

We laugh at stories like this one. But the truth is, many times our fears result from imaginary thoughts, things that will never happen or come true. Satan is a relentless adversary, and he loves to fill our minds with fearful thoughts. He knows if he can frighten us enough, he will stand a good chance of paralyzing us spiritually and physically.

When you come up against a fear-producing situation, immediately pray for God's wisdom and protection, admit your inner struggle, and then stand your ground against the enemy's tactics, for God has said:

Do not fear, for I am with you;
Do not anxiously look about you, for I am your God.
I will strengthen you, surely I will help you.
    (Isa. 41:10 NASB)

Dear Lord, You are with me in every situation. I will not be paralyzed by fear. You will strengthen and help me.

SCRIPTURE READING: Matthew 5:43–48
KEY VERSE: Hebrews 12:15

Looking carefully lest anyone fall short of the grace of God; lest any root of bitterness springing up cause trouble, and by this many become defiled.

Jesus was specific about forgiving those who hurt us. The reason? He never wants us to become ensnared by bitterness. Members of the early church knew the score when it came to abuse. Many suffered beatings, verbal attacks, and even death, all because they were followers of Jesus Christ.

Today, the lines of abuse often form a tangled web of violence and betrayal. Many times those who seek to harm you have been victims of abuse themselves.

At first, Jesus' admonishment may appear hard to swallow: "You have heard that it was said, 'You shall love your neighbor, and hate your enemy.' But I say to you, love your enemies, and pray for those who persecute you in order that you may be sons of your Father who is in heaven" (Matt. 5:43–45 NASB).

In praying for those who hurt you, you are not saying you condone their actions, nor do you say you deserve their abuse. No one deserves mistreatment. You focus the attention of your heart on Christ because He is your source of inner healing and protection.

No matter how difficult your situation appears, Christ is in it with you; and He will make a way of escape. Even the most horrifying incident can become something for His glory when you turn to Him.

> *I lift up to You all those who have hurt and abused me. Take the bitterness, dear Lord. I rejoice that even the most horrifying incidents of my past can be used for Your glory.*

SCRIPTURE READING: Psalm 18:16–19
KEY VERSE: Psalm 57:1

Be merciful to me, O God, be merciful to me!
For my soul trusts in You;
And in the shadow of Your wings I will make my refuge,
Until these calamities have passed by.

King Saul spent years consumed with the idea of ending David's life. At a time when he should have been basking in the blessings of God, Saul was obsessed with one notion—kill the son of Jesse, so Saul's position as Israel's king would be secure.

The issue was not a wrongful act or a betrayal by David. It involved Saul's jealousy and inability to submit to God's authority. David had to be very careful in his actions. One vengeful act could jeopardize his future as Israel's king.

By refusing to react to Saul's anger, David found a place of rest in God's presence. He was not drawn aside by negative thoughts or feelings of inadequacy, but instead sought strength and refuge under the wings of God (Ps. 91:4).

God did not immediately deliver David. Years passed before he sat on Israel's throne. Yet God watched over His servant and protected his every move. The process of molding David's heart into one of godly principle and character began in the brokenness of life.

No matter what you face, God has a plan for you. Ask Him to show you where to go from here. David prayed,

The LORD was my stay.
He brought me forth also into a broad place;
He rescued me, because He delighted in me. (Ps. 18:18–19 NASB)

Father, I know You have a plan for me. Show me where to go from here. Bring me forth into a "broad place" where I can serve You in a greater capacity.

SCRIPTURE READING: Exodus 3

KEY VERSE: Exodus 3:14

God said to Moses, "I AM WHO I AM." And He said, "Thus you shall say to the children of Israel, 'I AM has sent me to you.'"

Few of us would think of Moses as having low self-esteem. But read his answer when God told him that he would be the one to lead Israel out of bondage: "Who am I, that I should go to Pharaoh, and that I should bring the sons of Israel out of Egypt?" (Ex. 3:11 NASB).

Even after God confirmed His support, Moses continued to struggle: "Please, Lord, I have never been eloquent, neither recently nor in time past, nor since Thou hast spoken . . . for I am slow of speech and slow of tongue" (Ex 4:10 NASB).

If you have ever felt this way, you are not alone. However, God has a course mapped out for your life, and all the inadequacies in the world will not change His mind. He will be with you every step of the way. And though it may take time, He has a celebration planned for when you cross over the "Red Seas" of your life.

Moses was right. He had nothing to say on his own. But the moment he trusted the Lord to be his support, things changed—seas parted, pillars of fire rose in the night, and water flowed from rocks.

In God's eyes there are no losers, only lives being changed for His glory. The cure for inferiority is the staff of God's righteousness. Grasp it and move forward to meet the challenge He has placed before you.

I confess my feelings of inadequacy, Lord. I know You have a plan for my life and You will be with me each step of the way. Give me courage to cross the "Red Seas" of my life.

SCRIPTURE READING: John 3:14–19

KEY VERSE: John 3:17

God did not send His Son into the world to condemn the world, but that the world through Him might be saved.

God doesn't want you battling with feelings of shame. He has given you His Holy Spirit as a seal of your transformation from death (sin) to a new life (saved, sanctified, and cleansed) in Jesus Christ.

When temptations come and you yield to sin, feelings of shame are sure to follow. Your conscience springs to action any time it is violated. That is one way you know what you have done is not in line with God's will for your life.

There is only one way to handle shame: take it immediately to Jesus Christ. Ask Him to show you what you have done, if anything, and to help you obey His leading in confession and submission to His Word.

As a believer you stand forgiven before His throne. However, there will be times when you make wrong choices, and then you need to be willing to admit the mistakes. Never forget: God's forgiveness was applied to your life at the cross when Christ died for your sins past, present, and future.

When you have Jesus, you need never allow guilt or shame to dominate your life. He accepts you just the way you are. You cannot disappoint Someone who knows all about you and loves you just the same. This is God's love for you.

Lord, reveal the source of my shame so that I can deal with it. Thank You that You know all about me and love me just the same.

SCRIPTURE READING: Romans 7:15–25
KEY VERSE: Romans 7:19

For the good that I will to do, I do not do; but the evil I will not to do, that I practice.

You are a believer. The deepest yearning of your heart is to know, serve, and please God. But before you trusted Christ, you had a severe problem with anger. You still do. Before salvation, you grappled daily with depression. Now as a believer, you still are easily discouraged.

So what do you do? You commit yourself to study the Bible, pray regularly, memorize Scripture dealing with your particular albatross, read books, and listen to tapes.

What is the result? Sometimes temporary conquest but almost always eventual relapse. It all can lead to a very frustrating circle of resolve and regret. Why does this seem to be such a common experience?

Although you became a new spiritual creation in Christ at salvation, your mind, emotions, and habits were not automatically transformed. Once saved, you realize that these old patterns are not compatible with your new identity. Your natural response then is to do all you can to improve your behavior.

Such effort is admirable and makes you feel a little less guilty, but it doesn't work very well. The root cause requires a radical approach to your familiar problem-solving techniques.

I cannot do it in myself, dear Lord. Replace my self-effort and my problem-solving techniques with Your power. Let me learn to walk by faith.

SCRIPTURE READING: Ephesians 2:1–10
KEY VERSES: Ephesians 2:8–9

By grace you have been saved through faith, and that not of yourselves; it is the gift of God, not of works, lest anyone should boast.

No one would know it by your appearance, but inside you are frustrated—not with the circumstances beyond your control, but with your performance.

Your supervisors at work judge you to be successful, and your family is pleased with your level of involvement at home. The volunteer fundraiser you led at church raised even more than the projected dollar amount. Still, you can't shake the feeling that you have not done enough. A standard is out there, but you haven't reached it yet: *Maybe with a little more effort. . . .*

If this is frequently a sample of your thoughts, you might be struggling under the weight of perfectionism. Perfectionists drive themselves to do more and be more all the time, in an endless quest to gain approval. In every situation, even noncombative ones, perfectionists seek to have control by coming out on top.

To rid yourself of this consuming drive and put striving for excellence into healthy perspective, you must learn to acknowledge and rest in the acceptance you have in Christ. Remember, He died for you when you had nothing to offer and nothing to prove. You cannot earn His love by good performance, and you cannot lose it when you fail.

Learn to rest in His achievement.

Let me learn to rest in You, dear Lord. Thank You that I am not accepted on the basis of performance. I can't lose, even if I should fail today!

SCRIPTURE READING: Philippians 4:10–13
KEY VERSE: Philippians 4:12

I know how to be abased, and I know how to abound. Everywhere and in all things I have learned both to be full and to be hungry, both to abound and to suffer need.

You probably know people who live in a state of constant agitation. Even on a good day, they seem to be slightly irritated. Something isn't quite right—the weather, their hair, their schedule, their plans for the weekend, their bank account. And though they are believers and in general are emotionally well balanced, it is not unusual for them to voice some kind of complaint.

At the heart of their lingering frustration is a basic lack of contentment. They have not comprehended the lesson that Paul learned: "For I have learned to be content in whatever circumstances I am. I know how to get along with humble means, and I also know how to live in prosperity; in any and every circumstance I have learned the secret of being filled and going hungry, both of having abundance and suffering need" (Phil. 4:11–12 NASB).

So much of what you deal with on a daily basis are things you cannot change, either problems with people or environments over which you can exert no influence. You can respond in two ways: by grumbling and letting the frustration level rise, or by giving thanks for blessings received and looking ahead with peace and hope.

Hold on to this promise: "I can do all things through Him who strengthens me" (Phil. 4:13 NASB).

> *Dear Lord, help me accept the things I cannot change. Help me replace my grumbling and frustration with an attitude of praise and thanksgiving.*

SCRIPTURE READING: Matthew 11:27–30
KEY VERSE: Matthew 11:30

My yoke is easy and My burden is light.

When an old worn-out tire is left on a car, the result is often a blowout on the highway. You've seen it before—shredded rubber everywhere. If someone had taken care of that tire a little sooner, the whole mess could have been avoided.

Do you ever feel like a tire that is about to burst apart? Or one that already has? If so, you may be headed for emotional, spiritual, and physical burnout. Here are some steps to help you evaluate your situation:

Get away and reappraise your life. Take some time off, as much as possible, and make a list of everything you perceive to be an obligation. Write down how much time and energy each activity takes.

Look for a pattern. Are you more involved in career or hobbies? Do you balance work and play? What preference do you give to spiritual activity?

Ask God to give you insight on His priorities. What other people think doesn't matter; what God wants you to do is of primary importance.

Through His Word and the guidance of the Holy Spirit, He will show you what areas need adjustment. Before pressure makes you pop, go to the One who gives true rest to your soul, and He will steer you away from collapse.

> *Lord, I want to take time right now to appraise my life. Show me the patterns that need to be adjusted. Give me insight into Your priorities. Give me the courage to change.*

SCRIPTURE READING: Ephesians 1:3–11

KEY VERSE: James 4:17

To him who knows to do good and does not do it, to him it is sin.

Lack of obedience is one of the greatest hindrances to discovering God's plan for your life. Like a child, you sometimes exhibit selective hearing; that is, you hear only what you want to hear.

If you are seeking to know God's will in a certain matter, but an area of disobedience is present, do not be surprised if God appears silent. Faith and obedience go hand in hand. He wants you to follow in faith what He has taught you up to this point.

All of the Lord's principles and directions have a special function in shaping your life and character to be more like Christ's. In fact, God's ultimate goal is to conform you to the image of His Son. When you choose to ignore some part of what He is trying to teach you, you sin and hinder His growth process and remain unprepared for what He has in store (James 4:17).

The key to understanding His will for you is coming to the point where you want what God wants more than you want what you desire. In other words, you value His plans more than your own. You know that His way is the best way, no matter how good other options look. When you demonstrate this understanding by willing obedience, your ears are tuned to hear His voice.

Heavenly Father, I know Your way is best, no matter how good the other options appear. Attune my ears to Your voice. Make me willing to obey.

SCRIPTURE READING: Hebrews 12:1–15

KEY VERSE: 1 John 4:20

If someone says, "I love God," and hates his brother, he is a liar; for he who does not love his brother whom he has seen, how can he love God whom he has not seen?

In *The Weight of Glory,* C. S. Lewis wrote:

To forgive the incessant provocations of daily life—to keep on forgiving the bossy mother-in-law, the bullying husband, the nagging wife, the selfish daughter, the deceitful son—how can we do it?

Only, I think, by remembering where we stand, by meaning our words when we say in our prayers each night "Forgive us our trespasses as we forgive those that trespass against us." We are offered forgiveness on no other terms. To refuse it is to refuse God's mercy for ourselves. There is no hint of exceptions and God means what He says.

Not forgiving someone who offends you doesn't mean that you lose your salvation, but your refusal to forgive discolors your experience of God's grace. By not weeding out the roots of bitterness as they spring up, you will soon be controlled by the full-blown fruit of unforgiveness.

Have you ever seen a kudzu vine? One little tendril when it takes root grows at an astonishing pace. If left to grow unchecked, the vines engulf trees and choke them off from the sunlight. Efforts to clean up the vines must be absolutely thorough, because the tiniest piece of root left in the ground will start the process all over again.

Don't let the smallest grudge or littlest insult have room to grow. Take it to the Lord immediately.

Father, reveal any grudges I am harboring—any unforgiveness or bitterness. I want to forgive, even as You forgave me. Come, weed the garden of my spiritual life.

June 24

SCRIPTURE READING: Ephesians 4:26–32
KEY VERSE: Ephesians 4:32

Be kind to one another, tenderhearted, forgiving one another, even as God in Christ forgave you.

The two friends argued and then went their separate ways without reconciling their differences. That evening neither could sleep. The Bible instructs us to settle our differences before we part: "Be angry, and yet do not sin; do not let the sun go down on your anger, and do not give the devil an opportunity" (Eph. 4:26–27 NASB).

There are obvious reasons why God wants you to solve a disagreement quickly. For one, when you bring the right kind of closure to a hurtful matter, you free yourself and the other person emotionally and spiritually. Those who refuse to extend forgiveness are the losers. Nothing soothes a guilt-worn conscience like the forgiveness and love of God.

When you forgive others, you do what Jesus did for you. You also align your life with His standard of obedience. Forgiveness is not always easy, but it is essential to emotional and physical health. God promises to personally deal with those who have harmed you (Rom. 12:19).

However, many people refuse to wait on Him. They want vengeance, and they want it now. If this is your attitude, ask God to remind you of how your life looked to Him before He saved you. Even if you were six or sixty, you, like all people, deserved death. Yet through the work of His wondrous grace and forgiveness, you were given eternal life.

Dear Lord, help me learn to handle disagreements in a proper manner. Remind me of how my life was before You saved me so that I can show compassion to others who are offensive to me today.

SCRIPTURE READING: Luke 10:38–42

KEY VERSE: Philippians 3:10

That I may know Him and the power of His resurrection, and the fellow-ship of His sufferings, being conformed to His death.

Martha had chosen to prepare the evening meal. No one forced her to do it. In fact, if we examined the situation, we would find that Martha really didn't mind the work. She loved receiving praise for her cooking.

Yet here was the scenario: Jesus was in the front room of the house talking to those gathered near Him. Martha was rushing around the cooking area in the back of the house. All was fine until she discovered her sister was missing. A quick check of the courtyard provided no clue to Mary's whereabouts. With her jaw set to reprove her sister, Martha stormed by the doorway to the front room.

When she spotted Mary sitting near the feet of Jesus, envy and jealousy took control of Martha's heart: "Lord, do You not care that my sister has left me to do all the serving alone? Then tell her to help me" (Luke 10:40 NASB).

All of us have fought similar feelings. While God understands our weaknesses, jealousy is intolerable to Him. Why? For one, it proves that we are more interested in taking care of ourselves than in taking care of our love relationship with Him. Jesus told Martha, "Mary has chosen the good part, which shall not be taken away from her" (Luke 10:42 NASB).

Make every effort to rid your life of envy and strife. Let God bless you in the way He has chosen. Set the focus of your heart on Him, and rejoice that He greatly loves you.

Lord, remove envy and strife from my life. I focus my heart on You today. I choose the good part. Release me from the tyranny of the urgent to do the truly important.

SCRIPTURE READING: 1 Samuel 18
KEY VERSE: 1 Samuel 18:5

David went out wherever Saul sent him, and behaved wisely.

Everything was going well for young David. Saul had given him a position of authority. He also had access to the king's household and often spent his evenings in the king's presence. Saul gave no indication of having any envy toward David. Yet both jealousy and envy were brewing within the king's heart.

The only way jealousy can flourish is to have an acceptable atmosphere in which it feels at home and can grow. In reality, jealousy is a symptom of a deeper problem. And while it needs to be dealt with swiftly, you also need to ask God to show you the root cause of any envy that has set up shop in your life. Usually pride is the taproot of jealousy, envy, and strife.

Saul was pleased with David's allegiance until one day when he returned from war and overheard the people shouting: "Saul has slain his thousands, / And David his ten thousands" (1 Sam. 18:7 NASB). As a result of their cheers, Saul's need for acceptance evolved into a toxic jealousy that ruled his life until his death.

Only Christ can free you from the stronghold of pride and its cousins, jealousy and envy. If this is an area of concern in your life, be honest about it. Tell the Lord you want nothing to do with anything that keeps you from enjoying His fellowship. Pray that He will remove any hint of jealousy so that you may live free in Christ Jesus.

Pride, jealousy, strife—take it all, Lord. Free me from the strongholds of these emotions. I don't want anything to prevent me from enjoying fellowship with You.

SCRIPTURE READING: James 1:2–8
KEY VERSE: James 1:2

My brethren, count it all joy when you fall into various trials.

Scholars believe the book of James was one of the first New Testament books to be written. The apostle James wrote to believers forced to live outside Jerusalem. Because of the political and religious unrest of the city, Roman officials banished the early Christians.

Up until that point, they enjoyed worshiping in the temple. Peter, James, and John had been with them on a daily basis—teaching and encouraging them in the faith. James knew that their exile would become a point of discouragement and doubt. Therefore, he dealt with those issues immediately in the opening of his letter.

When trouble comes, one of the first things you want to do is to guard against doubt. Faith helped those believers get through such horrendous times, and many times that is all you and I have to combat discouragement. Through Jesus Christ, it is more than enough.

The church survived those dark times to become what it is today. Without those tenacious believers, we would not have the heritage of faith we so richly enjoy. Who is the beneficiary of your faith? Is it a son or daughter, a niece or nephew? Maybe a grandchild needs to see your faith in Christ. When you place your trust in the Lord, He always comes through in a mighty way.

When doubt floods my soul, let my faith kick in, Lord. Help me survive the dark times so that I can pass on the heritage of my faith to others.

SCRIPTURE READING: 2 Samuel 2:1–4
KEY VERSE: 1 Thessalonians 5:24

He who calls you is faithful, who also will do it.

Is there something you have been praying about for a long time? You know that your request is in keeping with God's will. You've checked the Scriptures to make sure you are on target, and God has confirmed that you are. Each verse the Holy Spirit brings up underscores God's faithfulness and ability to answer your prayer. However, your request seems to go unanswered.

God anointed David king over Israel when he was a lad and fresh out of service in his father's sheep field. Yet he did not assume the kingship until several years later. God may give you a promise and then allow you to go through a time of waiting for Him to bring it to completion.

That is when you face the greatest temptation to doubt Him. You wonder what He is doing, and you question His reasoning. Thoughts such as *Has God forgotten His promise?* run through your head as you worry over doing the right thing. Doubt is the breeding ground for confusion and fear.

Faith is the atmosphere in which hope and joy flourish. If God has promised to do a certain thing, it will be done. Little faith says, "I think God will do it." Perfect faith says, "It is already done in Christ Jesus. All I have to do is wait for God's perfect timing."

Never give up; with God all things are possible. You may be standing on the brink of a tremendous blessing.

> *I reject confusion! My request is already answered through Christ Jesus! Thank You, Father, that all I must do is wait for Your perfect timing.*

SCRIPTURE READING: Psalm 35:1–4
KEY VERSE: 2 Timothy 2:24

A servant of the Lord must not quarrel but be gentle to all, able to teach, patient.

What bugs you? Whether it's a neighbor who enjoys mowing his lawn at 7:30 on Saturday morning or a coworker who snaps her gum all day or a mate who always forgets to pick up after himself or herself, you are forced to deal with nagging irritations.

The most important principle to remember if you are to deal with minor irritants successfully is to view them as helpers in your spiritual growth. Each time you confront an abrasive person or circumstance, you must either lay down your personal rights or enforce them. That involves a denial of self and a yielding to the lordship of Christ.

Your choice in such situations advances your growth in godliness or neutralizes it.

You choose the way of humility and servanthood as Jesus did, or you proclaim your selfishness.

Tough choice, isn't it? But if you realize that each irritation is an opportunity for the expression and release of the Christ-life within you, then you can view such occasions as stepping-stones rather than stumbling blocks.

Irritations reveal the true nature of self. Accepting them as God's agents for maturity and obedience allows them to scrape away the layers of pride, ego, and selfishness and reveals the pearl of genuine spiritual beauty.

I am easily irritated, Lord. I confess it! Let me view every irritation as an opportunity for the release of Your life within me—to use them as stepping-stones rather than stumbling blocks.

SCRIPTURE READING: 1 Corinthians 3:1–17
KEY VERSE: Matthew 6:24

No one can serve two masters; for either he will hate the one and love the other, or else he will be loyal to the one and despise the other. You cannot serve God and mammon.

A veteran U.S. senator humorously tells how his late father used to describe fence-sitters: "My daddy told me there isn't anything in the middle of the road except dead skunks and a yellow line."

His reference was obviously political, but the same principle applies in the spiritual dimension: compromise with worldly, fleshly standards does not please us or God.

And that is exactly where the carnal Christian finds himself: trying as best he can to walk a spiritual middle of the road where he can blend his bent toward self with faith toward God. God described such a state in more graphic terms: "I know your deeds, that you are neither cold nor hot. . . . So because you are lukewarm, and neither hot nor cold, I will spit you out of My mouth" (Rev. 3:15–16 NASB).

Why such disgust? Because Jesus must be acknowledged as Lord of all. Receiving Christ is the step on a brand-new course of life that can be run only by wholehearted Christians as we trust Christ to express His life through us.

If you are attempting to hold on to a lifestyle that denies the absolute lordship of Christ, realize the danger, and ask Him to take total possession and control of your life.

I refuse to compromise, Father. Take total possession and control of my life. Replace my selfishness with the Christ-life.

July

THEME: The Fish Gate
REPRESENTING: Christian witness
KEY VERSE: Matthew 4:19

He said to them, "Follow Me, and I will make you fishers of men."

SCRIPTURE READING: Exodus 3

KEY VERSE: Exodus 3:4

When the LORD saw that he turned aside to look, God called to him from the midst of the bush and said, "Moses, Moses!" And he said, "Here I am."

God called Moses to a task that required a tremendous commitment. Once he accepted the challenge, there was no turning back. He could not lead the nation of Israel out of Egypt and then decide he had made a wrong decision.

True commitment changes a person's life forever. It changed Moses. Once he committed himself to God's call, everything else became insignificant.

However, it was not always that way. It took forty years of molding and reshaping Moses' character before he was ready for the mission God had for him. Then one day a flash of light on the side of Mount Horeb caught his eye. A bush was ablaze; yet the fire did not consume it.

When Moses stepped toward the burning bush, he took a step toward a lifelong commitment. Before that moment, his eyes were on his flocks, his family, his hurts, and his desires.

The Bible tells us, "When the LORD saw that [Moses] turned aside to look, God called to him." That was Moses' point of commitment—the turning of his heart to the things of God.

Has God placed a burning bush in your life, but you are afraid of the commitment? Moses could have avoided the call, but he never would have known the wonder of the holiness of God. Nothing is worth missing God's wonderful plan for your life.

Heavenly Father, I turn aside right now in renewed commitment to You. Change my focus from myself—my job, my hurts, my desires—to Your purposes. Nothing is worth missing Your plan for my life.

SCRIPTURE READING: Exodus 4:10–17
KEY VERSE: Exodus 4:12

Now therefore, go, and I will be with your mouth and teach you what you shall say.

Moses thought he was the wrong man for the job. Why should a pharaoh listen to a man who had spent the last forty years tending sheep?

However, God reminded Moses of his true identity: "Who has made man's mouth? Or who makes him dumb or deaf, or seeing or blind? Is it not I, the LORD?" (Ex. 4:11 NASB). In other words, God put Moses' attention and focus back on Him.

Not one detail of Moses' life or background had escaped God's attention. Moses belonged to God alone. The Lord created him specially for His purposes, called him, and promised to supply everything for the tasks ahead.

You can understand your identity and the unique works that God has planned for you only when you identify yourself fully with Jesus Christ. You are an eternal part of God's family. Insecurity, emptiness, and purposelessness have no place in your life—the Lord provides fulfillment and direction.

Do you feel inadequate or unprepared for a specific challenge? Is the threat of failure eroding your faith? Remember that God is sovereign and gives you the strength and wisdom for what He asks you to do. He calls you to step out in obedient faith, letting Him handle the details.

I feel inadequate for the challenges ahead, O God. The task is great, and the threat of failure looms. But I step out in faith, knowing You will give me the strength and wisdom to accomplish what You have asked me to do.

SCRIPTURE READING: Hebrews 13:20–21
KEY VERSE: Mark 2:17

When Jesus heard it, He said to them, "Those who are well have no need of a physician, but those who are sick. I did not come to call the righteous, but sinners, to repentance."

Jesus told us in Mark 2:17 that He did not come to the healthy. Instead, He came to the sick. In the Greek, *sick* is used metaphorically of mental ailments.

The people of Jesus' day were in need of much more than a physical touch. They were in need of a Savior. They struggled with depravity. Instead of worshiping God in purity, they often were bound to the darkness of their day. Paganism and legalism were just two of the infirmities plaguing them.

Once they were set free, Jesus commissioned them for service. He told them to go and share what God had done for them:

- The woman caught in adultery told of God's forgiveness.
- The demon-possessed lad told of Christ's deliverance.
- Mary told of the Savior's unconditional love.
- Matthew shared how he had been freed from greed.
- And Peter spoke of God's restoration.

That was how the gospel spread, by the testimony of those Jesus touched and healed. It is also how God equips us for service. Believers, once mentally insensitive to the things of God, are freed to share the hope of Jesus Christ.

Your life is a living testimony of the healing power of God. Ask Him to show you how you can share His victorious truth with someone today.

> *My life is a living testimony to Your power, O God. You changed every-thing! Show me how to share Your saving power with someone today.*

SCRIPTURE READING: Matthew 20:25–28
KEY VERSE: Matthew 20:16

So the last will be first, and the first last. For many are called, but few chosen.

It wasn't easy for Peter to restrain himself. He was a natural leader, and leaders lead others. However, the events of Christ's last week on earth shattered any dreams Peter might have had concerning self-glory and leadership.

He watched in frustration as the Savior wrapped a towel around His waist and began washing the disciples' feet (John 13). When He approached Peter with the basin of water, the disciple recoiled: "Lord, You shall never bathe my feet!"

Jesus was firm in His reply, "Peter, don't you understand? Unless you allow Me to do this, then you will have no part of Me."

A restless silence stood between them. God was confronting the motive of Peter's heart. Peter didn't understand the ways of God, and he wasn't ready for service. It takes both humility and grace to serve others. It also takes the same to allow others to serve you. Peter's life was still on the drawing board. Soon he would learn firsthand of God's grace through the painful trial of humility.

Jesus said to the disciples: "If you want to be first, you must first learn to be last." The only way you will develop a servant's spirit is to treasure this truth deep within your heart.

Lord, I need the grace to serve and be served by others. Give me a humble spirit. Let me learn how to be last.

SCRIPTURE READING: 2 Corinthians 5:14–21

KEY VERSE: 2 Corinthians 5:17

If anyone is in Christ, he is a new creation; old things have passed away; behold, all things have become new.

Those who met Jesus were changed eternally:

- The man born blind
- The woman who anointed His feet with oil
- The man He healed of leprosy
- And the Pharisee who came to Him by night
- No one meets Jesus and remains the same. Even Judas after the betrayal cried, "I have betrayed an innocent man" (Matt. 27:4, author's paraphrase).

Either you accept Jesus as the Messiah and become reconciled to God, or you reject Him and live a life of separation and denial. No matter how you view it, anyone who encounters Christ is changed.

Sin once separated you from God; but Jesus, being God's Son, broke the power of sin through His death, burial, and resurrection. When you accept Him as your Savior, God reconciles you eternally to Himself. Reconciliation is the goal of salvation.

Yet the message of reconciliation does not stop here but continues through you to reach others who have never heard the truth of the gospel. Nothing has changed since the call of the Great Commission. God reconciles you to Himself that you might have a ministry of reconciliation.

The words He spoke to His disciples at the Resurrection are the same words He speaks to you today. You are His channel of reconciliation to a lost and dying world.

I have been reconciled to You, Father—and I thank You! Now help me be a channel of reconciliation to this lost and dying world.

SCRIPTURE READING: Isaiah 6:1–8
KEY VERSE: Isaiah 6:8

I heard the voice of the Lord, saying:
"Whom shall I send,
And who will go for Us?"
Then I said, "Here am I! Send me."

The days in which Isaiah lived were filled with sinful peril. Israel worshiped many gods and adhered to all kinds of evil. When sin surrounds you, you rarely notice its silent gathering. Such was the case with the prophet Isaiah.

It is true; he should have known better than to overlook Israel's compromise. He was a priest of God and served daily in the temple. He knew the value of holiness. Yet sin in its quiet deception had stolen a place in his heart.

The day he stood in the presence of God with heralds of seraphim hovering above him was his day of reckoning. God was looking for one man, one voice, to carry His truth to the people. Who would go for Him? Who would answer His call?

The startling presence of holiness brought the prophet to his knees. As he cried out at the reality of his sin, the seraphim rushed to cleanse his lips with coals taken from the altar of God.

Has God called you to a certain task, but the memory of past failures holds you back? Take heart; He is near. Get on your face before Him. Tell Him the ways you have failed, and He will cleanse you.

One of the most wondrous attributes of the heavenly Father is His mercy in forgiveness. Will you, like Isaiah, answer His call?

I want to answer the call, dear Lord. Erase the failures of my past. I reconsecrate my life to You right now. Here I am—send me!

SCRIPTURE READING: John 13:1–5
KEY VERSE: John 13:35

By this all will know that you are My disciples, if you have love for one another.

If given a choice to serve or be served, most people would opt for the latter choice. The notion of servanthood, though not a repulsive idea, is certainly not a natural affinity. Although we stress quality service and attention to consumers in the commercial world, our private world is heavily weighted toward control and power.

Yet the call to servanthood is distinctly Christian; for Christ Himself, the Sovereign of the universe, came to serve, even to the point of death. A clue to His mission of suffering and service is found in the Upper Room Discourse. John described the scene as Christ stooped to wash the dusty feet of His disciples: "Jesus, knowing that the Father had given all things into His hands, and that He had come forth from God, and was going back to God, rose from supper, and laid aside His garments; and taking a towel, He girded Himself about" (John 13:3–4 NASB).

Jesus was secure in His identity as God's Son and in His destiny. The mantle of servanthood was not a threat but a fulfillment of His mission.

You can serve others when you are secure in your relationship with the Father. When you minister to others, you do so in His name and demonstrate the reality of Christ in you.

Father, make me secure in my relationship with You. Then send me to minister to others in Your name, to demonstrate the reality of Jesus Christ.

SCRIPTURE READING: Matthew 23:1–12

KEY VERSE: Matthew 23:11

He who is greatest among you shall be your servant.

Those who chose roles in our nation's government during the colonial days did so on the noble basis of public service. Compensation was small, and recognition was not the determining motivation.

How interesting that our notion of public service has eroded through the centuries. Now those elected to govern are usually motivated by greed or power. Once they are in office, their energies are focused on the maintenance of their position, not service to their constituency.

However, biblical servanthood is always cloaked in the garment of true humility. It is not self-seeking. Its real value lies not in pleasing or helping the one served, but in honoring the Master and reflecting His character.

Do you serve others so that you can be recognized for your efforts? Do you serve to gain position or acknowledgment?

You can maintain such humility only by cultivating an intimate relationship with the servant heart of Jesus Christ. The dearer Jesus is to you, the more you are enveloped in His holy humility. The more in awe you are of God, the less likely you are to succumb to pride.

Do not let a servant spirit be corrupted by corrosive motivations. Keep close to Christ, and you will gladly take towel in hand without regard to the outcome.

> *Heavenly Father, purify my motives for service. Help me take the towel of servanthood in hand and not worry about the outcome.*

SCRIPTURE READING: Philippians 3:1–11
KEY VERSE: Philippians 2:17

If I am being poured out as a drink offering on the sacrifice and service of your faith, I am glad and rejoice with you all.

The gift of serving Christ in the small, often unnoticed realms of life is the true testament of devotion to the Lord. Oswald Chambers wrote of the importance of serving God in *My Utmost for His Highest:*

Are you willing to be offered for the work of the faithful—to pour out your life blood as a libation on the sacrifice of the faith of others? Or do you say "I am not going to be offered up just yet, I do not want God to choose my work. I want to choose the scenery of my own sacrifice; I want to have the right kind of people watching and saying, "Well done."

It is one thing to go on the lonely way with dignified heroism, but quite another thing if the line mapped out for you by God means being a door-mat under other people's feet. Suppose God wants to use you to say, "I know how to be abased"—are you ready to be offered up like that?

Are you ready to be not so much as a drop in the bucket—to be so hopelessly insignificant that you are never thought of again in connection with the life you served? Are you willing to spend and be spent; not seeking to be ministered unto, but to minister? Some saints cannot do menial work and remain saints because it is beneath their dignity.

I want to serve You, Lord—to minister rather than seek to be ministered to. I offer up my life to be used to reach others. Make me willing to do even menial tasks in Your name.

SCRIPTURE READING: 1 Samuel 16:1–13
KEY VERSE: Acts 13:36

David, after he had served his own generation by the will of God, fell asleep,
was buried with his fathers, and saw corruption.

A former military commander spoke of the dignity and honesty that should grace the life of any individual. "When I stand before God," he said, "He won't ask me for my résumé."

His remark is profoundly simple and relevant. While we tirelessly work at enhancing our performance, God is concerned with a far more accurate barometer—the heart.

This should give hope and inspiration to any man or woman who wants to be used by God. You don't have to possess a college degree, attend a megachurch, or master the Greek and Hebrew languages of the Bible. God's requirement is a pure heart, a hunger and thirst to know and serve Him without consideration of reward.

David became king of Israel because through failure, bedlam, adversity, and challenge, his heart was bent toward God. When he sinned, he repented and asked God's forgiveness. When he was helpless and in distress, he called out to God for help. He felt no sense of embarrassment before others because of his passionate love for God.

Whoever you are, God can and will use you in an eternal, meaningful way if you maintain childlike faith and dependence on Him. That is His primary requirement for spiritual greatness.

Heavenly Father, I'm here today for a heart exam. Create in me a pure
heart that hungers and thirsts to know and serve You. Like David, I
want to be a person after Your own heart.

SCRIPTURE READING: 1 Corinthians 1:26–31
KEY VERSE: Exodus 4:12

Now therefore, go, and I will be with your mouth and teach you what you shall say.

Have you ever thought about the people God uses? If you took a heavenly roll call, the group would include an Egyptian castaway turned sheepherder, a shepherd boy whose best friends were criminals, an abandoned widow and her mother-in-law, a broken older woman whose only home was the temple, a carpenter whose hands were cracked and calloused, a common Jewish girl, a brawny fisherman, a tax collector, a prostitute, and a prideful Pharisee.

You may be thinking, *What a group! Looks as if God would have chosen people of nobility.* The truth is, He chose those very people, common in social status but uncommon in spirit, to change the course of history.

They may have appeared foolish by the world's standards, but they were wise by God's. He takes the world's hand-me-downs and molds them into precious instruments of His loving grace.

Common people doing uncommon things. God isn't looking for polished social giants; He is looking for people who are available and willing to trust Him.

Whatever your past holds, it is no match for God's grace. Tell Him you are available to be used by Him, and you will be surprised at the work He gives you to do.

> *Father, I am so thankful that You use ordinary people—just like me! I want to let You know, Lord, I'm available!*

THE REQUIREMENTS OF SERVANTHOOD

SCRIPTURE READING: Luke 19:1–10

KEY VERSE: Luke 19:10

The Son of Man has come to seek and to save that which was lost.

The most striking feature about Jesus during His earthly ministry was His unceasing servanthood mind-set. Though He was full deity, His life was a pure reflection of a humble servant.

Since you are created to be conformed to the image of Christ, you should increasingly demonstrate the attributes of a genuine servant. That will occur as you take on the following characteristics:

Awareness. Are you alert to the needs of others around you? Are you sensitive to their hurts, dreams, problems?

Availability. Do you take so much time meeting your own needs that you have no time for others? You have to make time to serve.

Acceptance. One reason you don't serve lovingly is that you have a hard time accepting others. You look at their faults instead of seeing them through the eyes of the Father.

Abiding. If you are to serve others, you must have something to give. You can give time and love to others only as you depend on Jesus daily and draw your strength and wisdom from Him.

Abandonment. Jesus said that if a man is to find his life, he must lose it (Matt. 10:39). What He meant was that you should cease trying to call attention to yourself and instead concentrate your concern on others.

> *Dear Lord, make me aware of the needs of others, and let me be more accepting of them. I want to abide in You, drawing strength and wisdom for each task You give me to do. Make me available. I want to lose my life and find it in You.*

SCRIPTURE READING: Matthew 28:18–20

KEY VERSE: 1 John 2:2

He Himself is the propitiation for our sins, and not for ours only but also for the whole world.

In his book *In the Gap,* David Bryant coins a term to identify the Christian's reluctance for missionary involvement:

Underneath disinterest in world outreach, underneath small missions budgets or limited personnel and the scandal of billions yet unreached, hides a culprit I call "pea-sized Christianity."

There is a pea-sized box called convert Christianity—life in Christ gets no bigger than making it safely inside the kingdom.

Or there's character Christianity—life in Christ gets no bigger than pulling one's own spiritual act together.

When life in Christ is no bigger than the warm, secure fellowship I have each week with my good Christian buddies, I'm in a box of cloister Christianity.

Or when life in Christ is no bigger for me than getting nicely settled in a good paying job after graduation, then I'm trapped in career Christianity. Many of us are groping around the box of church Christianity—the Sunday school picnic, the choir's Christmas pageant.

In summary, when my Christian experience expands no further than my salvation or small group or church or future, it's pea-sized. When my activities don't link me to the reaching of the earth's unreached people, I've succumbed to pea-sized Christianity.

Dear Lord, deliver me from pea-sized Christianity. Expand my focus, and bring me into harmony with Your divine purpose of reaching the world with the good news of the gospel.

SCRIPTURE READING: 1 Corinthians 4:8–21
KEY VERSE: John 4:35

Do you not say, "There are still four months and then comes the harvest"?
Behold, I say to you, lift up your eyes and look at the fields, for they are
already white for harvest!

Francis Schaeffer, the late Christian thinker and theologian, said the two greatest enemies of the modern church in America are "personal peace and affluence." He was describing the prevailing indifference that envelops the body of Christ today. Christians become complacent when they are preoccupied with meeting only their needs instead of reaching out to others.

The church in America is wealthy and prosperous. But believers in many countries are imprisoned for their faith or punished with loss of their jobs. Christians in Africa and developing countries are poor. Wherever we live, there are emotional, spiritual, and physical needs, but we must first lift our eyes to the fields (John 4:35).

Complacency is also nurtured when we settle for the wisdom of our age instead of becoming "fools for Christ's sake" (1 Cor. 4:10 NASB). Paul said he had "become as the scum of the world, the dregs of all things" (1 Cor. 4:13 NASB).

Following Christ calls for radical discipleship—denying self and discarding the wisdom of this world for the wisdom of God. Have you allowed God to disturb your comfort zone?

Father, disturb my comfort zone. Change my focus from personal peace
and affluence to the harvest fields of the world. Make me a radical
disciple.

SCRIPTURE READING: 2 Timothy 4:1–5
KEY VERSE: 2 Timothy 1:5

When I call to remembrance the genuine faith that is in you, which dwelt first in your grandmother Lois and your mother Eunice, and I am persuaded is in you also.

One day when the starter was injured, Steve, a second-string quarterback, not only took over but also led the team to a convincing win. "I knew my time would come one day," Steve said. "I spent my time on the bench—always watching and observing—so I would be ready when the opportunity arrived."

We all endure seasons of spiritual idleness when our service for Christ appears slack. Opportunities seem few; demand for our input is slight. If we allow such occasions to dull our spiritual fervor, however, we will not be ready to minister when the door of service opens.

Spiritual readiness in the dry season is necessary for usefulness later, meaning you cultivate your relationship with Christ Jesus through daily prayer and searching of the Scriptures. Your purpose is to know and glorify God. That should be your passion, regardless of your ministry opportunities.

Spiritual readiness also means you daily apply the truth you discover through fellowship with the Lord and study of the Scriptures. You apply publicly what God's Spirit teaches you in your private devotions.

You are faithful in the little things. Then when the demand arises, you will be fully prepared—equipped for the task through Christ's presence within you.

Prepare me, Lord. Make me faithful in the little things. Let me daily apply the truth of Your Word to my life. Equip me for service so that when the opportunity arises, I'll be ready.

The Power of Your Personal Testimony

SCRIPTURE READING: John 4:34–38

KEY VERSE: Psalm 145:6

Men shall speak of the might of Your awesome acts,
And I will declare Your greatness.

Your personal testimony of knowing Christ as Savior and Lord is an effective tool for evangelism and edification. To many, the Bible is antiquated and irrelevant. But people can relate to what God has done, and is doing, in your life.

Whether your conversion to Christ was a quiet living room or Damascus Road experience is insignificant. What matters is that you had an encounter with a personal God that changed your way of thinking and your life.

That encounter is a tangible means of personalizing and manifesting the reality of Christ and His Word—one that the Holy Spirit can use to authenticate the message of the gospel. Even other Christians can be encouraged through your testimony. Many can identify with your struggle of unbelief and doubt. Still others can relate to your continuing discovery of God's truth as a growing Christian, motivating them to continue the race begun at salvation.

Never be shy about telling someone else what God has done for you. God may use it in ways you never dreamed.

O God, I praise You for what You have done in my life. Now give me
the ability to share it with others—powerfully, forcefully, and persua-
sively.

You are the light of the world. A city that is set on a hill cannot be hidden.

Most Christians are engaged in very ordinary occupations in everyday circumstances. But in each commonplace and average day, we have an opportunity to achieve greatness, to let the light of Jesus Christ illumine our usual circumstances.

Jesus said, "You are the light of the world."

"Me?" you reply. "Plain, simple, struggling me—the light of the world?"

Jesus is never wrong. You are the earthly radiance of the presence of Jesus Christ because the Light of the World, Jesus, indwells your spirit with His. The Light of life resides in you from the moment of salvation. It is the light of truth. It is the light of hope. It is the light of peace. It is the light of love. It is the light of joy. It is the light of confidence.

Why? Because Jesus is all of these things and more, your responsibility is to let your light shine before others (Matt. 5:16). Let the light out. Do not bottle it up in unbelief, irritability, doubt, anger, bitterness, and other such stifling emotions.

Jesus will make His presence known to others around you in a very real way. Just abide in Him daily, and He will make Himself known.

> *Dear Lord, remove everything that would dim Your light through me. I want to shine brightly for You, illuminating the darkness of the world around me.*

SCRIPTURE READING: Ephesians 2:8–16
KEY VERSE: Ephesians 6:8

Knowing that whatever good anyone does, he will receive the same from the Lord, whether he is a slave or free.

Many fine, moral, nice people in the world bring good cheer to others, but leave no divine imprint. The interesting thing about Christians is that our light—our good works and words—is to shine in such a way so as to "glorify [our] Father in heaven" (Matt. 5:16).

Your light, your witness, should reflect on the person and character of Jesus Christ, attracting others to His uncommon presence. Your works should bring attention not to yourself but to God, casting His ways in sharp relief to the familiar ways of the world.

Your enthusiasm in your tasks should reflect your passion to serve God. That zeal should spring forth in the mundane projects, the obscure times, and the relatively boring jobs. Your enthusiasm points to the origin of the zest, a desire to glorify Christ in all you do.

Your light also shines uniquely when you do your work with excellence. You are faithful in the little things that others ignore; you go above the mediocre and walk the second mile.

Your enthusiasm and excellence in the familiar routine unveil the inner presence of Jesus Christ for the world to see.

Give me enthusiasm, O God—even in the routine, mundane things of life. Let my work be marked with excellence. I want to glorify You in everything I do.

SCRIPTURE READING: Mark 10:46–52
KEY VERSE: Matthew 10:32

Whoever confesses Me before men, him I will also confess before My Father who is in heaven.

Today, as you shop at the grocery store, work in the office, volunteer at school, or do any other routine activity, you will encounter many different people. Each one is a unique individual with an astounding array of personal needs—love, money, friendship, wisdom, courage, among others.

But every human being has one need in common: a personal relationship with Jesus Christ—Savior, Lord, and Friend of all who believe in Him. The joyous truth is that every believer possesses the Person who can meet that universal need.

You may not be able to help people financially. You may not live in close proximity to establish friendships. You may not have the material resources to supply their practical needs. But you can introduce them to Jesus Christ, the only One who can provide for every need, meet every demand, care for every hurt.

Jesus is the Answer. If you know Him, you can tell others about Him in a variety of ways: over a cup of coffee, through a tract, a suggestion to attend church or listen to a religious broadcast.

Everybody needs the Lord. Share Him as His Spirit leads you, and He will meet their needs as no other can.

Lord, I want to start today. Give me the opportunity to share You with others—then help me take it!

SCRIPTURE READING: 1 Corinthians 2:1–5

KEY VERSE: Isaiah 66:2

"For all those things My hand has made,

And all those things exist,"

Says the LORD.

"But on this one will I look:

On him who is poor and of a contrite spirit,

And who trembles at My word."

Humility is the key to an effective witness for Jesus Christ. No one knew that any better than the apostle Paul. With an educational background that rivaled the philosophers of his day, Paul said when it came to the things of God his knowledge was as nothing.

You may think that you can dazzle a person into God's kingdom with your Bible knowledge and memorized verses. However, if you fail to have a humble spirit, God cannot bless your efforts.

People need to see Jesus Christ—not a perfect saint, but a Christian who has been saved by His grace and who wants to share a humble testimony with others. If you will open yourself up to be used of God for His witness, in His way, you will be surprised at the opportunities He will bring to you.

Ask Him to give you basic tools from His Word. Lean on Him to provide the strength to overcome any fear the enemy may use to prevent you from telling others of His love.

There is only one message the world needs to hear: Jesus Christ our Savior, Jesus Christ our Lord, Jesus Christ our life, Jesus Christ our sufficiency for all things.

May He lead you in your witness for Him today.

O God, the world needs Your message. Help me overcome my fear, my

shyness, and my apprehension. Let me be Your witness.

SCRIPTURE READING: John 20:19–23
KEY VERSE: John 20:21

Jesus said to them again, "Peace to you! As the Father has sent Me, I also send you."

God gave Jesus a very clear mission—to seek and to save those separated from Him by sin. It was the same mission Christ gave His disciples, and it is the one He gives us today.

Many people spend a lifetime trying to understand their calling, but God's call is clear. We are to be missionaries of His love and grace to a world bound by sin and shame.

When you accepted Christ's death as payment for your sins, you also accepted the Father's call—to tell others of His forgiveness. It may take you across the country, around the world, or across the office or neighborhood.

The mission and its message are clear—freedom from the penalty, power, and presence of sin for all who place their trust in Jesus Christ. Christ never calls you to fulfill His mission in your own strength. As the Father sent Jesus with a clear understanding of His purpose and power, He sends you with the same understanding.

Lack of knowledge of the gospel is the greatest hindrance to God's mission. Ask Christ to give you a love for His Word that comes from the Holy Spirit. The insight you gain will serve as a beacon of hope not only to you but also to those the Father brings your way. May you know the wonder of His call today.

Heavenly Father, give me a clear understanding of Your purpose and power. Whether it is around the world or across the street, I want to fulfill Your mission.

SCRIPTURE READING: Luke 9:57–62

KEY VERSE: Luke 9:62

Jesus said to him, "No one, having put his hand to the plow, and looking back, is fit for the kingdom of God."

Jesus was committed to the Father's mission, even to the point of death. If you plan to answer the call of Christ, you must be committed to His mission.

Lack of commitment may cause you to waver, become fearful, and eventually quit. Peter sank while walking on the water because he took his eyes off the Savior and became consumed with his surroundings.

Jesus told His disciples that no one who puts his hands to the plow and then looks back at what might have been is fit for the kingdom of God. Commitment is everything to Him. If you are not fully committed to Christ, you will never be committed to His mission.

Many people fail to answer God's call because the commitment seems too great—the requirements too stiff. You may never understand God's motive in calling you to a certain task, but you can be sure He has a purpose and a wonderful plan in store for you. Obedience is always the prelude to blessing.

Jesus was and still is fully committed to you. Are you committed to Him and His call? If so, praise Him for His work in your life, and then ask Him to give you wisdom and insight into your personal mission.

O God, make me committed to You with the same level of commitment You have toward me. Raise me up in Your strength to fulfill my personal mission in this world.

SCRIPTURE READING: 1 Samuel 3:1–21
KEY VERSE: 1 Samuel 3:10

Now the LORD came and stood and called as at other times, "Samuel! Samuel!" And Samuel answered, "Speak, for Your servant hears."

You have probably known people who insist on serving God on their own terms. Before they even ask God in prayer what He wants them to do, they already have their plans mapped out. Before long, otherwise good and noble projects go wrong, and they don't understand why. Charging ahead without seeking the Lord's will, or ignoring His counsel, almost always brings negative consequences.

Hophni and Phinehas performed worship ceremonies in the temple according to their own wishes. Because they were more concerned about having relationships with the temple women and getting the best pieces from the sacrifices, God eventually allowed them to be killed.

Samuel, however, learned how to listen to God's voice and how to respond. Just as Eli had told him, when Samuel heard God's call in the night, he answered, "Speak, for Thy servant is listening" (1 Sam. 3:10 NASB). Samuel was ready to hear and obey whatever his Master told him; he waited for the Lord's command.

Do you seek God's instruction, or do you try to do His work in your own strength? For whatever He asks you to do, He provides the plan and the power to accomplish it. God's work done God's way means sure success.

Heavenly Father, I want to do Your work in Your way. Show me Your plan, then give me the power to accomplish it.

SCRIPTURE READING: 2 Corinthians 11:22–28

KEY VERSES: John 10:27–28

My sheep hear My voice, and I know them, and they follow Me. And I give them eternal life, and they shall never perish; neither shall anyone snatch them out of My hand.

The young convert shook his head in disbelief. He thought becoming a Christian would somehow inoculate him from future trouble. Christianity does not provide immunity from heartache and trouble. However, in the heartache, God promises never to leave us. His protection and wisdom are available to all who are His. Jesus said, "My sheep hear My voice, and I know them, and they follow Me; and I give eternal life to them, and they shall never perish; and no one shall snatch them out of My hand" (John 10:27–28 NASB).

In 2 Corinthians 11, Paul provided an extensive list of the personal trials he faced as a result of his love for Christ. Several times he was beaten to the point of death. Many times he was rejected and ridiculed for his desire to further the kingdom of God.

What was the driving force behind his life? What kept Paul from giving up? A passion for God—the very thing that sustains you when fear and adversity threaten your existence.

A passion for God goes beyond fondness. It is a love for God that is constant, regardless of circumstances. With a passion for God you never want to walk away from what God has given you to do. But if you should, you know you can come home because God has a passion for you, and God's love never grows cold.

O Lord, give me a passion for You and Your purposes. Let it burn within me. May its flame never grow dim.

SCRIPTURE READING: Colossians 1:24–29
KEY VERSE: Colossians 1:28

Him we preach, warning every man and teaching every man in all wisdom,
that we may present every man perfect in Christ Jesus.

In Colossians 1:28, Paul wrote, "We proclaim [Christ]" (NASB). The word *proclaim* means "to tell others" about Jesus. But how can you effectively do this if your heart is divided and you lack a true passion for God?

The world is filled with various passions—a passion for sports, food, personal achievement, money, recognition—the list could go on. Many people reason that God is not interested in what they do outside church. But Jesus had a different answer: "To love the Lord your God with all your heart is the greatest commandment" (Matt. 22:36–37, author's paraphrase).

He told His disciples: "To obey is better than sacrifice." Some Jews took great pride in offering sacrifices. They believed it was sufficient in uprighting their lopsided relationship with God. However, they offered the sacrifices out of a desire to be noticed by others.

Do you have a true passion for God? Is He your first thought in the morning, your constant companion throughout the day, and your last thought at night? Do you consider what He wants for your life above your personal desires?

You may achieve good things, but you will never fully experience Christ until your passion is for Him and Him alone.

> *You and You alone—that is my cry, O Lord. I want Your will, even*
> *above my desires. Give me a heart to love and serve You.*

SCRIPTURE READING: Philippians 2:1–11

KEY VERSE: Galatians 5:13

You, brethren, have been called to liberty; only do not use liberty as an oppor-
tunity for the flesh, but through love serve one another.

Philip Yancey, an insightful Christian author, reflected in a *Christianity*
Today article on the discrepancy between those who bask in the limelight
and those who toil in seeming obscurity:

> My career as a journalist has afforded me opportunities to inter-
> view diverse people. Looking back, I can roughly divide them into
> two types—servants and stars.
>
> The stars include NFL football greats, movie actors, music per-
> formers, famous authors, TV personalities, and the like. These are
> the ones who dominate our magazines and our television programs.
>
> I have also spent time with servants. People like Dr. Paul Brand
> who worked for twenty years among outcasts—leprosy patients, the
> poorest of the poor in rural India. Or the health workers who left
> high-paying jobs to serve with Mendenhall Ministries. . . . Or relief
> workers in Somalia, the Sudan, Ethiopia, Bangladesh, or other such
> repositories of world-class suffering.
>
> But as I now reflect on the two groups—stars and servants—the
> servants clearly emerge as the favored ones, the graced ones. They
> work for low pay, long hours, and no applause, "wasting" their tal-
> ents and skills among the poor.
>
> But somehow in this process of losing their lives, they have
> received the peace that is not of this world.

Lord, make me a servant instead of a star! Let me immerse my life in
fulfilling Your purposes. Though I toil in obscurity, I know I will not
lose anything—I'll gain!

SCRIPTURE READING: 1 Corinthians 4:1–7
KEY VERSE: 1 Timothy 1:5

The purpose of the commandment is love from a pure heart, from a good conscience, and from sincere faith.

The Corinthian church's bickering over personality and popularity was all quite ridiculous to Paul. He described both himself and Apollos in this humble way: "Servants of Christ and stewards of the mysteries of God" (1 Cor. 4:1).

That is, in essence, what every Christian is—regardless of level of spiritual maturity. We are servants because Jesus is Lord and Master of all. Those who aspire to leadership in the body of Christ have a divine prerequisite: ever-increasing servanthood. None of us should labor with the idea that others will admire us.

We are stewards because Jesus is the Owner and Giver of all: "For who regards you as superior? And what do you have that you did not receive? But if you did receive it, why do you boast as if you had not received it?" (1 Cor. 4:7 NASB).

Jesus has given us abundant and eternal life in His name. As our Maker and Redeemer, He has endowed us with natural and spiritual gifts. He has equipped us with the Holy Spirit and His Word. He teaches us, leads us, and reveals His ways to us. He is the Source of all. That removes all grounds for haughtiness and bragging in the Christian life. Paul, the chief of all sinners, knew it better than most (1 Tim. 1:15).

Do you?

Dear God, help me never lose sight of the fact that I'm only a steward of my gifts and abilities. I want to use the resources You have given me to the best of my ability.

SCRIPTURE READING: Colossians 3:12–25
KEY VERSE: Colossians 3:23

Whatever you do, do it heartily, as to the Lord and not to men.

In a watershed survey dealing with moral and ethical behavior for the *Wall Street Journal,* a 1983 Gallup Poll uncovered some astonishing results. The survey stated: "The results show the churched to feel somewhat more likely than the unchurched that charging a company for a cab ride is wrong, but other differences are of only marginal significance. . . . In the case of other types of behavior—lying, cheating, and pilferage—the differences are not significant or of marginal significance." It's no wonder that the business world sees little compelling evidence that Christianity is a practical, valid faith for all of life, not just Sunday morning.

Because He is Lord of our lives, God's wisdom, grace, and counsel are available for all of life, making us salt and light through the methods and quality of our work.

God has given work supreme dignity. It was His idea. He has called you to work. Whatever the nature of your job, the reality of your faith is communicated.

Christianity works in the workplace. Ask Christ to equip you to be His witness to your coworkers, and your job will become not just a career, but a calling.

> *Heavenly Father, help me reflect Your truth through my conduct and integrity in the marketplace of this world. Make me salt and light through the quality of my work.*

SCRIPTURE READING: 2 Corinthians 2:14–16
KEY VERSE: 1 Peter 2:12

Having your conduct honorable among the Gentiles, that when they speak against you as evildoers, they may, by your good works which they observe, glorify God in the day of visitation.

A great deception of our media-saturated age is that a person has to be prominent or visible to be influential. Jesus taught quite the contrary. Standing on a rural hillside with a few thousand farmers, fishermen, carpenters, and other men and women of humble background, He pronounced them as the "salt of the earth" and the "light of the world."

Jesus brings the same message to you. You are valuable and worthy in His eyes, created as His workmanship for a lifetime of good works that will demonstrate the reality of the kingdom of God to a blind and captive world.

Realize your worth in Christ. You were not created or saved by accident but by His design, to be used for His purposes, which will have eternal consequences.

Each day, on the bus, in the office, at the school, over the fence, you influence others for Christ. They see your love or your irritability. They hear your gracious comments or sarcastic remarks. The presence of the risen Christ is reflected or obscured.

Whoever you are, whatever you do, wherever you are, Christ can use you today. Accept your worth to Him and your value to others. Your life is a fragrance of the indwelling Christ.

Dear Lord, make my life count for You. You created me to be used for Your purposes, and I know there are eternal consequences involved. Help me to reflect Your presence.

SCRIPTURE READING: John 1:1–34

KEY VERSE: John 1:4

In Him was life, and the life was the light of men.

John described Jesus as the Light of the World, for "in Him was life, and the life was the light of men" (John 1:4). In actuality, Christ was God's first missionary. He was the bearer of redemption, of sins forgiven, and of God's grace for all humanity.

His words of acceptance and love moved men and women to immeasurable points of commitment to God. Their lives were changed, their hopes renewed, and their hearts made pure, all because they heard the gospel message and believed in God's Messenger.

When Jesus died on Calvary, His earthly mission was complete. Salvation's pathway was no longer closed. Instead, all of heaven was opened to everyone who would trust in God's Son.

As a Christian, you are His chosen light of hope to a world bound in the darkness of sin. You cannot escape the call of His commission. You may not be called to an overseas mission field, but as a child of God, you are called to carry the light of the gospel to those around you.

You are a missionary to the people in your office, in your family, on the commuter train, on the airplane, and in the garden club. Wherever there is darkness, Jesus wants you to shine His light of love and salvation.

> *Lord, You were a missionary, and Your mission is complete. Help me fulfill my mission. Raise me up to bear the light of Your Word to the darkest recesses of this sinful world.*

SCRIPTURE READING: Luke 24:44–51

KEY VERSE: Acts 1:8

You shall receive power when the Holy Spirit has come upon you; and you shall be witnesses to Me in Jerusalem, and in all Judea and Samaria, and to the end of the earth.

For a moment he studied the crowd moving toward the front of the church. Then with sweaty palms and a nervous feeling in the pit of his stomach, he stepped out into the aisle. As he walked to the front of the church, the words of "Have Thine Own Way" comforted him.

Standing at the altar, he suddenly felt a small hand slip inside his. In looking down he saw the face of his seven-year-old daughter. "I will go for Jesus, too, Daddy," she said and beamed a smile. As he lifted his eyes, he saw his wife holding their eighteen-month-old son. She said, "Darling, we'll all go for Him." He knew the moment meant total surrender to the will of God.

But so much had happened in the past. So many tears. So many words spoken in haste and anger. Could Jesus see past the years spent in sin and denial? Could God really be calling them to carry the light of His gospel halfway around the world?

Yes. God uses people with hearts turned toward Him. Past sins and failures are forgiven. He abides in the immediacy of the moment. When we open our hearts in obedient faith to His will, He uses us. Jesus has a job for you to do, and no one else can take your place.

Will you go for Him? Will you answer His call?

Yes, Lord, I'll answer the call. I'll leave the past behind. Send me. Use me. I'm ready to go.

August

THEME: The Fountain Gate

REPRESENTING: The work of the Holy Spirit

KEY VERSES: John 7:37–39

On the last day, that great day of the feast, Jesus stood and cried out, saying, "If anyone thirsts, let him come to Me and drink. He who believes in Me, as the Scripture has said, out of his heart will flow rivers of living water." But this He spoke concerning the Spirit.

SCRIPTURE READING: John 16:7–15

KEY VERSE: John 15:26

When the Helper comes, whom I shall send to you from the Father, the Spirit of truth who proceeds from the Father, He will testify of Me.

Although the Holy Spirit is defined to a degree by His various roles—teacher, guide, and helper—His identity rests on three truths:

First, the Holy Spirit is God. In several instances, the Holy Spirit is referred to as "the Spirit of God."

Second, He is one with God, the third person of the Trinity. As such, He possesses the inherent nature and character of God. The Greek word for "another" in John 14:16–17 is literally translated "another of the same kind." Thus, the Holy Spirit is God Himself, omnipotent (Job 33:4), omnipresent (Ps. 139:7–10), and omniscient (1 Cor. 2:10–12).

Third, since the Holy Spirit is a person, He is God. The Holy Spirit likewise is marked by a distinct personality. He is not an "it." He has a will (1 Cor. 12:11), emotions (Eph. 4:30), and intellect (Rom. 8:27).

As a person, the Holy Spirit can be resisted, lied to, and grieved. The Holy Spirit is life. The Holy Spirit helped birth the universe (Gen. 1:2). Christ was conceived by an act of the Holy Spirit. The believer is given God's life through His indwelling, and the abundant life is possible only through His activity.

Heavenly Father, during the coming days, reveal Your Holy Spirit to me in a new way. I want to live the Spirit-filled life.

SCRIPTURE READING: Acts 19:2–6

KEY VERSE: Zechariah 4:6

He answered and said to me:
"This is the word of the LORD to Zerubbabel:
'Not by might nor by power, but by My Spirit,'
Says the LORD of hosts."

A sense of enigma often surrounds the biblical teaching on the Holy Spirit. Our concept of God the Father is firmly established. Our perception of the Son, Jesus Christ, is clear. But when it comes to identifying the Holy Spirit, our description and understanding are often muddled.

However, apart from a firm grasp of the Holy Spirit's identity and function, it is unlikely we will make any visible progress in the spiritual realm. Ignorance of His work and ministry has stymied the growth and joy of millions of Christians through the ages. Misconceptions of His activity have led equal numbers down the disillusioning path of false doctrine.

Defining Him in the context of personal experience has diluted and distorted His unchanging nature and function. Examining the Scriptures, you can discover the identity and work of the Holy Spirit. In the process, you can lay a foundation for a new dimension in Christian living that transforms your thoughts, motivations, and behavior through His supernatural influence.

Heavenly Father, lay a foundation for a new dimension of Christian living in my life. Through Your Spirit, transform my thoughts, motivations, and behavior.

SCRIPTURE READING: John 14:16–26
KEY VERSE: John 14:16

And I will pray the Father, and He will give you another Helper, that He may abide with you forever.

In John 14:16, Jesus called the Holy Spirit a Helper. In the Greek this word is *Parakletos,* or "Comforter." It suggests the giving of aid much like a legal counselor or advocate would do. The sense in which *Parakletos* is used means "to come alongside another while giving strength and encouraging support." The Holy Spirit is God's personal representative here on earth. He is the third person of the Trinity.

Jesus knew the void within the hearts of His disciples would be great after He returned to the Father. Therefore, God in His greatness and compassion sent the Holy Spirit to comfort the followers of Christ, and He is still with us today. He is our Guide to all truth and our personal Advocate and Comforter before the throne of God.

A. B. Simpson asserted,

The Holy Spirit is not to us now what He was under the Old Testament, purely the Spirit of Deity, but He is, if we can understand what it means, the Spirit that dwelt in the human and divine Christ; the Spirit that (if we may say it with reverence) was softened and in some sense humanized by union with Jesus . . . and so Jesus received Him and spoke all His words and did all His works through the Spirit; and now He gives to us the very same Spirit that dwelt in Him.

This is your peace and strength—knowing that whatever you face, God faces it with you through the Holy Spirit.

Holy Spirit, You are my Advocate. Thank You for representing me. I know that whatever I face today or in the future, I am not alone.

SCRIPTURE READING: John 3:5–8

KEY VERSE: Romans 8:9

You are not in the flesh but in the Spirit, if indeed the Spirit of God dwells
in you. Now if anyone does not have the Spirit of Christ, he is not His.

A. T. Robertson writes in *Word Pictures in the New Testament:* "The
entire earthly life of Jesus was bound up with the Holy Spirit from His
birth to His death and resurrection." Seriously consider this truth: If the
presence of the Holy Spirit was essential for the birth, ministry, and resurrection of God's Son, then how essential is the Spirit's presence in the
believer's life?

Apart from the Holy Spirit's active participation, a person cannot be
born again (John 3:5–6). The Holy Spirit's presence authenticates an individual's membership in God's family (Rom. 8:9).

The power of God's Spirit is the only means by which you can live a
consistently productive spiritual life. The Spirit of God produces
Christlikeness, enabling you to experience the supernatural life of Christ
in your practical world of relationships, obligations, conflicts, and challenges (Gal. 5:16).

Jesus was conceived, anointed for ministry, and raised by the power of
the Holy Spirit. Likewise, your spiritual conception, life, and eternal destiny are all secured by the Holy Spirit. Are you depending daily on Him?

Heavenly Father, the ministry of Your Holy Spirit is essential in my
life. Let Your Spirit bring the supernatural into the practical world of
my relationships, obligations, conflicts, and challenges this day.

SCRIPTURE READING: 2 Corinthians 3:1–6

KEY VERSE: 1 Corinthians 3:16

Do you not know that you are the temple of God and that the Spirit of God dwells in you?

The incarnate Jesus was Immanuel—God with us. As His crucifixion neared, He spent His last hours with the disciples explaining that the gift of the Holy Spirit would be the divine agent of God's presence following His death and ascension.

Because you are a believer in Jesus Christ, God is with you always through the indwelling presence of the Holy Spirit. You are never alone. You are never helpless. You are never comfortless. The presence of the Holy Spirit is unceasing. Once you are saved, His residence is permanent. The Holy Spirit will never be taken from you.

The presence of the Holy Spirit is unconditional. His presence does not depend on your performance. When the joy of the Lord fills you to the rim, when the depths of despair overwhelm you, He is there.

Knowing that, you should feel great security in the Spirit's unceasing and unconditional presence. It should also encourage you. Through the Holy Spirit, God is intimately involved with every detail of your existence.

Thank You, Lord, that I am never alone. I am not helpless. I am not without comfort. The presence of Your Spirit is always with me. Unconditionally. Unceasingly.

SCRIPTURE READING: Romans 8:26–30

KEY VERSE: Acts 13:2

As they ministered to the Lord and fasted, the Holy Spirit said, "Now sepa-
rate to Me Barnabas and Saul for the work to which I have called them."

A friend asks you to pray for her deteriorating marriage—you really do
not know how to pray.

A telephone call comes in the night with distressing news about your
father's illness—the words are lost in tears.

When you do not know what to say, how to pray, or what the needs
are, the Holy Spirit is your greatest ally.

In His omniscience—He knows the need.

In His omnipotence—He is able to help.

In His omnipresence—He is involved in their lives.

The Holy Spirit also knows the mind of the Father. He can pray
according to the will of God for every person, in every circumstance.
Your part is to present the person or petition to the Father, admitting your
ignorance and helplessness.

You must also deeply desire God's answer for the dilemma. When you
do, the Spirit of God can take your vague requests and intercede before
the Father on others' behalf (and yours). If something has baffled or perplexed you, trust in the supernatural, intercessory ministry of the Holy
Spirit. His advocacy is imminently effective.

I can't handle this day alone, Lord. That is why I am so grateful for
Your Spirit. Reveal Your Spirit to and through me today.

SCRIPTURE READING: 1 John 5:6–8

KEY VERSE: Job 32:8

There is a spirit in man,
And the breath of the Almighty gives him understanding.

Catherine Marshall in her book *The Helper* provided keen insight into the Holy Spirit's intercessory role:

Unquestionably, all of us need massive help with praying aright. So set is our flesh against praying at all that the Helper's first task is to create in us even the basic desire to pray. He is the One Who also spotlights for us the prayer-need or topic for prayer by creating a "concern" within us.

Then the Helper has to uncover for us the essence, or kernel, of what it is we really want. Usually, the true desire at the heart of our prayer petition is buried under debris that obscures and muddles the real issue.

It is also the Helper's task to show us the blockages in the way of a given prayer-petition: any self-seeking, our desire to control, any resentments and unconfessed sin, etc.

He is also the One who gives us His own prayer faith; also His fervor to replace our tepid love and caring.

As we recognize our ignorance about praying aright and our helplessness, and actively seek the Spirit's help, our prayer life becomes the anteroom to amazing adventure.

As I wait before You this morning, Lord, let Your Spirit intercede through me. As I lift my requests to You, reveal the true desires of my heart. Remove the things that hinder the flow of Your life through me.

SCRIPTURE READING: Ephesians 4:25–32

KEY VERSE: 1 Thessalonians 5:19

Do not quench the Spirit.

The fire of the Spirit burns continuously to work the will of the Father. However, His flame is not often seen in our behavior because of a "quenching" of His activity. The Spirit can be resisted. His promptings can be ignored. His inner stirrings can be doused.

How do you quench the Spirit?

The Spirit is quenched when you fail to spend consistent time in God's Word. The Scriptures were authored by men under the inspiration of the Holy Spirit. The primary way that the Spirit communicates to you is through the Bible. How can you hear His voice, understand His ways, or carry out His desires if you neglect His Word?

The Spirit is also quenched when you stubbornly cling to a bad habit, a willful sin, or a carnal desire. The Spirit seeks to makes you holy. That is why He is the *Holy* Spirit. Holiness, however, is not attained unilaterally. It involves your cooperation and your obedience to His cleansing and conviction.

Are you resisting Him at a point? Have you turned a deaf ear to His urgings? His fullness, blessing, and power are yours the instant you obey.

Lord, I don't want to quench Your work in me. Make me responsive to the conviction of Your Holy Spirit. Holy Spirit, make me holy.

SCRIPTURE READING: Hebrews 3:7–19
KEY VERSE: Hebrews 3:15

It is said:
"Today, if you will hear His voice,
Do not harden your hearts as in the rebellion."

When he was five years old, he responded instantly to your voice.

When he was ten years old, he waited until your instructions were repeated at least two or three times.

By the time he was a teenager, he ignored you.

Such is also the danger when you stifle the Holy Spirit's gentle voice.

He nudges you to avoid gossip and grumbling. You listen, but fail to obey. He brings Scriptures to your mind repeatedly; you are convicted, but gradually lapse into your habit. Over time, your spiritual sensitivity is dulled. The Word of God no longer penetrates your soul, much less brings pangs of conscience.

A hardened heart and numbed conscience are the dangerous consequences of regularly muffling the Holy Spirit's persistent voice. If you procrastinate or have disobeyed so consistently that God's Word no longer convicts or delights you, then you are in the perilous process of quenching the Spirit.

Quickly repent. Confess your sin, your habit, your neglect, and thank God for His restored fellowship.

Surrender your rights to His lordship, asking Him to shape you into His image. Listen and respond instantly to the Spirit's voice.

Soften my heart, Father. Make me immediately responsive to the voice
of the Holy Spirit.

SCRIPTURE READING: John 15:1–8

KEY VERSE: John 15:5

I am the vine, you are the branches. He who abides in Me, and I in him, bears much fruit; for without Me you can do nothing.

Have you considered why a peach tree bears peaches, not apples, or why a pear tree bears pears, not bananas? It is because the life of the fruit is inseparably bound up in the tree itself. The sap that flows through the vine and into the branches determines the identity.

Just as surely, God's life within each believer produces Christlike character. We are the branches that live in union with the Vine, Jesus Christ.

The life within that determines the godly fruit you bear is the Holy Spirit. He is the divine sap that seeks to reproduce the spiritual qualities of godliness.

You can be kind to ungrateful people because the Holy Spirit is unfailingly kind. You can love all people because the Holy Spirit is love. You can be patient in trials because the Holy Spirit has boundless patience.

"I want to experience the life of the Holy Spirit, but I cannot. I try, but I fail!" you exclaim.

Do not despair. Failure is the first step to victory. Abiding in the Vine, allowing the Holy Spirit to reproduce Christ's character, begins with humble surrender and dependence.

Father, let me view my failures as the first step to victory. You are the Vine; I am the branch. Let Your divine essence flow through me to reproduce the spiritual qualities of godliness in my life.

SCRIPTURE READING: Galatians 5:16–25
KEY VERSE: Galatians 5:16

I say then: Walk in the Spirit, and you shall not fulfill the lust of the flesh.

Notice Jesus' words when He described the abiding life:

"If anyone does not abide in Me . . ."

"If you abide in Me, and My words abide in you . . ."

"If You keep My commandments . . ."

Bearing Christlike character is not automatic. You are in union with the Vine and indwelt by His Spirit, but the process of developing godly fruit is conditional.

Christ's character is reproduced in you as you not only live by the Spirit, but also "walk by the Spirit" (Gal. 5:25 NASB). "Walking by the Spirit" is consciously depending on the power of the Holy Spirit. Dependence on the Holy Spirit is unabashed anticipation that He will conform you to the image of Christ.

"Walking by the Spirit" is turning over each area of your personality to His control. You do not become Christlike all at once. It is a process that allows the Spirit of God to transform your thoughts and conduct.

The Holy Spirit will not overwhelm you. Rather, He will reveal a specific area that He desires to change. Your responsibility is to obey at each step.

Make me continually conscious of my dependence on the power of Your Spirit, Lord. I turn over each area of my personality to Your control. Transform my thoughts and conduct. Help me cooperate with the process.

SCRIPTURE READING: 1 Corinthians 12:1–11
KEY VERSE: 1 Corinthians 12:14

In fact the body is not one member but many.

Imagine that someone asked you to build a home and provided you with the architect's drawing and all the necessary building materials: bricks, wiring, Sheetrock, and so forth. Only the proper tools were missing—no hammer, nails, saw, or pliers.

Sometimes, the Christian life can seem as frustrating. God's Word tells us what to do—outlines His plans for living—but we do not seem able to get the job done.

At this juncture, we must depend on the indispensable ministry of the Holy Spirit. As our divine Helper, God's Spirit gives us the tools to accomplish the Father's will in one significant area—spiritual gifts.

Just as there are a variety of workers involved in building a home—plumbers, electricians, roofers, framers, carpenters—so there are a variety of Christians involved in building up the body of Christ. God has a place for you in His church. He has a job for you to do. He has provided you with the heavenly tools to do it right. Do you know your spiritual gift? Are you enjoying your part in building His body, using His special enablement?

> *Lord, You are the Giver of divine gifts. Through Your Holy Spirit, You have given me the right tools to get the job done. Use me to build Your kingdom.*

SCRIPTURE READING: 1 Corinthians 12:12–31
KEY VERSE: Romans 12:6

Having then gifts differing according to the grace that is given to us, let us use them.

Discovering your spiritual gift is the first step toward a lifetime of rewarding service in God's kingdom. This discovery is not mysterious, arduous, or convoluted. God does not work to confuse you. He wants you to know and exercise your spiritual gift.

Your spiritual gift (or gifts) is usually in accord with your unique set of personal inclinations. If you like helping others, service is probably your motivational gift. If you enjoy study and investigation, teaching is more than likely your gift. If others consistently benefit from your counsel and correction, the gift of exhortation is a good place to start in your search.

The second best indicator of your spiritual gift is the verification of others. If you like teaching, but no one learns, you had better reconsider. If you enjoy leading, but no one follows, leadership and administration are not your calling.

Ask God today to reveal your spiritual gift or gifts. Examine your likes and dislikes, and seek the input of others. Above all, remember your gift is given and determined by the Spirit and is to be used to bring glory to God.

> *Lord, I know You have a job for me to do. Reveal my spiritual gifts, then enable me to use them for Your glory.*

SCRIPTURE READING: Acts 1:1–8

KEY VERSE: Acts 1:8

You shall receive power when the Holy Spirit has come upon you; and you shall be witnesses to Me in Jerusalem, and in all Judea and Samaria, and to the end of the earth.

Immediately before Jesus' ascension, the disciples eagerly asked the resurrected Savior His intentions for Israel: "Lord, is it at this time You are restoring the kingdom to Israel?" (Acts 1:6 NASB).

Jesus never answered their query, informing them instead of the imminent, personal ministry of the Holy Spirit: "You shall receive power when the Holy Spirit has come upon you" (Acts 1:8).

We all have piercing questions we would like answered. But we are not to be overly occupied with them. Our real need is for power to enjoy and experience the abundant Christian life. Our most pressing demand is the divine enabling to know and follow Jesus Christ.

Jesus made it clear. What the apostles needed and what we need today is the power of the Holy Spirit.

Are you experiencing the power of the Holy Spirit on a consistent basis? Are you aware of His equipping and enabling in matters that are too difficult for you?

As God's child, you are indwelt by the Holy Spirit. He will release His power through you to meet every demand, every problem, every emergency, every circumstance. Just call on His name.

Heavenly Father, release Your power through me today. I want to meet every demand, problem, emergency, and circumstance through the power of Your Holy Spirit.

SCRIPTURE READING: Ephesians 3:14–21
KEY VERSE: Ephesians 3:16

That He would grant you, according to the riches of His glory, to be strengthened with might through His Spirit in the inner man.

As Great Britain faced the German might alone in the initial stages of World War II, Prime Minister Sir Winston Churchill sent this urgent but concise message to President Franklin Roosevelt: "Give us the tools, and we will finish the job."

The power of the Holy Spirit is the supernatural tool God has given to equip and enable each believer. The power of the Holy Spirit is to do the work God calls you to accomplish.

Serving others, loving even your enemies, building up one another in the faith, sharing Christ, and exercising your spiritual gifts are possible only through the Holy Spirit's enabling ministry. Trying to do such tasks in your own wisdom and strength and by your own methodology will eventually lead to failure and burnout.

The power of the Holy Spirit is also available for you to become the person God wants you to be. How can you possibly be loving, kind, gentle, patient, joyous, self-controlled, or peaceful apart from the Spirit's help?

Depend daily on Him, and the task of becoming Christlike and building His kingdom can be achieved.

I've tried it in my own strength and failed. Lord, I need Your enabling power to accomplish the task. I'm depending on You today.

SCRIPTURE READING: Galatians 6:7–9

KEY VERSE: Galatians 6:8

He who sows to his flesh will of the flesh reap corruption, but he who sows to the Spirit will of the Spirit reap everlasting life.

You are driving on a long trip to visit your folks for Thanksgiving. In the backseat, friction is rising between your ten-year-old and twelve-year-old. You have a decision. Will you lose your temper and discipline the children, or will you firmly correct them with your emotions under the Spirit's control?

Such are the constant choices each individual makes to "walk in the Spirit." It is not a mystical experience but practical submission to God's will in everyday circumstances. Walking in the Spirit is thus a cultivated lifestyle, learning to act and react under His direction and influence rather than being controlled by temperament or personality.

Each day brings increasing cooperation with the Spirit's will and power. You can walk in the Spirit one trusting step at a time. Begin with the next decision you must make.

One step at a time—and let me take it under the control of Your Spirit, O God. Teach me to act and react under Your direction. Make me Spirit led instead of temperament controlled.

SCRIPTURE READING: Colossians 3:5–10
KEY VERSE: Colossians 1:10

That you may walk worthy of the Lord, fully pleasing Him, being fruitful in every good work and increasing in the knowledge of God.

Walking in the Spirit certainly is not as simple as one, two, three; but a pyramid of biblical truth can help you keep step with His cadence.

When you walk in the Spirit, you are doing what God tells you to do. That entails a consistent reading and hearing of God's Word and obedience to His commands. You progressively discover what the Spirit of truth reveals through the Scriptures.

When you walk in the Spirit, you are doing what God says to do and how He says to do it. Learning God's methods comes only through systematic, persistent study of God's Word. It is not enough to read His truth. You must investigate, explore, and examine His principles.

Finally you walk in the Spirit when you do what God says, how He says to achieve it, and why He says to accomplish it. You apply the *why* through deliberate meditation on God's Word. You read and study, but then you delight in, revel in, and ponder the awesome truths designed to glorify Christ that it reveals.

Keep these cornerstone tenets in focus each day, and walking in the Spirit will become natural for you.

Heavenly Father, through Your Spirit, reveal to me today the what, how, and why of each situation. Help me apply the principles I learn in solitude to the hectic arena of my everyday life.

SCRIPTURE READING: 1 Corinthians 13
KEY VERSE: Galatians 5:25

If we live in the Spirit, let us also walk in the Spirit.

Have you ever held someone's hand as you walked along together? You surely noticed how important it is to maintain the same stride. You can't walk too slowly and you can't walk too fast, at least not without pulling your hand away.

That is what Galatians 5:25 is talking about when it says "walk in the Spirit." The New International Version captures the original Greek flavor of the word *walk* here: "Since we live by the Spirit, let us keep in step with the Spirit." The word picture is one of "walking in line with." When you are not following your fleshly urges to walk at your own pace, you feel the direct guidance of the Holy Spirit step by step along the way.

When you walk in harmony with the Spirit, the fruit of this relationship is evident. It makes sense that the fruit of the Spirit is the subject of other verses of Galatians 5. Which of these do you see in your attitudes and behavior: love, joy, peace, patience, kindness, goodness, faithfulness, gentleness, and self-control? It is truly an awesome list. As you think through these attributes, it's crucial to remember that they are not products of a decision to try harder. God keeps your feet on His good path when you keep in step with Him.

> *How often I have walked my own way, O Lord. Forgive me. I want to keep in step with Your Spirit. Set my feet on Your path and keep them there.*

SCRIPTURE READING: 2 Thessalonians 2:13–17
KEY VERSE: 1 Thessalonians 4:7

God did not call us to uncleanness, but in holiness.

You are born again by God's Spirit when you believe in Christ's atonement for your sins. That is salvation, a singular decision with eternal permanence.

You are also sanctified by the same Spirit of God. But unlike salvation, sanctification is a lifelong process. In *The Pursuit of Holiness*, Jerry Bridges describes the joint venture of holy living:

> The farmer knows that unless he diligently pursues his responsibilities to plow, plant, fertilize, and cultivate, he cannot expect a harvest at the end of the season.
>
> In a sense he is in a partnership with God and he will reap its benefits only when he has fulfilled his own responsibilities.
>
> Farming is a joint venture between God and the farmer. The farmer cannot do what God must do and God will not do what the farmer should do.
>
> We can say just as accurately that the pursuit of holiness is a joint venture between God and the Christian. No one can attain any degree of holiness without God working in his life; but just as surely, no one will attain it without effort on his own part.

> *Holiness—it's a joint venture, Lord. I cannot do what You must do, and You will not do what I should do. Help me cooperate in the process.*

SCRIPTURE READING: 1 Peter 1:13–21

KEY VERSE: 1 Peter 2:2

As newborn babes, desire the pure milk of the word, that you may grow thereby.

The moment you embrace Christ as Savior you become holy and blameless in God's sight; your sins are forgiven by the blood of Christ. Yet salvation is only the starting block for a life of holiness. Your holy state, or position, as a new creature in Christ must be continually appropriated as you grow in holiness.

Think of humanity as an analogy. When a child is born, he is a human being in the fullest sense. However, his entire life is spent developing physically and emotionally, authenticating his humanness.

As you grow in holiness, you demonstrate the reality of your new identity as a saint, or "holy one." Although you must apply all your faculties to experience growth in holiness, the Holy Spirit is always the Change Agent for holy living. External observance of religious traditions will not make you holy. Good works will not make you holy. Avoidance of certain activities will not make you holy.

Do you want to be holy? Remember that God has already accepted you as His holy child, and then depend on the Holy Spirit to dynamically and continuously make you a partaker of God's divine, holy nature.

> *Heavenly Father, I want to live a holy life. I realize I cannot do it in myself. I cannot change myself. But You can. I'm depending on Your Holy Spirit to make me a partaker of Your divine, holy nature.*

SCRIPTURE READING: 1 Corinthians 2:6–16
KEY VERSE: Psalm 32:8

I will instruct you and teach you in the way you should go;
I will guide you with My eye.

The most vital area of truth into which the Holy Spirit guides you is the knowledge of God Himself. His holiness, love, faithfulness, wrath, judgment, mercy, grace, patience, power, and numerous other attributes are unveiled for you. Without the Spirit's aid you could never see God for who He is.

The Spirit also reveals the truth about humankind. The Spirit of God convicts the unbeliever of sin and the estrangement from God. The Holy Spirit underscores human depravity and the desperate need for a Savior. Apart from the Spirit's enlightenment, you are blinded by pride and conceit. After you become a Christian, the Spirit continues His ministry of conviction and illumination, not to condemn, but to enlighten and correct.

In addition, the Holy Spirit highlights God's truth about His specific instructions for living. He clearly shows you the pattern for family harmony, the proper motives for business, the guidelines for getting along with neighbors and enemies, and the principles for ethical and moral conduct. Let the Holy Spirit guide you into His truth for your special need today.

Holy Spirit, guide me in the way of truth today. Reveal it; teach it;
apply it. I submit to Your instruction.

SCRIPTURE READING: Romans 8:28–30

KEY VERSE: John 3:17

God did not send His Son into the world to condemn the world, but that the world through Him might be saved.

C. S. Lewis wrote in *Mere Christianity* that God has a common objective in each Christian's life:

Salvation is the changing from being confident about our own efforts to the state in which we despair of doing anything for ourselves and leave it to God. I know the words "leave it to God" can be misunderstood, but they must stay for the moment. The sense in which a Christian leaves it to God is that he puts all his trust in Christ: trusts that Christ will somehow perfect human obedience which He carried out from His birth to His crucifixion: that Christ will make the man more like Himself and, in a sense, make good his deficiencies.

In Christian language, He will share His sonship with us, will make us, like Himself, sons of God.

This is what God is up to in good and bad, adventure and drudgery, favor and misfortune. He wants you to be like Christ, and He equips you with the Holy Spirit to make you progressively so. In all things, God is working to help you enjoy completeness in Christ and become like Jesus in word and deed. This is God's remarkable doing, and the common events of each day work toward this eternal purpose.

Heavenly Father, let me look beyond the common events of this day to see Your greater eternal purpose. Make me like Your Son, Jesus Christ. Empower me with Your Holy Spirit so that Christlikeness will become a reality in my life.

SCRIPTURE READING: Psalm 23
KEY VERSE: 1 Corinthians 10:11

All these things happened to them as examples, and they were written for
our admonition, upon whom the ends of the ages have come.

A major function of the Holy Spirit is to guide God's children. But too often the leadership of the Spirit is ascribed to methods and sources of which the Father has no part.

In *Knowing God,* J. I. Packer helps us to understand the fundamental error and make the proper course correction:

Earnest Christians seeking guidance often go wrong about it. They look for a will-o'-the-wisp; they overlook the guidance that is ready to hand, and lay themselves open to all sorts of delusion.

Their basic mistake is to think of guidance as essentially inward prompting by the Holy Spirit, apart from the written Word.

The true way to honor the Holy Spirit as our guide is to honor the Holy Scriptures through which He guides us. The fundamental guidance which God gives to shape our lives . . . is not a matter of inward promptings apart from the Word but of the pressure on our consciences of the portrayal of God's character and will in the Word. . . .

The Spirit leads within the limits which the Word sets, not beyond them.

O Lord, I haven't passed this way before. Guide me this day by Your
Holy Spirit. Lead me within the limits set by Your Word. Don't let me
stray beyond them.

SCRIPTURE READING: Acts 16:6–10
KEY VERSE: Psalm 31:3

You are my rock and my fortress;
Therefore, for Your name's sake,
Lead me and guide me.

The eyes of America turned westward in the 1800s as settlers and explorers streamed into the vast frontier. Most were familiar only with states and land east of the Mississippi River. Therefore, they required a knowledgeable guide for the oceans of grass prairies, the weeks of desert, and the maze of mountains. Thus did men like Christopher "Kit" Carson and William Frederick "Buffalo Bill" Cody become cultural legends as they safely led thousands, including the U.S. military, to their destinations.

Each Christian has an infallible guide within, the person of the Holy Spirit. He is responsible to navigate you in God's direction.

You are completely ignorant of the future, but the Holy Spirit is all-knowing. He knows how your decisions today fit into His will for your tomorrows.

The Holy Spirit wants to guide you into a more intimate relationship with Christ. His express purpose is to glorify the Son of God (John 14:26). He also desires to guide you into the truth of God. The truth sets you free, and God's Word is truth. It should come as no surprise then that the Spirit uses Scripture as His primary tool of guidance.

Do not worry or fret. Gather information, pray, search the Word, and ask God to lead you. He will not fail you.

Dear Father in heaven, I don't know the future, but I rest in the knowledge that You do. You know how each decision I make today prepares me for Your will tomorrow. Lead me.

SCRIPTURE READING: 1 Corinthians 1:26–29

KEY VERSE: 1 Corinthians 1:27

God has chosen the foolish things of the world to put to shame the wise, and God has chosen the weak things of the world to put to shame the things which are mighty.

God has equipped you for every good work. The presence of the Holy Spirit is His guarantee that no matter what you face, He is committed to providing the power and strength you need to accomplish the task, get through the hurt, and end up victorious in Him.

D. L. Moody had only a fifth-grade education, but he became one of the greatest evangelists of our time. He was never ordained to the ministry, yet God used him to lead thousands to the saving knowledge of Jesus Christ. The book *More Than Conquerors* tells us that "during the nineteenth century when mass media consisted of only printing presses and public oratory, more than 100 million people heard or read the gospel message of D. L. Moody. The evangelist spoke to at least 1.5 million in London during four months in 1875, long before radio and television."

God chooses the weak things to shame those who think they are strong (1 Cor. 1:27–29). There is only one way God can be glorified in your life, and that is through your willingness to lay aside your ability, talent, and personal desires in order to follow Him in obedience. Sacrifice and submission lead to a life of tremendous hope, freedom, and eternal joy.

D. L. Moody could do nothing apart from the Savior. And what he did through the power of the Holy Spirit can never be duplicated.

Here they are, dear Lord—all my natural abilities, talents, and personal desires. I give them all to You. A great exchange, so that Your glory can be revealed through me.

SCRIPTURE READING: Luke 22:31–62

KEY VERSE: Acts 2:14

Peter, standing up with the eleven, raised his voice and said to them, "Men of Judea and all who dwell in Jerusalem, let this be known to you, and heed my words."

The night of the Lord's Supper, Peter told Jesus: "Lord, with You I am ready to go both to prison and to death!" (Luke 22:33 NASB). A short time later as Jesus struggled in prayer in the Garden of Gethsemane, Peter could not stay awake long enough to pray for the One he called Master. With the betrayal and Jesus' arrest, Peter found himself hovering beside a small courtyard fire outside Caiaphas's house. There three times he denied knowing Jesus.

"Peter said, 'Man, I do not know what you are talking about.' And immediately, while he was still speaking, a cock crowed. And the Lord turned and looked at Peter. And Peter remembered the word of the Lord, how He had told him, 'Before a cock crows today, you will deny Me three times.' And [Peter] went out and wept bitterly" (Luke 22:60–62 NASB).

Hours earlier, Peter said he would die for Jesus. Yet when the time came for him to stand beside the Lord, he denied knowing Him. It was not within Peter's ability to withstand such an attack of the enemy. Jesus knew Peter would rely on his own ability and fail.

In the book of Acts, Peter was completely transformed. God's Spirit was alive within him. The power you have in Christ is all you need to stand securely in the midst of the fiercest battle, the deepest sorrow, the longest wait. What Peter could not do on his own, he did mightily in the Spirit of God, and you can too!

Thank You, Father, that through the power of Your Holy Spirit, I can stand the fiercest battle, the deepest sorrow, the longest wait. What I cannot do on my own, I can do through You.

SCRIPTURE READING: Ephesians 5:8–14
KEY VERSES: Ephesians 5:9–10

(For the fruit of the Spirit is in all goodness, righteousness, and truth), find-ing out what is acceptable to the Lord.

What kinds of sounds do you hear in a grape arbor or other fruit orchard? You can probably hear birds chirping, the wind rustling through leaves, and many other usual outdoor sounds.

What you do not hear is the sound of the vines or trees groaning and straining. The plants are not laboring to produce their fruit; the fruit comes out of their branches naturally as a part of the growing process. The vine does not have to concentrate on producing grapes. When the vine is healthy and has all the water and nutrients it needs, the grapes come forth.

Jesus compared your life to the branches on a grapevine. He said: "I am the vine, you are the branches; he who abides in Me, and I in him, he bears much fruit; for apart from Me you can do nothing" (John 15:5 NASB).

The secret to fruit producing is as basic for you as it is for a real grapevine: stay planted in the Vine, and focus all of your energy and attention on being there, or abiding, in Christ. Worship Him, praise Him, meditate on His words, seek solitude in Him, and let yourself be absorbed into His purposes.

Through the power of the Holy Spirit, who bears testimony that you are planted into the Vine, your "grapes" will grow. Your fruit is a direct reflection of the quality of your relationship with Christ.

Make me a healthy spiritual vine, dear Lord. Let the fruit of my life reflect the quality of my relationship with You. Teach me to abide.

SCRIPTURE READING: Psalm 139
KEY VERSE: Psalm 139:23

Search me, O God, and know my heart;
Try me, and know my anxieties.

If we are honest, we must admit that at least subconsciously, if not overtly, we prefer the pleasant over the painful, the comfortable over the distressful. Despite this decidedly normal human disposition, we will stumble badly through the Christian journey if we adopt these longings as our chief aim.

Christ's goal for your life transcends this limited perspective. He has something far more sublime in mind for you—to make you productive in the work of His kingdom. This involves a process Christ termed *pruning,* a continual trimming of your character and habits that are unproductive for your personal growth as a believer.

It can be painful at times, even severe when the pruning lops off sensitive areas. But whatever God sees as detrimental to your fruitfulness and well-being, He will seek to sever. The tools of Providence may be sharp, but loving hands hold them.

Perhaps you can identify an area that God's Spirit has surfaced as deleterious to your spiritual health. Cooperate with the Husbandman. Though it may be trying for a time, God's goal is to grow you into the image of Christ. In this kind of pain, there is godly gain.

> *I don't like it, Lord—but I need it! Prune the unproductive branches of*
> *my life. I know it may be difficult, but I want to cooperate with the*
> *process. I rejoice that through my pain, there will be gain.*

SCRIPTURE READING: Galatians 5:1–13
KEY VERSE: Galatians 5:1

Stand fast therefore in the liberty by which Christ has made us free, and do not be entangled again with a yoke of bondage.

Jesus knew that on their own the disciples, and all believers, did not have the power and spiritual resources necessary to be His witnesses throughout the earth. In every dimension of our lives, the Holy Spirit releases power within us to be witnesses to God's truth, and only by submitting to the Lord's leadership through the Spirit do we find wholeness. Jack Hayford observes in *The Power and Blessing*:

In the judgment of some, "a life of submission" sounds like a page out of a handbook for membership in a religious order. . . . In fact, in much of today's church, many have almost sanctified the notion of autonomy, of independence, of "I can do just about whatever I want, because of my freedom in Christ."

In terms of spiritual reality, we are made free. But our liberty in Christ isn't a program of perpetuating self-rule in the soul. Our "freedom" is (1) to free us from practicing sin, (2) to free us from smallness of soul, and (3) to free us from a "Lone-Ranger" order of independence which proposes "me" as the singlehanded controller of everything in my life.

The spirit of submission, lived out in biblical terms, proposes that God could, in fact, use other people to teach me. . . . I'm exposing myself to the possibility that at times these "others" will adjust and correct me in the spirit of love.

I'm free in You, Lord. Free from sin. Free from smallness of soul. Free from selfish independence. Your Spirit has made it possible. Thank You for my liberty.

SCRIPTURE READING: 2 Corinthians 10:1–5
KEY VERSE: 2 Corinthians 10:4

The weapons of our warfare are not carnal but mighty in God for pulling down strongholds.

The power of the imagination—it has created the greatest inventions of all time, the most heartwarming stories, and the solutions to countless everyday problems. The imagination can also be a source of trouble, even as every aspect of your life is touched by the urge to give in to sin. Have you ever found yourself contemplating ideas you knew were not pleasing to the Lord? What was your response?

The Lord knows all too well how your thought life can lead you astray of His purposes and desires. That is why the Bible has so much to say about where you allow your mind to be and the concepts with which you fill it.

If you struggle in this area—and we all do—write down the following verses and commit them to memory. Then when certain alluring notions threaten to overcome your thoughts, you will have God's truth to conquer them.

Gird your minds for action, keep sober in spirit, fix your hope completely on [God's] grace. (1 Peter 1:13 NASB)

Whatever is true, whatever is honorable, whatever is right, whatever is pure, whatever is lovely, whatever is of good repute, if there is any excellence and if anything worthy of praise, let your mind dwell on these things. (Phil. 4:8 NASB)

Holy Spirit, I prepare my mind to face this day. I choose to dwell on the things that are true, honorable, right, pure, lovely, good, excellent, and worthy of praise. Jesus is all these things, so I will keep my mind fixed on Him.

SCRIPTURE READING: Ephesians 5:1–20
KEY VERSE: Ephesians 5:18

Do not be drunk with wine, in which is dissipation; but be filled with the Spirit.

The subject of many current science fiction films and programs is that of alien invasion and control. Few things are more frightening from a worldly perspective than the thought of nonhuman creatures taking over humans and making them function as aliens.

Regardless of what you think of science fiction, you can recognize the fundamental fear that these programs reflect: the loss of control. Many people find it important to maintain the feeling that they are in charge of their lives and all decisions, and the chance of losing any of that autonomy is scary.

Yet when the Bible speaks of being controlled by the Holy Spirit, the meaning is entirely different. Being controlled by the Spirit is not something to be afraid of; you do not become a robotic creature unable to think or act independently. The Spirit indwells you and fills your spirit, but He never insists on control. In fact, by deciding not to listen and pursuing your own course, you can effectively drown out His gentle voice.

Paul told the Ephesians: "Be filled with the Spirit, speaking to one another in psalms and hymns and spiritual songs, singing and making melody in your heart to the Lord." Yielding to the Spirit's control results in beautiful praise to God and a spirit filled with joy and renewed purpose, and that's nothing to be afraid of.

Dear heavenly Father, I want Your Spirit to have authority in my life so that my conduct and character will glorify Your name. Come now, Holy Spirit, and take complete control.

September

THEME: The Prison Gate

REPRESENTING: Deliverance

KEY VERSE: Isaiah 45:2

I will go before you
And make the crooked places straight;
I will break in pieces the gates of bronze
And cut the bars of iron.

SCRIPTURE READING: Psalm 106
KEY VERSE: Psalm 119:25

My soul clings to the dust;
Revive me according to Your word.

We usually do not seek freedom until we are miserable in our bondage. Sin's pleasures can control us for many years, decades, even a lifetime. It is not until we realize the extent to which sin controls us that we cry out for release.

Some would say it is too late to be delivered from the bondage of such masters as lust, alcohol, drugs, fear, anger, and/or inferiority. But with God our helplessness is our first step on the road to freedom. God places us in the awkward, uncomfortable position of helplessness.

Too many of us do not fully receive our freedom in Christ because we will do almost anything to avoid such a predicament. We enjoy the feeling of control. We detest the notions that we cannot stop our drinking, cannot halt our immorality, cannot conquer our fears, cannot heal our marriages, and cannot discipline our children.

Perhaps you view helplessness as weakness—as admission that you are inadequate to solve your dilemma or to do anything apart from Christ, who said, "Apart from Me you can do nothing" (John 15:5 NASB). But in God's eyes and along His route to spiritual freedom, your feelings of helplessness are the birth pangs of a miracle.

I feel helpless, O Lord, but I take this word as a personal message to
me today. I believe I am experiencing the birth pangs of a miracle!

SCRIPTURE READING: John 8:30–36
KEY VERSE: Galatians 6:14

God forbid that I should boast except in the cross of our Lord Jesus Christ,
by whom the world has been crucified to me, and I to the world.

The winds of freedom blow hard in our world today. Politically oppressed, Communist bloc countries continue to demolish imprisoning walls and topple the icons of brutal dictators. Countries are dropping the shackles of ideologies that have padlocked individual freedom for the sake of state control.

Yet even when freedom is achieved, the once golden promises of liberty are tainted by painful new realities. Democracy is not a panacea. New leaders are not messiahs. The gains of social crusades are often short-lived. In each case, freedom is defined as what allows a nation, a group, or a person the right to pursue and obtain selected goals. It involves the removal of external barriers to self-fulfillment.

But true freedom is spiritual, within the human heart. It is the removal of the universal oppressor—sin—whose great infection lies in the bosom of every man and woman. It cannot be earned or legislated; it can be received only as a gift from God.

God's freedom, liberation of the soul from sin's tyranny, can be enjoyed behind barbed-wire walls, within prison camps, or in the midst of injustice. It cannot be stifled, regulated, or imprisoned. That is freedom worth pursuing.

Thank You for true freedom, Lord. I am free from the tyranny of sin.
I praise You that my freedom cannot be stifled or regulated by any force
in this world.

SCRIPTURE READING: John 10:7–15
KEY VERSE: John 10:10

The thief does not come except to steal, and to kill, and to destroy. I have come that they may have life, and that they may have it more abundantly.

Freedom—some people spend a lifetime seeking it. They may endure tremendous hardships waiting for it. Yet they bear the cost because the alternative of oppression is too horrible to accept.

Christ Jesus was and is the Great Emancipator. He came to set men and women free, not from political or military tyranny but from the far worse grip of sin.

When you embraced Christ as your Savior, Lord, and Life, you were liberated immediately from the penalty of sin—eternal death. Its mastery over you was shattered instantaneously and permanently.

That was only the beginning. Christ came not only to loose you from sin's penalty but also to unshackle you from its power that still seeks to enslave your emotions, will, and personality.

"I came that they might have life, and might have it abundantly," Jesus declared (John 10:10 NASB). Was He only joking? Did He really mean that you can attain a life that is surpassingly free from the chains of habits and fears and worries?

Did Christ ever speak a false word? No, He wants you to be free to experience the most wonderful life you can imagine—His life expressed through your personality. Are you ready to learn how?

Thank You for the abundant life, O Father. Let me learn to walk in the freedom secured by the death of Your Son, Jesus Christ.

SCRIPTURE READING: Psalm 20
KEY VERSE: Psalm 20:6

I know that the LORD saves His anointed;
He will answer him from His holy heaven
With the saving strength of His right hand.

Many times what we think will lead to freedom ends up leading to bondage. In his book *Living Free in Christ,* Neil Anderson discusses our freedom as God's children:

The most practical, present benefit of being a child of God is freedom. Being a servant of sin is bondage; being a servant of God is freedom.

As one who belongs to God, we have freedom in three ways:

First, we are free from the law. The law says "don't do this" in order to be righteous, but Galatians 5:1 says, "it is for freedom that Christ has set us free. Stand firm, then, and do not let yourselves be burdened again by a yoke of slavery." . . . Living by the Spirit gives life and liberty.

Second, we are free from the past. "Because you are sons, God sent the Spirit of His Son into our hearts, the Spirit who calls out, 'Abba, Father.' So you are no longer a slave, but a son." As children of God, we are no longer products of our past; we have a new heritage.

Third, we can be free from sin. The only means by which we are capable of doing this is to realize that we have been bought with a price and that the Holy Spirit now lives in us, enabling us to live our lives for Him, free from sin's bondage.

But the choice is still ours. Say no to sin, and you will experience a freedom that our lost world can only dream of knowing.

I am free from the law. I am free from the past. I am free from sin. I
make the choice, O Lord, to live in Your freedom.

SCRIPTURE READING: 1 Corinthians 1:1–9
KEY VERSES: 1 Corinthians 1:7–8

So that you come short in no gift, eagerly waiting for the revelation of our Lord Jesus Christ, who will also confirm you to the end, that you may be blameless in the day of our Lord Jesus Christ.

Sin had infiltrated the ranks of the Corinthian church. Members of the congregation knew of the situation, yet they had done nothing to right it.

Paul wrote his letter with the purpose of correcting the sin before it became a stumbling block. Each of us at some point will fall short of God's plan. This, in fact, is the very definition of sin: missing the mark that God has set as a standard for us to live by.

But instead of condemning and lashing out at the church, notice how Paul chose to address the congregation: "To the church of God which is at Corinth, to those who have been sanctified in Christ Jesus, saints by calling, with all who in every place call upon the name of our Lord Jesus Christ" (1 Cor. 1:2 NASB).

Paul expressed the truth about God's love for His people. He reminded them of their position in Christ and how they had been sanctified and separated by their faith. It was also a reminder of God's personal love for us. When sin enters our lives, we suffer.

Paul refused to give the enemy an inch, and you should do the same. Where there is a problem of sin, God has a solution, and that is forgiveness through the shedding of His Son's blood at Calvary. Freedom comes when you turn to Him and ask Him to apply His forgiveness to your life.

Lord, I don't want to give the enemy one inch of territory in my life. Cleanse me from every sin that would ensnare me in bondage. Let me walk free.

SCRIPTURE READING: John 20

KEY VERSE: John 20:29

Jesus said to him, "Thomas, because you have seen Me, you have believed. Blessed are those who have not seen and yet have believed."

One of the reasons Jesus came to earth, apart from humankind's need of salvation, was to correct our view of God. He came to change our perspective of our Father's love. The disciples had tremendous freedom in His presence. They witnessed His miracles and felt secure whenever they were with Him.

After the Crucifixion, their view changed. Suddenly fear gripped their hearts. It was only at the sight of Jesus that their fears subsided. One of the greatest truths you can learn, in addition to God's eternal, unconditional love for you, is that He will never leave you.

Jesus assured the disciples of this very thing, but their human capacity to understand His words was limited. No one had ever trusted God in that way before. Think about it. Jesus who was God in the flesh was with them day in and day out—eating, sleeping, talking, and even laughing. Then in a horrendous turn of events, He was gone. However, death could not hold Him.

The freedom the disciples gained in the presence of the risen Lord is something you, too, can experience. Christ lives in you through the power of the Holy Spirit. Every need, every question you have, can be answered. He is available and longs for you to come to Him. What glorious freedom this brings! Someone is near who cares about your every struggle.

Heavenly Father, You have the answer to every question. You have the answer to every need. You are available to me today. Thank You for the glorious freedom this knowledge brings.

SCRIPTURE READING: John 14:1–6
KEY VERSE: Matthew 7:13

Enter by the narrow gate; for wide is the gate and broad is the way that leads to destruction, and there are many who go in by it.

A highway designed to exacting specifications gives us the freedom to drive. Medicine formulated with precise chemical components gives us the freedom to enjoy its benefits. In every instance the truth—accurate, unbending—is the foundation for lasting success.

It is the same with the spiritual realm. The eternal, unchanging, applicable, divine truth sets us free to enjoy God and experience His blessings.

That truth is Christ and His Word. When you have Christ within and when you abide in (live in, meditate on, internally assimilate) His unerring Word of truth, you are on the road to freedom in your emotions, will, intellect, family, job, relationships, and future.

Your constant battle is against the deceiver, the devil. His tactics always are to distort and twist the truth. He is the cursed liar who seeks to enslave the inner person. The devil tells you, "You are no good. God cannot possibly be pleased with you. You will never amount to anything. You cannot measure up to others. You cannot overcome this habit."

This master liar can be overcome only by the truth of God as revealed in His Word and applied by the Holy Spirit.

Dear Lord, help me to abide in Your truth. To meditate on it. To assimilate it. I want to be able to overcome every lie of the enemy with the truth of Your Word.

SCRIPTURE READING: Psalm 51

KEY VERSE: Psalm 51:6

Behold, You desire truth in the inward parts,
And in the hidden part You will make me to know wisdom.

In Psalm 51, David's psalm of contrition, he declared the words of today's key verse. God's truth, woven richly into your innermost being, is the foundation for freedom. God wants His truth to sink deep to establish His perfect wisdom in your mind and heart.

When you understand the truth of your position in Christ, you understand that you are sealed by the Holy Spirit—that you are secure in the family of God. No act or thought can ever alienate you from the love of God. You no longer have to depend on others or other things for your identity. You belong to Christ; You are His and He is yours.

When you understand the truth of your personhood in Christ, your feelings of inferiority can dissolve. You are of infinite worth to God who died on your behalf.

It is not your income level or social status that determines your value; it is God's estimation of your life. You are so valuable to Him that He desires your company for all eternity.

When you understand the truth of your possessions in Christ, any incompetency or inadequacy you may feel is overcome. You have everything you need in the indwelling Christ. He makes you adequate for every demand.

Your truth is the foundation of my freedom. Father, thank You that I
have everything I need in the indwelling Christ. I am adequate for
every demand.

SCRIPTURE READING: Romans 1:18–25
KEY VERSE: Ephesians 5:8

You were once darkness, but now you are light in the Lord. Walk as children of light.

Satan is always at work, seeking to blind the minds of men and women. His darkest work is to obscure our lost condition due to our sin and our need for Jesus Christ as our Savior, Lord, and Life.

When the devil fails in this endeavor, he does not retire. Rather, he is operating constantly to cause us to exchange "the truth of God for a lie" (Rom. 1:25 NASB). We do so when we allow the wrong thoughts of our childhood years to influence us.

Perhaps you could never please your father. Now you have a difficult time understanding how you can please your heavenly Father.

You exchange the truth of God for a lie when you adopt the distorted cultural views of society rather than the authority of the Scriptures. The world endorses the concept of rights; God talks about responsibility. The world sees sex as a mere physiological function without moral implications; God created sex for pleasure and procreation within the context of marital fidelity.

Is there any area of your past or present life in which you have accepted the lies of others about yourself instead of agreeing with God's standard of truth about you once you are His child? If so, embrace God's truth.

I reject every deception of the world around me. I embrace Your truth gladly, dear Lord, for it is the only thing that will set me free.

SCRIPTURE READING: 1 Corinthians 15:44–49
KEY VERSE: Hebrews 11:1

Faith is the substance of things hoped for, the evidence of things not seen.

The reality of our physical existence is undeniable. Each day we awaken to a world that is filled with pain and joy, clouds and sun, failure and success, problems and opportunities. One of the greatest troubles we have with internalizing the freedom that comes from God's truth is comprehending the reality of the spiritual world.

We know our problems are real. Cancer makes us sick. Our work makes us angry. The checkbook is in the red. Our relatives shun us. Our children rebel. Comprehending the reality of the spiritual world and how it can affect our problems is the real test.

Listen to the insight of A. W. Tozer offered in *The Pursuit of God*:

Our trouble is that we have established bad thought habits. We habitually think of the visible world as real and doubt the reality of any other.

We do not deny the existence of the spiritual world, but we doubt that it is real in the accepted meaning of the word.

The world of sense intrudes upon our attention day and night for the world of our lifetime. The world of sense triumphs. The visible becomes the enemy of the invisible; the temporal, of the eternal.

Help me internalize Your truth, dear Lord. I reject the negative thoughts that plague my mind. Fill me with the truth that sets me free. Let me focus on the reality of the spiritual world instead of the fleeting things of the temporal world around me.

SCRIPTURE READING: John 15:1–7
KEY VERSE: Isaiah 55:9

> *As the heavens are higher than the earth,*
> *So are My ways higher than your ways,*
> *And My thoughts than your thoughts.*

The truth does not liberate us automatically. All of us can testify to knowing the truth but failing to experience its power.

When Jesus said the truth would set His hearers free, He preceded that declaration with: "If you abide in My word, then you are truly disciples of Mine" (John 8:31 NASB). Two crucial principles are involved in the emancipation of your spiritual being.

First, you must abide in the Word of God. To abide means "to continue in." Bondage to sin and deception did not come overnight, and neither will your sense of liberty. You have to allow the Spirit of God to pour His truth into your inner person over time. He will free you with His truth, but you must be exposed to it repeatedly.

Second, you must be a learner. That is the meaning of the Greek word for disciple. Since God's ways are higher than yours (Isa. 55:9), you have to humble yourself, admitting that you lack the wisdom or strength to save yourself.

Truth is learned in all fields of endeavor, and it is no different in the spiritual realm. The truth will set you free as you look to God and in His Word with an eager, open heart, wanting all He will provide.

> *Dear heavenly Father, I want to experience the power of Your truth.*
> *Help me to abide continually in Your Word. Make me a disciple, will-*
> *ing to walk in Your ways.*

SCRIPTURE READING: Psalm 119:129–35
KEY VERSE: Psalm 119:170

Let my supplication come before You;
Deliver me according to Your word.

How can the truth set you free? Behind the generation of electricity for a home or business is the power of nuclear physics. Behind the power of an automobile engine is the power of spontaneous combustion. In each instance the power of the truth substantiates the action.

For the Christian, behind the truth of the Scriptures is the power of the living God. His power saved you. The same power of God underwrites every word of the Scriptures. When you believe His Word for handling everyday obstacles, His same divine power works on your behalf.

When Jesus spoke, things happened—diseases healed, demons vanquished, sins forgiven, seas calmed. His power can conquer every fear, every doubt, every habit, every inordinate passion, every trembling heart, every lonely soul.

Whatever holds you in bondage cannot withstand the power of the Warrior of the Ages. You can have hope this very hour because the power of God is behind His truth and will work on your behalf as you embrace and cling to the Lord Jesus Christ. The risen Christ can and will liberate you from any bondage if you call on His all-powerful name.

Father, reveal Your power in me. Conquer every fear, doubt, habit, or
inordinate passion. Comfort my lonely soul and still my trembling
heart.

SCRIPTURE READING: Mark 9:14–27

KEY VERSE: Mark 9:23

Jesus said to him, "If you can believe, all things are possible to him who believes."

You must receive the truth of the Scriptures in order to be free from the bondage of insecurity and inadequacy. *Webster's Dictionary* defines *receive* as "to take in through the mind or senses; to permit to enter; to take or come into possession of." Truth can be rejected; it can be held at arm's length.

First, you have to receive God's truth into your inner person. Pride in your resources can hinder that reception. God is a Gentleman; He will not force His ways upon you. You must open the door of your mind and heart to Him.

Second, you must believe the truth of the Scriptures. Believing means that you trust God enough to step out on His promises. You cannot just assent to the Word of God; you must rely on, lean on, and let Him implement His Word in your life so that Christ Jesus—who is the truth (John 14:6)—can set you free.

Belief is action. Since God tells you in His Word not to worry (Phil. 4:6), you must stop fretting. Since He says you are valuable in His eyes (John 3:16), you must lay aside your ideas about a lack of self-worth. When you receive and believe God's authoritative, liberating truth, you have entered the doorway of freedom.

I receive Your truth. I believe Your truth. I act upon it today, dear Lord, as I walk through the doorway of freedom.

SCRIPTURE READING: John 16:13–15
KEY VERSE: Genesis 1:26

God said, "Let Us make man in Our image, according to Our likeness; let them have dominion over the fish of the sea, over the birds of the air, and over the cattle, over all the earth and over every creeping thing that creeps on the earth."

Imagine this scene: a young boy lives in a small frame house in the inner city. He is surrounded by poverty and crime. His days are filled with emptiness and despair. There seems to be no way out. He does poorly in school because he has no motivation.

One afternoon a gentleman knocks on the door. He shares staggering news—the young boy is a direct descendant of a writer of world renown.

From that moment on, the boy is never the same. He studies hard; he goes to the library; he helps his parents. Yet all that is changed is his view of himself.

Do you see why it is so important to see ourselves in the light of God's truth? We are not plain Joes and Janes; we are God's sons and daughters. We are not rescued sinners with streaks of goodness; we are saints—the holy people of God. We are not the same, ordinary people we were before we received Christ; we are entirely new creations.

There has been a radical change. You are now an heir with Christ. All that God has is yours as you receive His blessings humbly by faith (John 16:13–15).

How do you see yourself today? Lonely, inadequate, defeated, afraid? The truth of who you are in Christ will set you free.

I am free in You, dear Lord. Help me to see myself as You see me. Thank You that I have been radically changed and I am an heir with Your Son, Jesus Christ.

SCRIPTURE READING: John 13:31–35

KEY VERSE: Proverbs 27:17

> *As iron sharpens iron,*
> *So a man sharpens the countenance of his friend.*

The art of being a friend is a delicate one, involving honesty, sharing, forgiveness, and much more. That is why Scripture is so full of admonitions concerning how we are to treat one another in love and respect.

Besides the obvious ways of hurting one another, there are other traps to avoid. Pamela Reeve discusses a major one in her book *Relationships:*

Another common problem in friendships develops when one person tries to control the other. The deeper the friendship grows, the more vulnerable we become at any level. But the intimate relationship in particular provides fertile ground for the stronger personality to control the one who yields more easily.

This type of manipulation can occur on both conscious and subconscious levels. Yet whatever form that control may take, it's poison in a relationship. It may be quick poison or it may be slow poison, but it will always weaken and often kill a friendship.

What kind of friend are you? Are you so afraid of losing a relationship that you attempt to manipulate the other person into liking you? Do you give the person space to make his or her choices? How do you respond to disappointment when the person lets you down? It's important to evaluate these issues honestly and ask the Lord to make you a selfless and supportive companion.

Dear Lord, free me from manipulation. Don't let me be controlled by others. Don't let me seek to control others. Make me a selfless and supportive friend and companion.

SCRIPTURE READING: 1 Peter 1:18–23

KEY VERSE: John 17:17

Sanctify them by Your truth. Your word is truth.

A formidable enemy of the truth of Christ is feelings. You feel unworthy—even though God says you are made in His image (Gen. 1:26–27) and called by His name (Acts 2:21).

You feel insignificant—even though everything you do can be done to the glory of God and used by Him to accomplish His sovereign purposes (Col. 3:17).

You feel unloved—even though God says He cares for you as a shepherd cares for his sheep (John 10:11).

You must learn sooner or later to move past your feelings and instead lean on the indisputable fact of God's Word. How can you do that?

The best way is to compile a list of Scriptures dealing with the troubling emotions that beset you. If you are depressed, you should take a week or so to find Scripture passages dealing with God's joy and His comfort. Then you should write them down so that you can carry them with you.

When these feelings assault you, you should turn to the Scriptures and read them aloud. You should tell the Lord Jesus Christ that you choose to believe His truth rather than your emotions. Then you should praise Him for His answer.

Refuse to budge. Your feelings may linger, but they eventually will crumble under the weight of God's mighty truth.

> *Father, sometimes I feel unloved, unworthy, and insignificant. But these are only feelings—not facts. I choose to believe Your truth rather than my emotions.*

SCRIPTURE READING: Romans 12:1–2
KEY VERSE: Proverbs 23:7

For as he thinks in his heart, so is he.

Computers may appear much the same to the eye, but they function in thousands of different ways. The critical distinction is always in the software—the internal programming that performs multitudes of discriminating tasks.

Christians, persons who have received the Spirit of God at salvation, have entered God's kingdom. They are new spiritual creatures (2 Cor. 5:17), but they retain the memory banks of previous years. Habits, thoughts, inclinations, and affections can still influence behavior as before.

That is exactly why too many Christians live in such a miserable state. They do not want to return to their former state, but on the other hand, they cannot enjoy their new standing as children of God.

Yet there is hope. Your internal being—mind, emotions, will—can come under the influence of the Holy Spirit who now indwells you. Your old mental grid system can be replaced by an entirely new set of thoughts and behavior through the power of God's truth.

A new way of living is possible when you view life from God's perspective and His truth takes up residence in your inner being. Real victory and genuine godliness take root and bear the unmistakable fruit of a Christ-filled life.

> *Heavenly Father, please reprogram my internal computer. Replace all the old thoughts and behavior patterns with the fruit of a Spirit-filled life.*

SCRIPTURE READING: 1 Corinthians 8:1–13
KEY VERSE: Galatians 5:13

You, brethren, have been called to liberty; only do not use liberty as an opportunity for the flesh, but through love serve one another.

When you receive Christ as your Savior, you instantly step into marvelous liberty. No longer are you dependent on the approval of others for your worth. No longer do you seek to be justified by good works. Rather, you are free to worship and serve Christ as an adopted child.

Such emancipation can be intoxicating, however. Freedom is not without boundaries. Your actions must be aligned with the Father's loving will, and they must not be a hindrance to other Christians.

Responsible freedom as a child of God means you must view others as more important than yourself. Your actions may be scripturally permissible, but they may cause trouble for less mature believers. You must have genuine concern for their well-being even if it means discontinuing a particular activity or relationship.

Your salvation brought you into a new relationship with the body of Christ. You must always use your freedom responsibly for the growth and harmony of the entire body.

That is possible only when you regard your witness for the gospel of Christ to an unbelieving world above your personal preferences. You are free to do not as you want but as you ought under the constraints of agape love for Christ and for your brothers and sisters in Christ.

Set the boundaries of my freedom, O God, then make me willing to remain within these limits. Make me responsible to other members of Your body.

SCRIPTURE READING: Matthew 18:15–17
KEY VERSES: Matthew 5:23–24

If you bring your gift to the altar, and there remember that your brother has something against you, leave your gift there before the altar, and go your way. First be reconciled to your brother, and then come and offer your gift.

The woman was always one of the first to walk through the church doors on Sunday morning and one of the last to leave. Despite her regular giving to God's work, her consistent attendance, and service on various committees, there was an unmistakable coolness surrounding her. Townspeople often tried to warm up to her, and friends who knew her years ago forgave her abruptness.

An incident that happened between her and her best friend fifteen years before left her bitter, resentful, and angry. Time was not a healer. Neither was distance. Thinking that both could begin again, her friend had moved away, but that did not happen.

Unresolved emotions filter into the cracks and crevices of our hearts, spilling over to those around us. Before we know it, they have not only stolen our joy, but also blocked our view of God.

Forgiveness is the only force strong enough to break the bondage of anger or any other unresolved emotion. Jesus knew that in order for us to enjoy our relationship freely with the heavenly Father, there would have to be forgiveness. It cost Him everything, but He paid the price.

Is there someone in your life you need to forgive today?

You forgave me. Thank You, Lord! That frees me to forgive others. Through the power of Your Holy Spirit, I forgive _____ right now.

SCRIPTURE READING: Philippians 4:4–9
KEY VERSE: Philippians 1:6

Being confident of this very thing, that He who has begun a good work in you will complete it until the day of Jesus Christ.

What's your attitude toward life? About people, work, and family? Whatever your disposition, it eventuates from your thought processes. And how you think and what you think about have a tremendous influence on your outlook.

Part of the fantastic good news of salvation is that Christ has come into your life to give not only a new destiny, but a new disposition as well. The apostle Paul wrote that you are "transformed by the renewing of your mind" (Rom. 12:2 NASB).

God desires to revolutionize your mind as well as your soul! Why? Because He knows that your thoughts are the breeding ground for behavior and attitude. Change your thinking and you'll ultimately change your ways.

You're not hostage to your past or to your current conditions. The Holy Spirit is a supernatural Change Agent who can surmount any and all entrenched mental configurations.

You can indeed change. God is now, even at this moment, at work in you to bring about the transformation: "He who began a good work in you will perfect it until the day of Christ Jesus" (Phil. 1:6 NASB). If you are willing, God will make it happen.

Find specific verses of Scripture that provide God's perspective on your particular situation. Memorize them, think repeatedly on them, and the transformation will be well under way.

Dear Lord, please change my thinking so that my ways can change. You have begun a good work in me, and I trust in Your promise to complete it.

SCRIPTURE READING: Ephesians 5:1–13
KEY VERSE: Ephesians 5:3

But fornication and all uncleanness or covetousness, let it not even be named among you, as is fitting for saints.

When God led His people into the promised land, He gave them specific instructions about how they were to live. He stressed the need to remain separate from their enemies (Deut. 6:14). Even in Old Testament times there was a variety of cultures, and each had its own value system.

The Israelites were to worship God alone. Other nations worshiped anything from the stars to the sun and moon. Their lives were polluted with all kinds of immorality. God knew if Israel disobeyed Him, their moral and spiritual purity would be compromised.

Paul discussed the same subject in Ephesians and instructed members of the early church to be imitators of God. In Ephesians 5:3, he wrote, "But among you there must not be even a hint of sexual immorality, or of any kind of impurity" (MOFFATT). Paul's instruction was clear: there was not to be even a fraction of impurity among them.

You are surrounded by temptation. Most of it comes to you in quiet ways—what you watch, what you hear, what you do when no one else is around.

The enemy's goal is much more than to mar God's creation. He wants to destroy your witness for Christ. As a believer, you are no longer bound by sin's power. Christ put an end to sin's reign at Calvary. Don't hesitate to call out His name whenever you face temptation of any kind (1 Cor. 10:13).

Temptation lurks at every turn, but You are there, O Lord, to show me the way of escape. I choose the narrow path that leads to freedom.

SCRIPTURE READING: Matthew 11:25–30

KEY VERSE: Psalm 119:32

I will run the course of Your commandments,
For You shall enlarge my heart.

All Paul had known as a boy growing up in a slum neighborhood was pain. Merciless beatings by his father, who ordered him never to cry, left him too bloody to crawl. By the age of ten, he was an accomplished thief and a hard drinker. At twelve, he murdered a woman as he took her money.

Juvenile prison and reform school didn't work. Punishment only made him sneer. It took the consistent nurture of a Christian couple and a friend who invited him to a Christian youth rally to help turn his life around. In his book *Too Tough to Cry*, Paul Powers tells about the night his screams of anger at God were met with unconditional love:

> At that instant, all of the hurt and pain of thirteen years that had been held inside welled up in my throat. "Oh, God, no, I'm going to cry . . . I'm going to cry . . . but real men don't cry."
>
> I couldn't hold it in any longer. I fell to the floor and began to cry. I wept and wept and continued to weep. It was like a dam had burst inside, and the tears poured out of me. I kept moaning, "Forgive me, forgive me. . . ."

Today, Paul is a pastor who ministers especially to children.

Does the horror of an abusive or bitter past have a choke hold on your heart? Do you feel incapable of loving or reaching out for help? Jesus is the only One who can heal that kind of crushing hurt and restore emotions.

Dear heavenly Father, as I wait in Your presence today, set me free
from the past. Heal the hurt. Restore my emotions.

SCRIPTURE READING: 2 Peter 2:4–22
KEY VERSE: 2 Peter 2:9

The Lord knows how to deliver the godly out of temptations and to reserve the unjust under punishment for the day of judgment.

Part of the deception of sin is the lie that you're in too deep to ever get out. You can feel so dirty, so soiled, so mired in its clutches that you begin to believe sincerely that there is no way out for you. With each small step toward freedom that you take, your feet seem to slide backward even more.

You must cling to God's power to free you from the bondage of sin. Self-effort is useless, and your human abilities of reason and emotion are clouded by the consequences of the very sin you are trying to escape.

Abraham's nephew, Lot, must have felt trapped in his sinful environment and polluted by it as well. Lot also probably experienced guilt from his sin, since he made the decision to move near the wicked cities.

The good news for Lot is the same hope you have today: "And if [God] rescued righteous Lot, oppressed by the sensual conduct of unprincipled men (for by what he saw and heard . . . while living among them, felt his righteous soul tormented day after day with their lawless deeds), then the Lord knows how to rescue the godly from temptation" (2 Peter 2:7–9 NASB).

God knows how to rescue you from the temptations you face right now. Through the power of Jesus Christ, you don't have to say yes to what you know is wrong. That is the liberating message of the Cross.

O God, I realize that my human abilities of reason and emotion are holding me captive to the very sins I long to escape. Give me the power to say no to temptation.

SCRIPTURE READING: Psalm 107

KEY VERSE: Romans 8:1

There is therefore now no condemnation to those who are in Christ Jesus,
who do not walk according to the flesh, but according to the Spirit.

Many people are bound by feelings of inadequacy. They struggle with low self-esteem and unworthiness. Your sense of self-worth comes from only one Source, the Lord Jesus Christ. He would never want you to view your life as being less than the very best in Him.

That is what He has in mind for you—the best. When God thinks of you, He thinks of His Son and what He did for you at Calvary. He never considers all the mistakes of the past or even those that will come in the future (Rom. 8:1). Instead, God focuses on your potential.

He does this because His love and forgiveness are greater than any sin. The Lord hates sin, but He certainly does not look at your life and think, *There's no way for Me to bless him or her because of what he or she has done.* God does not operate that way. Read Psalm 107 and discover afresh the chronology of Israel's mistakes and how God continued to love them.

Is this a license to sin? Certainly not, but it is truly an invitation to love and be loved by the One who loves you the most.

You may think it is too late for you. Nothing could be farther from the truth. This is the glorious freedom Christ brings.

When you fall, God provides a way of forgiveness. He lifts you up and gives you a new opportunity at life. Only Jesus Christ can truly set you free.

> *O Lord, I feel so inadequate. Please lift me up. Give me a new oppor-*
> *tunity at life—free from the shackles of unworthiness.*

SCRIPTURE READING: Matthew 7:13–14
KEY VERSE: John 14:6

Jesus said to him, "I am the way, the truth, and the life. No one comes to the Father except through Me."

A movie celebrity remarked during an interview that he had been reared in a Christian environment but he rejected Christianity as an adult. His rationale was: "There are billions of people on this earth. How can any one group of people make a claim that their way is the only way? I just can't believe that."

He is not alone in his thinking. Multitudes reject the notion that faith in the person of Christ is the only means by which they can approach God. "Surely," they reason, "the diverse throng of tribes, cultures, and nations cannot all be expected to walk the same spiritual path. They must have their own unique staircase to the heavens."

Logically carried to its conclusion, the way to God depends on individual preference. God then is approached in millions of ways, each way right in the eyes of the seeker. Absolute truth then is nullified. God is whatever we make of Him.

What if mathematics were subject to similar logic? Would two plus two equal five in Albania, sixteen in Norway, and eight in Canada?

The Bible strikes at the heart of such nonsense. It claims Christ is the only way because He is the true way, available for all people everywhere (John 14:6). Truth demands one way. Jesus is the way.

Dear Lord, there is one way to the truth that sets me free—and that is Jesus. I come Your way. Set me free in every area of my life.

SCRIPTURE READING: Psalm 69:13–18
KEY VERSE: Romans 8:15

You did not receive the spirit of bondage again to fear, but you received the Spirit of adoption by whom we cry out, "Abba, Father."

Throughout the ages men and women have fought for what they believed was freedom. Now that we have obtained a higher level of national security, the theme has shifted to how we can remain free.

But are we really experiencing true freedom? Everywhere we turn there are evidences of freedom granted and freedom abused.

Political leaders, exhausted from their flight to freedom without moral restraint in the seventies, now claim we must return to the moral values of our forebears. As a society, we have rejected values that even hint at morality. In a recent interview, one congressman stated that our nation no longer has any clear-cut "moral guidelines."

Jesus told us there is only one way to experience true freedom—by abiding in His truth. Freedom without moral restraint is not freedom; it is chaos. When we reject God's moral values, we trade freedom for bondage. We run the risk of becoming so comfortable in our sin, we refuse to take the way out when it is given.

Are you experiencing Christ's freedom, or are you living in bondage to the world's sin? When you come to Jesus, placing all your needs and expectations on Him, He grants freedom the unsaved only dream of knowing.

Heavenly Father, in a world seeking to be free of moral restraint, set me truly free by the power of Your Word. I want to experience Your freedom.

SCRIPTURE READING: Ephesians 1:3–14
KEY VERSE: Ephesians 1:7

In Him we have redemption through His blood, the forgiveness of sins, according to the riches of His grace.

In today's Scripture reading, the apostle Paul summed up our position in Christ. We are chosen of God, sealed by His grace through the redemption of our souls. No one is excluded from His presence. Those who seek eternal salvation find their deepest need met at His altar. Others who long for intimacy and a sense of belonging discover eternal love.

There is a freedom that comes from being loved and accepted by another. But for this to take place, you must first have an understanding of just how much God loves you. During your lifetime, you have probably experienced some form of rejection. A parent who walked away when you were young, abuse that came at the hands of another, or a spouse who suddenly lost interest and filed for divorce—each represents deep emotional hurts that can keep you bound in fear.

However, difficulties such as these also carry a tremendous opportunity for spiritual growth and freedom, especially when you refuse to become bitter and angry. God knows the hurts you have felt, and He wants to heal your life. Every heartache can be used to teach you more about His unconditional love and acceptance.

Jesus died for you. Even if you have never accepted Him as your Savior, He loves you. Today can be your first day of true freedom. Give Him your past hurts and failures, and He will set you free.

Lord, I rejoice that You can take every heartache of the past and every trauma of the future and use them to accomplish Your purposes. On the basis of this truth, I declare right now—this is my first day of true freedom!

SCRIPTURE READING: Romans 7:15–19

KEY VERSE: Romans 8:11

If the Spirit of Him who raised Jesus from the dead dwells in you, He who raised Christ from the dead will also give life to your mortal bodies through His Spirit who dwells in you.

Some former prisoners have a lot of trouble adjusting to the "life outside," especially if they have been incarcerated for many years. Even though the bars and restrictions are removed, their behavior patterns still reflect a lifestyle of imprisonment. Many are overwhelmed emotionally by the sudden flood of freedoms and seek ways to return to the life they knew.

When Jesus sets you free from sin, you are no longer held captive by sin's impulses and desires. You do not have to heed them, but many times, however, you may give a knee-jerk reaction when those desires assert themselves. Old habits die hard, and it's difficult to shake off living patterns that may be entrenched after a period of years.

Paul expressed this frustration in Romans 7:15–19: "For that which I am doing, I do not understand; for I am not practicing what I would like to do. . . . For the good that I wish, I do not do; but I practice the very evil that I do not wish" (NASB).

Living in the liberty that Christ gave you by His death at Calvary is a result of understanding that He gives you the power to say no to old ways. The call of sin is the empty shout of false bondage; Jesus' dying cry of "It is finished!" is your emancipation proclamation (John 19:30).

You can say with Paul: "Thanks be to God through Jesus Christ our Lord!" (Rom. 7:25 NASB).

Old habits die hard, Father, but I do want them to die. Help me shake off the negative patterns that have been entrenched in my life for years.

SCRIPTURE READING: Acts 2:14–36

KEY VERSE: Acts 2:14

Peter, standing up with the eleven, raised his voice and said to them, "Men of Judea and all who dwell in Jerusalem, let this be known to you, and heed my words."

Can you remember the first time you were truly excited about learning something new? Maybe it was the day you learned how to ride your first bicycle. For days you tried to pedal without tipping over, but you continued to fall. Finally one afternoon, it all came together and you knew exactly how to do it.

The disciples knew that feeling. Jesus had spent three years with them. His crucifixion had left them despondent and lonely. But the Resurrection changed their view. For the first time they grasped what He had been saying. Can you imagine what it was like to be with Peter when he finally understood?

Acts 2:14–36 provides this account. The man who stood up and spoke on the day of pentecost was not the same man who had denied Christ on the night of His arrest. What changed Peter was not merely being around Jesus; the indwelling of Christ's Spirit made the transformation complete.

Make Christ the focus of your days and the emphasis of your praise. He knows where He is leading you, and He is aware of all that is needed to make your life complete.

Neither should you become discouraged over the times you fall short of your expectations. Allow God to be in control, and you will discover freedom unlike any you have ever known.

O God, You are the focus of my life. You are all I need to make my life complete. You are in complete control. You are free to set me free.

SCRIPTURE READING: Romans 6

KEY VERSE: Romans 6:7

He who has died has been freed from sin.

Tens of thousands of East Germans have found freedom in Western Europe as communism's grip has loosened. Although they have rightfully celebrated their new status in the West, the East Germans still must face the same slavish masters of money, passion, and fear that we all must confront.

The truth of God alone sets you free (Eph. 2:13–16). Only God can penetrate the invisible boundaries of your spirit and soul and thereby rescue you from sin's rule.

As you relinquish your area of bondage to God, remember that the freedom you find in the Lord Jesus Christ will endure. It will stand fast.

The benefits of freedom in Christ may not be visible for a time. Anger may still flare; fear may still lurk in your mind; passion may still burn. But as you trust the Spirit of God to work in your life, results will come. The battle is yours to endure, yet the Holy Spirit will bring the victory. He is at work in your innermost being, even when you think all is lost. He will triumph as you trust in His strong arms.

Begin now to operate on the basis of God's truth as revealed in the Scriptures and as you are empowered by the Holy Spirit. The truth can set you free forever.

Your truth brings liberty. O Lord, let it penetrate the invisible boundaries of my spirit and soul and free me from sin's rule.

October

According to the grace of God which was given to me, as a wise master builder I have laid the foundation, and another builds on it. But let each one take heed how he builds on it. For no other foundation can anyone lay than that which is laid, which is Jesus Christ.

SCRIPTURE READING: Matthew 7:24–29
KEY VERSE: Psalm 1:3

> *He shall be like a tree*
> *Planted by the rivers of water,*
> *That brings forth its fruit in its season,*
> *Whose leaf also shall not wither;*
> *And whatever he does shall prosper.*

When looking for a builder to construct your home, your most important question is: "Are his homes well built?" The Scriptures refer to the importance of a well-crafted Christian life that can withstand the pressures of living.

The well-built life follows God's design. The beginning of a good home is a good architectural design. The solid Christian seeks to do the Father's will, not his own. Do you walk in the paths God has ordained, or do you continually insert selfish changes of direction?

The well-built Christian life has a solid foundation. That foundation is a love for and obedience to the Word of God. Anything built on personal preference will crack eventually. Adherence to biblical principles always brings lasting results.

The well-built Christian life is faithful in the little things. The attention to detail distinguishes a good builder. A loyal disciple of Christ is steadfast and careful in small as well as large things. You watch the tone of your voice as you talk to your family. You are courteous in snarled traffic and selective about what you watch on TV.

By having your heart bent toward God, your convictions based on God's Word, and your actions consistent, you will withstand the tests of time and tribulation.

> *O Lord, examine my spiritual foundations. I want my life to be built*
> *on solid principles that will enable me to withstand the test of time.*

No other foundation can anyone lay than that which is laid, which is Jesus Christ.

The fifty-five-story skyscraper began to sway and vibrate as the earth tremors grew more intense. The quake climbed to 7.0 on the Richter scale. Smaller buildings crumpled into unrecognizable heaps of rubble. When the shaking stopped and the thick dust cleared, the skyscraper was still standing.

Developers and contractors had planned for the worst, and their foresight paid off. Fortifying the structure with extra steel beams and a special shock-absorption coil system had cost thousands of additional dollars. But when the ultimate test came, their investment stood firm.

In His parable of the wise builder, Jesus made this very point: the foundation is everything. A life built on self-reliance and self-seeking motivations is destined for collapse. But a life based on the lordship of Christ and obedience to God's principles is unshakable.

Are you a wise builder, or have you settled for the sinking sands of convenience? Sometimes, following the Lord's direction may appear to be unprofitable, especially when you are criticized or ridiculed for doing so. But when the storms come, temporary rewards are blown away, and unwise builders are left with nothing.

Heavenly Father, I don't want to settle for the sinking sands of convenience. If I build on my self-reliance, I am destined for collapse. Let me build my life on the lordship of Your Son, Jesus Christ.

SCRIPTURE READING: John 1

KEY VERSE: John 1:29

The next day John saw Jesus coming toward him, and said, "Behold! The Lamb of God who takes away the sin of the world!"

When convicted serial murderer Ted Bundy publicly shared his religious beliefs days before his execution, many Christians doubted the reality of his conversion. Their reasoning was based not necessarily on his lack of sincerity or on erroneous doctrine but on the repulsiveness of Bundy's crimes. "How could someone who perpetrated such murders possibly be forgiven?" was their fundamental question.

This thinking fails to understand the complete inability of anyone to receive God's forgiveness apart from a personal faith in Christ's work on the cross. Humankind's greatest need is forgiveness of sin because all of us are guilty and separated from God. Good people are lost; bad people are lost. Moral people are guilty; immoral people are guilty.

When Christ died as our substitute at Calvary and paid sin's penalty, which is death, our righteous Judge was free to forgive us based on Christ's full payment. With the sin debt paid, humankind can receive God's pardon and gift of eternal life based completely and solely on Christ's redeeming work.

God saves a Ted Bundy or a good Sam on the same grounds: personal faith in Jesus Christ who shed His blood for the forgiveness of our sins—no matter how despicable they may be.

Dear Lord, thank You for the foundation of Your forgiveness. I can build my life on it. I have assurance of eternity through it.

SCRIPTURE READING: Mark 11:20–24
KEY VERSE: Mark 11:22

Jesus answered and said to them, "Have faith in God."

Although we may wish otherwise, the Christian life is a journey of faith. We like tangible evidence. We are comfortable with proven cause-and-effect scenarios. We turn the key, and the engine starts.

Faith is intangible. It is not so predictable. Yet faith is the unseen dynamic for Christian growth and living. It is the indispensable core of a vital spiritual existence.

And for good reason. Faith in God is His requirement for fruitful, enduring ministry. Faith is the barometer of genuine Christianity, which is a personal relationship with the Lord Jesus Christ.

When you express your faith in Christ for your particular needs or desires, you acknowledge your dependence on God. You are drawn intimately near Him as you believe in His purpose and provision. God wants your being—your entire personality—committed to Him, not to a cause or religion or philosophy.

Thus, faith is the highest expression of your allegiance to the Lord. When you place your faith in God, you confess your absolute trust in His personhood.

The Lord wants to fellowship with you. Do you place your faith in Him because you seek results or because you know Him and love Him?

Lord, I place my faith in You today—not because I'm seeking results for my desires, but because I know and love You. I humbly acknowledge my dependence on Your purpose and provision.

SCRIPTURE READING: Psalm 33
KEY VERSE: Psalm 33:21

Our heart shall rejoice in Him,
Because we have trusted in His holy name.

One significant problem concerning faith is reliance upon personal experience. Although the Lord's answers are cause for celebration, you must be careful not to base your confidence on individual cases.

Many foundational principles govern faith's exercise. God always responds to faith in a manner that glorifies Him. You were created to glorify the Lord, but not all of your requests are designed to honor Him.

God alone knows how to answer you so that His provision magnifies His name above all else. That is why He meets your needs often in unusual or unexpected ways. In such instances you know the Lord has worked sovereignly, and your praise is amplified. God always responds to your faith so that you are conformed to the image of Christ.

Though marred by sin, you are being molded into Christlikeness. Thus, God's focus is greater on transforming you into Christ's image than on answering your requests. That explains why your prayers sometimes seem to go unanswered. The omniscient Lord understands exactly how you can be shaped into Christ's image. When you place your confidence in God, your faith depends on His criteria, not yours.

Magnify Yourself in me today, Father. Let my faith depend on Your
criteria, not mine. I place my confidence in You.

SCRIPTURE READING: Ephesians 6:10–18

KEY VERSE: Ephesians 6:16

Above all, taking the shield of faith with which you will be able to quench all the fiery darts of the wicked one.

With an increasing emphasis on the occult evident in society, it is easy to forget that Satan's most effective weapons are two ancient foes—doubt and discouragement. How many Christians have been spiritually defeated because they lost heart by the sabotage of these evil ambassadors? Too many fail to press on in their relationship with Christ because they give in to the insistent demands of doubt and discouragement.

Although doubt and discouragement are strong enemies, God has given you the means to resolve this problem: "In addition to all, taking up the shield of faith" (Eph. 6:16 NASB). Firm, unwavering confidence in the Lord keeps the powers of darkness at bay. Satan is thwarted when the shield of faith is raised against him.

Doubt says, "I don't think so." Faith says, "God is able."

Discouragement says, "It's hopeless." Faith says, "With God, all things are possible."

You may be in a situation where you have almost given up. Your strength is failing; your outlook is grim. Take up the shield of faith. Put the matter squarely into the Lord's hands and believe that He is in control. When Satan attacks, the shield of faith will rout him.

Heavenly Father, doubt says to me today, "I don't think so"—but I declare in faith, "You are able!" Discouragement dictates, "It's hopeless"—but I proclaim, "With You, all things are possible!"

SCRIPTURE READING: Numbers 13–14
KEY VERSE: Proverbs 24:10

If you faint in the day of adversity,
Your strength is small.

Of the millions of men, women, and children who trudged through the wilderness, only two (Caleb and Joshua) saw "the promise" of the promised land. The millions suffered a faith failure.

Like the sinning Israelites, we, too, hesitate when we face a challenge, allowing the obstacles to frighten and even immobilize us. We don't reach our objectives, and our faith sags instead of stretching us.

The key to a growing, confident faith is a consistent focus on the power and might of God. Caleb and Joshua saw imposing giants—as did the rest of the Israelite spies—but they measured them against the power of the most high God.

The focus that develops faith to tackle life's challenges comes from sustained, concentrated meditation on the Word of God. Remember God's instructions to Joshua: "This Book of the Law shall not depart from your mouth, but you shall meditate in it day and night" (Josh. 1:8).

Joshua and Caleb kept their gaze on God in an unwavering faith in His Word. Then when the challenge came, they drew their conclusions on the basis of God's unlimited resources, not theirs.

Nourish your faith for tomorrow's challenges by renewing your mind in God's Word today.

Nourish my faith today, O Lord, that I will be equipped to face tomorrow's challenges. Teach me to measure every "giant" of my life against Your mighty power.

SCRIPTURE READING: Jude 17–23

KEY VERSE: Colossians 2:7

Rooted and built up in Him and established in the faith, as you have been taught, abounding in it with thanksgiving.

Massive concrete buildings are imposing structures. However, the inner, invisible steel reinforcement rods provide the strength and sturdiness. Without this internal network, concrete would crumble and collapse.

Similarly most often unseen practices and habits reinforce faith in Jesus Christ. It begins by being faithful in the small things—repaying legitimate debts, keeping promises to your children, getting to work on time.

Genuine faith starts small and builds a foundation for the more pressing situations you encounter. It is nurtured in private seasons of prayer. Communion with God is a vital link to expectant faith.

Loving God is yet another interior bar of authentic faith. If you obey God only out of a sense of duty, you will do well. But if you obey Him because you love Him deeply and long to please Him, your faith will issue from an artesian well of passion that never runs dry.

Regular times of prayer are the rods of a sturdy faith. Confession, repentance, worship, and petition undergird any meaningful life of faith.

Build your faith each day with the disciplines that give your trust true stoutness and solidity.

Reinforce my faith, Father, as I wait before You right now. Let my faith spring from an artesian well of passion that will never run dry.

SCRIPTURE READING: Psalm 100

KEY VERSE: Matthew 6:33

Seek first the kingdom of God and His righteousness, and all these things shall be added to you.

A flaw in a product can go unnoticed for long periods of time before the defect finally emerges. Likewise, many believers can grow quite rapidly in their faith before a dormant spiritual fault is revealed in a time of testing. It is then that the most common defect is discovered—operating on personal agendas.

The goal of the Christian life is to exalt and worship the person of Jesus Christ. Faith in anything but His will is idolatry. Substituting your plans for His purposes is idolatry. Faith practiced solely for achieving your personal objectives, as noble as they may seem, is idolatry.

Paul's overwhelming ambition was to know and please Christ, to do everything to His glory. Is that your passion? Do you enter His presence with gratefulness, excitement, and reverence for Him?

It is all right to pray for personal needs and guidance, but all such requests are secondary to faith's primary aim—experiencing God's will for your life and personal communion with the Father. If God is accomplishing that purpose in your life, your faith will not be shaken even when the going gets rough. You will depend on God not to grant your every desire but to fulfill His purposes, whatever they may be.

Dear Father, I do not want any flaws in my faith. Create in me a pure faith so that when the going gets rough, my faith will not be shaken. Make the focus of my faith a passion to know and please You.

The Lord said, "If you have faith as a mustard seed, you can say to this mulberry tree, 'Be pulled up by the roots and be planted in the sea,' and it would obey you."

Would you like to have greater faith in God? The disciples did. They said to the Lord, "Increase our faith!" (Luke 17:5 NASB). The Master's reply to His disciples—and to every Christian who desires to please Him—was: "If you had faith like a mustard seed . . ." (Luke 17:6 NASB).

A mustard seed is very small. The contrast in Jesus' response was curious: His disciples wanted more faith, and Jesus used this seed as an example. The Savior communicated that they needed to use the faith they already had.

The road to a growing faith is to trust Christ each day for the small things of life. You may trust God for the amazing and fantastic, but you may not have learned to depend on Him in the everyday, practical areas. Are you trusting the Lord for the seemingly mundane things: help in the office and home, guidance in financial purchases, strength and a cheerful spirit for chores?

God has given you the fullness of His Son, Jesus Christ, through the indwelling of the Holy Spirit. As you learn to express your faith in His love and in His provision for life's daily grind, your faith will increase for the bigger challenges that await you.

O God, grow my faith as I face mundane things today—on my job, in my home, in all the detailed affairs of my life. Let me learn to express my faith in the daily grind so that it will be strong for bigger challenges in the future.

SCRIPTURE READING: Daniel 6:10–28
KEY VERSE: Psalm 103:19

The LORD has established His throne in heaven,
And His kingdom rules over all.

An unshakable faith is anchored in a living, unchanging, sovereign God: "For He is the living God . . ." (Dan. 6:26 NASB).

Your faith works because you trust in a personal, living God who hears your pleas and works on your behalf. The living God never sleeps or slumbers. There is no hour, day or night, when you cannot instantly and confidently approach Him. He lives.

"For He is the living God and enduring forever . . ." (Dan. 6:26 NASB).

Your faith is firm because God is from everlasting to everlasting. He is the same for every man, woman, and child of every generation, of every culture. His ways never change; His character is unalterable. He is the stability of our times.

". . . And His dominion will be forever" (Dan. 6:26 NASB).

Your faith is steadfast because God is sovereign, ruling over people and affairs to achieve His purposes. God is in control even when everything seems out of control. He overrules all evil, using even bitter, painful moments for divine good.

God lives. He lives forever. His kingdom and rule on earth are being established now and will be permanently installed upon His return. You can trust God without reserve or regret.

Unshakable faith—that's what I want, Lord. You are in control, even when everything seems out of control. I praise You that You are using everything that touches my life—both good and evil—for Your divine purposes.

SCRIPTURE READING: Colossians 3:1–4
KEY VERSE: Colossians 3:2

Set your mind on things above, not on things on the earth.

The apostle Paul spent a great deal of time writing to the early church about the mind-set of faith, how they should think as new believers in Christ. The message he shared with the church in Colosse was no exception. Because of its location, Colosse was a hub of activity and cultural expansion. Various philosophies dictated religious views and doctrines while young believers faced many challenges concerning their belief in God and His redemptive provision through Christ.

Paul exhorted them to set their minds on the things above, not on the things of this world. The reason was simple. When you focus on Jesus Christ and His truth and plan for your life, you are not easily swayed. You are firmly fixed and established in light of God's victory. Therefore, when disappointments, doubts, or temptations come, you know God is in control because your mind is set on His truth and principles.

Many believers at Colosse struggled spiritually because they allowed their minds to be drawn aside by false doctrines. Paul told them to think with their minds set on Jesus Christ. The same is true for you today. When your mind is focused on Christ, you have His perspective. That is your security and hope.

> *Dear heavenly Father, give me a mind-set of faith. Focus my attention on the eternal—Your truth, Your plan for my life. Turn my attention from the philosophies of this world, and establish my mind firmly on Your principles.*

HOW WELL DO YOU KNOW HIM?

SCRIPTURE READING: 2 Timothy 1:8–12
KEY VERSE: 2 Timothy 1:12

I know whom I have believed and am persuaded that He is able to keep what I have committed to Him until that Day.

A stranger approaches you at the bus stop one morning and asks you to invest $5,000 in his new business venture. Your swift response is negative, for you are unaware of the individual's identity or integrity. You will not place your trust in someone you do not know.

The same principle is at work in the spiritual realm. The more you know about Jesus, the more you will entrust into His care. How well are you acquainted with Jesus Christ? Do you know as much about Him as one knows about mountain climbing by reading books on the subject? Or do you know Jesus intimately as one who knows mountain climbing by ascending the summit of Mount Everest?

You can know Jesus for yourself by investigating the Word of God regularly, praying habitually about small and common needs, and obeying in the trifles of life. A vital faith in Christ is forged in the tiny corners of the home and heart. You see answers to prayers and observe Him at work in your life.

If you want great faith in Christ, set your heart to know and obey Him in the little tasks. Your faith will increase because you will "know whom [you] have believed" (2 Tim. 1:12).

> *Father, examine every aspect of my home life, my work, and my relationships. Shine Your light into the deepest recesses of my heart, for there a vital faith in You is forged.*

SCRIPTURE READING: Zechariah 4:6–10

KEY VERSE: James 1:5

If any of you lacks wisdom, let him ask of God, who gives to all liberally and without reproach, and it will be given to him.

Jim Elliot was a bright, articulate young man who left his home in the United States for the jungles of South America. In his mid-twenties he was killed by Indian spears, leaving behind his wife, Elisabeth, and a daughter.

Elisabeth used her deceased husband's diary as the source for her stirring book *The Shadow of the Almighty*. Thousands have testified to the book's influence in motivating them for mission service. By secular values, her husband accomplished little, dying young in a remote forest. But in God's eyes he was successful. He was one mighty in spirit, allowing the Holy Spirit to direct, guide, and energize his life.

People who are mighty in spirit can build enduring, rewarding lives whether they live in a high-rise or in the slums, whether they earn much or little money, whether they are known by many or few.

God's presence and reign in your life give you eternal significance. You can enjoy the gracious blessings that God gives without partiality to His children (James 1:5). Wherever you are—even if it is in the remote reaches of a tropical forest as Jim Elliot was—you can impact your world by being mighty in spirit.

Lord, I want to be mighty in spirit. I want to impact my world with Your power. Direct, guide, and energize my life to accomplish Your purposes.

SCRIPTURE READING: Proverbs 2

KEY VERSE: Hosea 6:3

Let us know,

Let us pursue the knowledge of the LORD.

His going forth is established as the morning;

He will come to us like the rain,

Like the latter and former rain to the earth.

You do not become mighty in spirit by setting your inner person on automatic pilot to drift through life. You must employ several basic disciplines if you are to experience the rewards of a Spirit-directed life:

The discipline of rejection. The Holy Spirit is opposed to the flesh, and the one who is mighty in spirit must constantly reject the competing values and passions of the world system, which is devoid of godliness.

The discipline of relationship. Wisdom flows from a pure, honest relationship with the Lord Jesus Christ. The legalist, moralist, and Pharisee are not mighty in spirit. Above all you must guard your heart and keep Jesus as your first love—singularly devoted to Him, not a cause.

The discipline of obedience. Being acquainted with Christ and His Word is not enough. Obedience is always the path to growth and blessing. Are you obeying what you know? The riches of heaven are yours when you obey the Word of God and the leading of the Holy Spirit.

The motivation for each of these disciplines is love of the Lord Jesus Christ. You want to be mighty in spirit because you adore Him.

Heavenly Father, I reject the values and passions of the world system.
I want to be singularly devoted to You, not just a cause. I want to walk
the pathway of obedience that leads to spiritual growth.

SCRIPTURE READING: Psalm 31
KEY VERSE: Psalm 31:15

My times are in Your hand;
Deliver me from the hand of my enemies,
And from those who persecute me.

Watching a football player lie motionless on the turf after a vicious hit is sobering. Almost universally feared, but usually unspoken, is the possibility of an injury that results in paralysis. Often these fears are relieved when the player is escorted off the field.

Far more damaging and much more prevalent is another kind of paralysis that sets in when we are faced with a decision. Multitudes are frozen in fear and confusion in the decision-making process. It is a form of bondage that God certainly does not desire.

You can be confident in any form of decision making because your trust is ultimately in the Lord Jesus Christ. You are responsible to gather facts, analyze them, and weigh alternatives. People hold you responsible for results also.

Having done your part, you can rest because the Lord is in control. You do not know the future; He does. Your times and decisions are in His hands as you trust in His guidance (Ps. 31:15). Even when the consequences of your decision are not what you envisioned, you still know that God works all things together for good to those who love Him (Rom. 8:28).

Lord, please guide my decisions as I build my life on You. Eliminate fear and confusion. Give me the mind of Christ as I gather facts, analyze them, weigh alternatives, set my goals, and accomplish them by faith.

SCRIPTURE READING: Hosea 6:1–4
KEY VERSE: Proverbs 20:6

Most men will proclaim each his own goodness,
But who can find a faithful man?

In certain sections of the country, a morning fog is almost a daily occurrence. The day begins with a heavy mist that dissipates within a few hours. The prophet Hosea described the Israelites' relationship with God in a similar way: "For your loyalty is like a morning cloud, / And like the dew which goes away early" (Hos. 6:4 NASB).

Loyalty is an essential ingredient in the relationship between us and God. In the Old Testament the Hebrew word for loving-kindness is translated as "loyal, faithful, steadfast love."

Despite our rebellion and sin, God kept His covenant love for us through the generations, fulfilling His eternal plan for reconciliation through the cross of Christ. In return, God expects the wholehearted allegiance of His followers.

Are you actively demonstrating your loyalty to Jesus Christ? Has your devotion to the Lord slackened over the years? Do you question God's care?

The Lord Jesus Christ is not as interested in your money or time or activity level as He is in your heart. He wants your wholehearted devotion that is not diminished by time or circumstances.

Almighty God, I declare my loyalty to You. I want to be faithful and steadfast. I pledge my wholehearted allegiance to You.

SCRIPTURE READING: Matthew 25:14–30
KEY VERSE: Matthew 25:21

His lord said to him, "Well done, good and faithful servant; you were faithful over a few things, I will make you ruler over many things. Enter into the joy of your lord."

The fast track for success is faster than ever. Employers complain that young people want to rise to the top as quickly as possible without any time-consuming layovers in areas they consider unnecessary.

Success in any area, however, does not come easily; and it is no different in the spiritual realm. If you want to do great things for God, you must be willing to endure the small things with patience. There are often seasons when the Lord prepares you faithfully for future challenges.

Responsibility is learned in the little things. Can God entrust a pastorate to one who is inconsistent in teaching a Sunday school class? Can He send someone overseas to the lost if he has not labored among the unsaved where he lives?

Responsibility is best learned on the backstage where you are diligent and faithful because you want to please the Lord, not other people. As you learn to labor consistently out of the limelight, God can challenge you with progressively more demanding opportunities. A responsible Christian is one whom God and other people can count on in any circumstance.

Are you faithful where He has placed you, or do you clamor for more? Persevere, and your future is bright.

Heavenly Father, I really do want to accomplish great things for You. Help me to be faithful in the small things.

SCRIPTURE READING: Nehemiah 1
KEY VERSE: Matthew 14:23

When He had sent the multitudes away, He went up on the mountain by Himself to pray. Now when evening came, He was alone there.

Sociological studies show that despite increased leisure time, Americans feel more pressured than ever. With increased freedoms and opportunities come more choices; with more choices, more decisions are required.

The key to living an orderly life in the midst of such frenzy is an established prayer life in which you can present your needs and agenda to the all-wise God. Nehemiah understood this foundational principle.

When he heard the news of Jerusalem's plight, he did not immediately organize a rescue squad or launch a new organization. Nehemiah's response was to pray: "I sat down and wept and mourned for days; and I was fasting and praying before the God of heaven" (Neh. 1:4 NASB).

For four long months, Nehemiah interceded on Jerusalem's behalf, asking God for direction and wisdom. Then when the time came to petition King Artaxerxes, Nehemiah's request was granted miraculously (Neh. 2:1–6).

Order in your life begins with the rule of the Holy Spirit and the outworking of God's plan. The discernment to implement His plan comes as you spend time in fervent prayer, seeking His mind and purposes.

Dear heavenly Father, I realize that order in my life begins with the rule of Your Holy Spirit—so please, come and rule and reign in my life. Implement Your plan and purposes. Bring order out of chaos.

SCRIPTURE READING: Exodus 14

KEY VERSE: Exodus 14:14

The LORD will fight for you, and you shall hold your peace.

We have to admit that we cannot be successful in eliminating an area of habitual sin, even with strong wills, discipline, and perseverance (John 15:5). That puzzles us because we think we usually can arrive at a successful conclusion. We think, *Why should this problem of lust or jealousy or greed be any different?*

The first step toward progress is a recognition that the battle is spiritual, not rational or behavioral (Eph. 6:13–20). You have allowed the power of sin to establish a spiritual stronghold, a fortified position in your inner person. You cannot conquer this stronghold by futile, ordinary means (2 Cor. 10:3–4).

You can be free by relying on these spiritual weapons—the living Word of God and the Holy Spirit's power. Since the battle is mainly in your mind, reading God's Word attacks the stronghold by infusing His truth, which will always prevail (1 Cor. 10:13; Eph. 4:12).

The Spirit of God, who brought you from death to life, also can demolish spiritual strongholds. His power is available as you depend upon His supernatural resources (Ex. 14:14; Rom. 15:13).

Identify your spiritual stronghold. Recognize that you are in a spiritual battle, and use the spiritual weapons the Lord gives you. They work!

> *Heavenly Father, through the power of the Holy Spirit and on the basis of Your Word, I claim victory over every spiritual stronghold in my life—and I thank You for the supernatural resources You have provided for me to fight my battles.*

SCRIPTURE READING: Romans 8:31–39
KEY VERSE: Galatians 2:16

Knowing that a man is not justified by the works of the law but by faith in Jesus Christ, even we have believed in Christ Jesus, that we might be justified by faith in Christ and not by the works of the law; for by the works of the law no flesh shall be justified.

People who doubt their salvation are miserable Christians and confusing witnesses to the unbelieving world. They are not portraits of "the abundant life" that Jesus Christ gives those who trust Him for the forgiveness of their sins.

How then do you slip into this anxiety-producing mind-set? By subtly shifting from grace to performance. By losing sight of the all-sufficiency of the Cross. Salvation is always "by grace . . . through faith" (Eph. 2:8 NASB). It is a gift from God.

Once saved, you may drift into a performance-based mentality, thinking your relationship with the Lord depends upon your conduct. This is heresy. Only God's grace saves you and keeps you saved. Your basis of acceptance before Him is the Cross where God the Father justified you (declared you not guilty) through His Son's death. You are accepted not on your merit but wholly on Christ's substitutionary death on Calvary. Once for all, Jesus died for all your sins for all time. When you are saved, your sins are forgiven—past, present, and future.

If you are wrestling with doubt over your salvation, look to the Cross. If you have received Christ by faith, you are eternally secure in the Savior. Nothing can alter that fact.

Dear Lord, I thank You that the foundation of my spiritual life rests on the assurance of my salvation. I am saved and sure. My sins are forgiven—past, present, and future!

SCRIPTURE READING: Hebrews 11:1–6

KEY VERSE: Luke 8:25

He said to them, "Where is your faith?" And they were afraid, and mar-
veled, saying to one another, "Who can this be? For He commands even the
winds and water, and they obey Him!"

Some people confuse the concept of faith with positive thinking, which it is not. Others project faith as the intense effort to attain something. "If he just had enough faith, he could have what he asks," they say.

These descriptions are foreign to the biblical portrait of faith, which is a confident reliance upon the faithfulness of God. It is not worked up by individuals but grounded in the very character and being of our Father in heaven.

Our faith is in God. When we are weak, we look to Him for strength. When we are afflicted, we look to the Lord for comfort. When we are in need, we look to Him for provision. When we want to see someone saved, we count on God's saving power.

Faith is the divine link that taps into the inexhaustible resources of eternal God, relying on His perfect wisdom, power, and love. God looks for men and women who will place faith in Him, depending on His sufficiency and adequacy.

Where is your faith placed today? Trust in the Lord Jesus Christ alone, and you will never be disappointed.

Lord, I don't have to work it up or pray it down. Faith is a divine link
You have provided. Thank You that my faith is grounded in Your char-
acter and not in my performance or abilities.

SCRIPTURE READING: Hebrews 11:23–27
KEY VERSES: 1 Peter 5:6–7

*Humble yourselves under the mighty hand of God, that He may exalt you
in due time, casting all your care upon Him, for He cares for you.*

You have prayed daily for your alcoholic son. You have trusted God for
your spouse's salvation for many years. You have sought the Lord for
healing from a serious disease for several months.

But your son still drinks, your spouse is still unsaved, and your illness
still lingers painfully. How do you hold on to your faith?

First, you must believe that God is at work. You may not see any evidence, but the Holy Spirit unceasingly labors for you. The Lord is changing you in the process, developing Christlike qualities in you.

Second, you must not forget that God cares. The Scriptures assure you
that the Lord cares so much that He executed His Son on your behalf
(Rom. 5:6). His love toward you is unfailing. Because the Lord cares, you
can cast your burdens on Him daily (1 Peter 5:6–7).

Third, you must rest in the assurance that God knows best. His wisdom is sure, even when it runs totally against your logical grain. He
knows when, how, what, where, and why. If you are to hold on to faith
during trials, you must renew your trust with fresh, daily reminders of
the Lord's absolute faithfulness, power, wisdom, and care.

*Father, I believe You are at work in the difficult circumstances of my
life. You really do care. You have not forgotten me. I rest in the assurance that You know best.*

SCRIPTURE READING: 1 Peter 1:3–9
KEY VERSE: 1 Peter 1:7

That the genuineness of your faith, being much more precious than gold that perishes, though it is tested by fire, may be found to praise, honor, and glory at the revelation of Jesus Christ.

Face it. You never will receive all you ask from God.

You will experience suffering that cannot be explained. You will be buffeted by volatile affliction. While on earth, you never will fully understand why you must go through trials. Your faith must be anchored in the eternal. You are assured that one day—maybe not on earth—your faith will be rewarded by your just Lord: "That the proof of your faith, being more precious than gold which is perishable, even though tested by fire, may be found to result in praise and glory and honor at the revelation of Jesus Christ" (1 Peter 1:7 NASB).

Faith sees past the physical world into what is invisible and eternal. Faith that rests on visible evidence is not faith at all.

You understand that sin has marred the world and that things will not be set straight until Christ Jesus comes again to establish His reign on earth. When you meet Jesus face-to-face, your wounds and sorrows will be replaced by His perfect peace and joy (Rev. 21:4).

Your faith will be rewarded one day—if not now. It is precious to the Lord, and it is your most valuable weapon in persevering on earth.

Father, each day my faith is on trial. Help me pass the tests, and let my faith result in praise, glory, and honor when Jesus returns.

SCRIPTURE READING: 1 Kings 18
KEY VERSES: Isaiah 55:8–9

"For My thoughts are not your thoughts,
Nor are your ways My ways," says the LORD.
"For as the heavens are higher than the earth,
So are My ways higher than your ways,
And My thoughts than your thoughts."

Elijah challenged the prophets of Baal with this stirring announcement: "Then you call on the name of your god, and I will call on the name of the LORD, and the God who answers by fire, He is God" (1 Kings 18:24 NASB). Here is the ultimate expression of faith: God will answer.

Have you prayed about a sick child, financial problems, or your marriage? God will answer. False gods never answer. The Lord always hears the prayers of His children and responds to our petitions. Of course, we do not know how He will reply or what His answer will involve. Our faith must rest in God's love, grace, and wisdom.

The test of your faith is that you have expectations but God has His heavenly plan. His ways are higher than yours (Isa. 55:9), and they are always for your welfare. Will you wait for His answer, or will you manipulate the circumstances to achieve your goals? Will you be satisfied with His response, or will you grow bitter and rebel because you did not get your way?

Burn this truth into your heart: God will answer. His ears and eyes are open to your requests and problems. Your faith can withstand the strongest doubts and unbelief when you are assured of His loving answer.

Thank You, Lord, that You will answer! It may not be when I want or
how I want—but You will answer. I place my faith in Your love, grace,
and wisdom.

SCRIPTURE READING: 1 Samuel 17
KEY VERSE: 1 Samuel 17:47

Then all this assembly shall know that the LORD does not save with sword and spear; for the battle is the LORD's, and He will give you into our hands.

A U.S. Army advertisement shares a father's advice to his son on bravery: "Courage is putting your fears aside and doing your job." That is good counsel, but the Christian can rephrase it: "Courage is putting your fears aside and doing your job through confidence in a faithful God."

David's courage in facing Goliath came from his steadfast focus on the might of Jehovah God: "You come to me with a sword, a spear, and a javelin, but I come to you in the name of the LORD of hosts, the God of the armies of Israel" (1 Sam. 17:45 NASB).

Putting your fears aside is not simple. Sometimes the more you look at the risks or possibilities, the more fearful you become. Only when your fears are placed in perspective against the background of a holy, powerful, caring God can they be dispelled and your courage bolstered.

Identify the task, person, or issue that frightens you. Run through the scenarios that might happen. Then consider the vastness of your infinite, merciful, mighty God. Can He help? Is He bigger than your problem? Does your foe trouble Him?

With a faith focused on the person of Jesus Christ, courageously tackle your Goliath—not in your might but in His. The battle is God's to win.

Heavenly Father, I put aside my fears to accomplish Your purposes through the power of Your might. You are greater than my foes. My battles are Yours to win.

Then the word of the LORD came to him, saying . . .

When we think of Elijah, we usually focus on his exceptional faith in God. Such believing faith is not the exclusive domain of prophets or disciples. Every Christian is called to live and walk by faith.

Notice how many times the phrase "the word of the LORD" occurs in 1 Kings 17. Elijah's mighty deeds are repeatedly preceded by this pronouncement.

For believers today, "the word of the LORD" is not delivered by angels or dreams or given orally. Rather, God's word is His revelation of truth in the Bible. Scripture is filled with the same divine significance that Elijah experienced when he heard "the word of the LORD."

Your faith is anchored in the eternal principles of God's Word whose Author is the Holy Spirit. That should bring an awesome sense of reverence and new anticipation as you approach this supernatural communication of God.

As such, it is the cornerstone for life-changing faith. Believe the Word, and you are saved from sin's penalty. Believe the Word, and you can be delivered from sinful strongholds. Believe the Word about any issue, attribute, or problem, and your faith in His truth will work miracles in your life.

> *Heavenly Father, what a privilege that the God of the universe should communicate to me! Thank You for Your Word, which guides and directs my life.*

SCRIPTURE READING: Genesis 12:1–5

KEY VERSE: Hebrews 11:8

By faith Abraham obeyed when he was called to go out to the place which he would receive as an inheritance. And he went out, not knowing where he was going.

Two children play in a yard. One mother cries, "Johnny, it's time to come home." Johnny hurriedly tells his friend good-bye and runs home. His companion Bill continues to play. Why did Johnny respond but not Bill? Because Johnny was related to the one speaking, while Bill was not.

Similarly your obedience to God's leadership is a validation that God is your Father and you are His child. When He requires your obedience to His conviction, guidance, and reproof, your compliance is evidence of your relationship with Him. You are still His if you do not obey, but God desires obedient children who are submissive to His will.

Also Johnny responded to his mother's command because of his love for her. When you obey the Father, you likewise give evidence of your devotion to Him. Loving God involves your consistent adherence to His Word and means your glad, prompt obedience.

Knowing that God seeks your obedience only for your benefit is the grounds for your loving allegiance. Even in correction, God's motivation is His love for you. If He is speaking to you about a specific action, let your obedience demonstrate your love as His child.

I love You, Lord, and I want to be an obedient child. I submit to Your will. Come, and take complete control.

SCRIPTURE READING: 1 Kings 11:1–8
KEY VERSE: Psalm 147:5

Great is our Lord, and mighty in power;
His understanding is infinite.

When we compromise on God's clearly stated truth, we dilute His standards. God knows best. Rationalize as we might, compromise is simply an attempt to bring God down a notch, to say that we really know what is best, which always leads to distasteful consequences.

When we compromise our convictions, we settle for less than biblical excellence. Obedience to revealed truth in the Bible allows us to maximize our God-given potential. Compromise reduces our effectiveness as God's servants and is the pathway to spiritual mediocrity.

Likewise, compromise is the precursor to entanglement and enslavement to sin. Compromise seems easy at first, but its long-term consequences are severe. Sin still seeks to master us, and what starts as a minor concession can become a major problem later.

If you are thinking about compromising on any of God's commandments, think again. You always lose when you compromise, for God will never change His Word.

Father, show me where I have compromised in my life. Reveal where I
am trying to rationalize my behavior. Redirect me from the road of
spiritual mediocrity to the pathway of excellence.

SCRIPTURE READING: Ephesians 4:17–24
KEY VERSE: Ephesians 4:24

And that you put on the new man which was created according to God, in true righteousness and holiness.

Oswald Chambers wrote in *Our Brilliant Heritage,*

The one marvelous secret of a holy life lies not in imitating Jesus, but in letting the perfections of Jesus manifest themselves in my mortal flesh. Sanctification is "Christ in you." It is His wonderful life that is imparted to me in sanctification, and imparted by faith as a sovereign gift of God's grace. . . .

Sanctification means the impartation of the holy qualities of Jesus Christ. It is His patience, His love, His holiness, His faith, His purity, His godliness, that is manifested in and through every sanctified soul. Sanctification is not drawing from Jesus the power to be holy; it is drawing from Jesus the holiness that was manifested in Him, and He manifests it in me. Sanctification is an impartation, not an imitation.

Many Christians run into difficulty when they work to imitate Jesus. They cannot do it and remain simple and pure in their spiritual focus. The key to living like Christ is found not in striving but in letting go of aspirations and seeking the Lord above all else.

When you pray to be holy, pray to be like Jesus. He lived life as a reflection of the Father. His holiness and purity were natural overflows that comforted and cared for all who were lonely and wayward in heart. He drew people to Himself not by being mechanical in His worship of the Father but by being a light of hope to a darkened world.

Christ in me! The very thought is overwhelming. Dear Lord, I draw upon the resources of this divine life flow within to walk in holiness today.

SCRIPTURE READING: Colossians 1:19–23
KEY VERSE: Colossians 1:23

If indeed you continue in the faith, grounded and steadfast, and are not moved away from the hope of the gospel which you heard, which was preached to every creature under heaven, of which I, Paul, became a minister.

F. B. Meyer urged, "Dare to trust Him; dare to follow Him! And discover that life, at His bidding, becomes the material of which an avenue is made to liberty."

Life in New Testament times was not easy. Once a church was established, Paul traveled to another city with God's message of salvation. New believers were left, often on their own, to meet, worship, and study the Word that had been spoken to them. Paul's letters were filled with the call to remain true to the faith and not to be swayed by false teachings, thoughts of discouragement, or feelings of temptation.

We think our world today is volatile, but the world in which the early church existed was under constant attack from outside forces. Paul could not be everywhere at once. Timothy and Silas and others did much to uphold the faith, but even they could not meet all the spiritual needs.

It came down to a matter of faith. Congregational minister Horace Bushnell commented, "If you go to Christ to be guided, He will guide you; but He will not comfort your distrust or half-trust of Him by showing you the chart of all His purposes concerning you. He will show you only into a way where, if you go cheerfully and trustfully forward, He will show you on still farther."

The foundation of your faith begins and ends with simple trust. Outside that there is no other truth.

Heavenly Father, sometimes I make things too complicated. Let me realize the foundation of my faith rests on simple trust in You. Lead me one step at a time.

November

THEME: The Gates of Praise

REPRESENTING: Thanksgiving, praise, and worship

KEY VERSE: Psalm 100:4

Enter into His gates with thanksgiving,
And into His courts with praise.
Be thankful to Him, and bless His name.

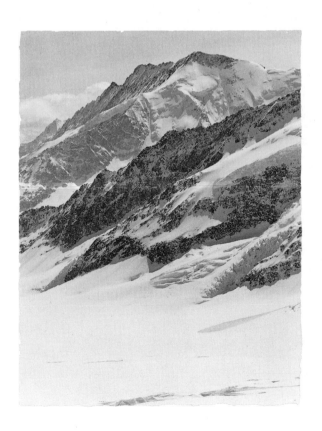

SCRIPTURE READING: Psalm 27:4–7
KEY VERSES: Psalm 92:1–2

> *It is good to give thanks to the LORD,*
> *And to sing praises to Your name, O Most High;*
> *To declare Your lovingkindness in the morning,*
> *And Your faithfulness every night.*

Hudson Taylor, who founded the China Inland Mission, is considered the founder of modern faith missions. The key to his faith and perseverance as he labored for many years in a foreign, hostile environment was a commitment to daily worship.

Early each morning, whether at home or on a journey, he would strike a match, light a candle or lantern, and proceed to enter God's presence with thanksgiving and praise. It was said of Taylor that before the sun ever rose on China, he was worshiping God.

If you are to cultivate the spiritual art and intimacy of worship, there must be a setting of the will. Until this happens worship will remain a mystery—an enigma. Add to that the weariness of the flesh, and worship will never flame into godly passion unless you, like David, desire this one thing: "To behold the beauty of the LORD, / And to meditate in His temple" (Ps. 27:4 NASB).

Prepare your heart for worship by an initial setting of your will. As you continue, you will ride the crest of swelling devotion to a majestic God.

> *Almighty God, I desire one thing—to behold Your beauty and medi-*
> *tate in Your temple. Stir the flickering embers of my spirit, and ignite*
> *a new passion for worship.*

SCRIPTURE READING: Psalm 34
KEY VERSE: Psalm 34:1

I will bless the Lord at all times;
His praise shall continually be in my mouth.

In her daily devotional book *Edges of His Ways*, Amy Carmichael noted,

I believe that if we are to be and to do for others what God means us to be and to do, we must not let adoration and worship slip into second place. For it is the central service asked by God of human souls; and its neglect is responsible for much lack of spiritual depth and power.

Perhaps we may find here the reason why we so often run dry. We do not give time enough to what makes the depth, and so we are shallow; a wind, quite a little wind, can ruffle our surface; a little hot sun, and all the moisture in us evaporates. It should not be so. . . .

Today if we will hear His voice, today, this morning, if we will draw near to Him, He will draw near to us. In the hush of that nearness . . . we shall forget ourselves, lost in the wonder, love and praise to Him. . . . The morning never disappoints us by not coming, neither does our loving God.

You may be hurting emotionally and find the thought of praise awkward. That's okay. God knows what you are up against. But if you will begin to praise Him, regardless of your circumstance, He will lift you up and give you strength to carry on.

Truly, You are great, O Lord. Help me look beyond the problems and
challenges of my circumstances to praise You today.

SCRIPTURE READING: Psalm 63

KEY VERSE: Psalm 63:4

I will bless You while I live;
I will lift up my hands in Your name.

When you are faced with a problem, it is deceptively easy to forget God. You may pray briefly or ask for prayers of others, but seeking God must be more than a casual pursuit. You become serious about seeking God and His purposes as you realize these crucial truths:

God cares for you. As the Good Shepherd, Jesus is intimately interested in your well-being. You are a sheep of His pasture and a person of His hand. Since He cares so passionately and personally for you, your decisions, actions, and thoughts are His concern as well. He has a plan for you that He is willing to make known as you seek Him and His kingdom first.

God is involved in everything. Because He cares and because He is sovereignly at work in your life, His involvement is unlimited. Your work, family, relationships, play, and other facets of daily living are His delight. The house you need, the job you desire, the spouse you are seeking—all involve the love and care of God. He watches over your life and desires for you to seek His counsel at every turn.

Are you seeking God and His face? Turn your attention to Him, and He will order your steps and strengthen your heart. Seek God, and all else will fall into place.

> *Lord, how thankful I am that You care for me and are involved in*
> *every detail of my life. Help me to seek You consistently, knowing that*
> *if I do, all else will fall into place.*

SCRIPTURE READING: Psalm 66
KEY VERSE: Psalm 66:8

Oh, bless our God, you peoples!
And make the voice of His praise to be heard.

Some basic building blocks can help you keep a reliable, scriptural perspective on the necessity of seeking the Lord.

First, you should develop consistent habits of seeking God in the ordinary rounds of life. Bringing your ordinary, seemingly mundane needs and problems to Him helps you to understand His sufficiency in times of true crises. God never fails you or forsakes you when you call out in desperation. He wants you to seek Him for who He is, cultivating a personal relationship with a God who loves you and cares for you as no other.

Second, you need to continue in the Word and in prayer. God speaks to you through the living words of the Scriptures. You do not have to wait on some "experience" when you have God's sure and clear Word. You must also talk to Him in prayer, pouring out your heart to Him, hiding nothing.

Third, you must do all these exercises of the soul humbly and honestly. Those who are secure in their own strength, capable in their own energies, have little reason to seek the Lord. However, because you realize your inadequacies and weaknesses, you come to God with an open, receptive heart in need of His supernatural help.

Seeking God ultimately gives you His adequacy for your inadequacy.

Lord, I come to You with an open and receptive heart. I seek Your face.
I need to exchange my inadequacies for Your adequacies, my weakness
for Your strength.

SCRIPTURE READING: Psalm 62
KEY VERSE: Psalm 62:8

Trust in Him at all times, you people;
Pour out your heart before Him;
God is a refuge for us. Selah

Not only is meditation on God's Word important for receiving His counsel and comfort, but it is essential for worship and fellowship with the Father. In *Knowing God*, Dr. J. I. Packer wrote about the benefits of meditation:

How can we turn our knowledge about God into knowledge of God? The rule of doing this is demanding but simple. It is that we turn each truth we learn about God into meditation before God, leading to prayer and praise to God.

Meditation is the activity of calling to mind, and thinking over, and dwelling on, and applying to oneself, the various things that one knows about the works and ways and purposes and promises of God.

It is an activity of holy thought, consciously performed in the presence of God, under the eye of God, by the help of God, as a means of communion with God. Its purpose is to clear one's mental and spiritual vision of God, and to let His truth make its full and proper impact on one's mind and heart.

Its effect is to ever humble us, as we contemplate God's greatness and glory, and our littleness and sinfulness and to encourage and reassure us . . . as we contemplate the unsearchable riches of divine mercy displayed in the Lord Jesus Christ.

O God, please turn my knowledge about You into knowledge of You.
I want to know You in ever-increasing intimacy.

SCRIPTURE READING: John 14:15–24

KEY VERSE: Philippians 3:12

Not that I have already attained, or am already perfected; but I press on, that I may lay hold of that for which Christ Jesus has also laid hold of me.

Is your relationship with the heavenly Father one of duty or delight? God, who is love, desires your fellowship with Him to be motivated by personal, growing, demonstrated love.

God is a person. Although He could have existed without creating humankind, He made us for Himself. He wants such an intimate relationship with you that He executed His Son for you so that you could be reconciled to Him forever.

As His child, you are free to love Him for all He is and for what He has done and will do for you. Each day is an opportunity to express your love for Jesus. You can love Him by telling Him so.

There is no such thing as true love in a marriage without verbal encouragement and praise. Likewise, God wants to hear the words of your lips that proclaim His excellencies. You can also tell Him you love Him by cheerful obedience. Work heartily at your task, knowing Christ is your Master. Carry out principles of Scripture He has laid on your heart. Serve others with compassion and understanding as Christ's ambassador on earth.

The more you know Christ, the more you love Him. The more you love Him, the more passionately you want to honor and praise Him. It is a divine circle of love filled with blessings.

Heavenly Father, the more I get to know You, the more I love You. I am overwhelmed by the love that You showed in offering up Your Son, Jesus, in my behalf. Make me an ambassador of Your love here on earth.

SCRIPTURE READING: Psalm 51

KEY VERSE: Psalm 51:15

O Lord, open my lips,
And my mouth shall show forth Your praise.

Most Christians sincerely desire to love God and please Him. Although if we are honest, we feel distant and detached from God at times.

Perhaps you have become entrapped in the hectic pace of work, school, family, or other meaningful obligations. Your times of communion with Christ have diminished.

Perhaps you have been ensnared by a sinful habit that you will not abandon, and your guilt is so overwhelming that you are ashamed to approach Christ. Whatever the reason for your broken intimacy with God, there is good news. Jesus waits to embrace you now in the arms of unconditional, divine love.

Stop today, take a deep breath, admit your misplaced priorities, and begin again to seek the kingdom of God. It may take time for feelings of intimacy to return, but fellowship can again be sweet.

If you have sinned, your guilt is washed away by the blood of the Cross. Confess your sin, receive His infinite forgiveness, and ask Christ to restore your soul. Once you are saved, no sin can keep you outside the love of God. He never condemns you.

God's mercies are new every morning. Great is His faithfulness. Return to Him, and the Spirit of God will rekindle your dimly burning wick.

Sometimes I feel distant from You, Lord. Rekindle my dimly burning
wick. Renew our intimate fellowship.

SCRIPTURE READING: Acts 2:46–47
KEY VERSE: Psalm 29:2

Give unto the LORD the glory due to His name;
Worship the LORD in the beauty of holiness.

Personal worship of God is a vital part of knowing Him. Likewise, corporate worship is an instrumental facet of healthy Christianity.

Corporate worship, the body of believers worshiping together, was common in the Old Testament. It was associated with the gathering of Israel for special feasts and ceremonies. It does not vanish in the New Testament but is the prominent feature of the body of Christ following pentecost.

The Holy Spirit who indwells each believer desires to honor Christ through public expressions of reverence. Corporate worship fosters unity and harmony, supernaturally removing barriers of division and discord. It is a powerful weapon against Satan's disruptive schemes.

Corporate worship underscores our uniqueness as God's people, placed in Christ and adopted in His family. We are not alone in this world. We have other brothers and sisters who share similar experiences. Worshiping together is a catalyst for the exercising of spiritual gifts that build up one another for fruitful Christian service.

If you are not worshiping together with a body of believers, ask God to direct you to a church. You will be encouraged, strengthened, and renewed for the daily battles awaiting you. Don't be a lone sheep.

Heavenly Father, thank You for the opportunity to worship together
with other members of Your family. Remove the barriers of division
and discord that would prevent me from exercising this glorious priv-
ilege.

SCRIPTURE READING: Matthew 17:1–9
KEY VERSE: Psalm 50:1

The Mighty One, God the LORD,
Has spoken and called the earth
From the rising of the sun to its going down.

In an instant, Peter, James, and John saw their Friend and Teacher as they had never seen Him before. Just a moment earlier, Jesus stood beside them in the plain clothes of a humble workman. Then suddenly He shone forth in brilliant, dazzling light like the sun, and His clothing glowed like fire.

What was the disciples' reaction? Immediate worship: "While he [Peter] was still speaking, behold, a bright cloud overshadowed them; and . . . a voice out of the cloud, saying, 'This is My beloved Son. . . .' And when the disciples heard this, they fell on their faces and were much afraid" (Matt. 17:5–6 NASB).

As God's glory engulfed them, they were stricken with a sense of His absolute holiness and prostrated themselves before Him, the almighty Lord of all. At first, Peter was focused on human effort, what they could do in their own strength to show their love. But Jesus had a bigger plan. The moment that Peter saw Him "unveiled" as sovereign God, his worship was transformed and centered on God alone.

How do you worship God? Do you recognize Him as the holy, all-powerful Lord of your life and submit to Him without reservation? You worship God properly when you see Him as He is.

Almighty God, it is my heart's cry to worship You. Reveal Yourself to me. Let me see You as You really are.

SCRIPTURE READING: Psalm 150
KEY VERSE: Psalm 150:6

Let everything that has breath praise the LORD.
Praise the LORD!

"Praise the Lord!" the psalmist repeated in his song to God. For God's mighty acts, for His excellent greatness and holy character, he praised the Lord with all his soul and being. You can almost feel the intensity and fervent energy as you read the words.

God created you to praise Him, to recognize Him as eternal, sovereign Lord and King of all creation. There are no other gods before Him, and none besides the Almighty deserve your adoration and deepest love.

When you pray, do you praise God before you bring Him your petitions? Is worship your primary concern? Learning to praise God is key to spiritual growth, to understanding who He is and how He works in your life.

It is difficult to pull your mind off personal problems and place it on God, especially when your heart is troubled. But by focusing on Him, you can see your life the way God does. You are aware of His grace and daily care, and your spirit is revitalized. Pride and self-reliance vanish in the face of an all-sufficient Lord.

Read and heed Psalm 147:1: "It is good to sing praises to our God." As you give God glory and honor, you experience His joy and peace in a fresh, transforming way.

> *I praise You, O God, for Your mighty acts, Your excellent greatness,*
> *and Your holy character. You are eternal, sovereign Lord and King of*
> *all creation. There are no other gods before You!*

SCRIPTURE READING: Psalm 96
KEY VERSE: Psalm 96:2

Sing to the LORD, bless His name;
Proclaim the good news of His salvation from day to day.

Sir Winston Churchill. Albert Einstein. Bill Cosby. President George Bush. Already your mind has formulated thoughts and opinions concerning these individuals, such as courage, genius, humor, and leadership. That is because a person's name reflects far more than mere identity. It suggests character and personality, the sum of each person's being.

Your worship experience can likewise be elevated through a new appreciation for the names by which God is called in Scripture. God's name is indicative of His personal essence. The psalmist wrote, "O LORD, our Lord, / How majestic is Thy name in all the earth" (Ps. 8:1 NASB).

Listed here are just a few of the names ascribed to God in the Bible along with the particular aspect of His character they reveal:

El Olam—the everlasting or eternal God. Refers to God's eternal existence (Gen. 21:33).

El Shaddai—God almighty. Refers to the all-sufficient power and might of God (Gen. 17:1).

El Elyon—God the Most High. Refers to the sovereignty of God (Gen. 14:18).

Jehovah—the Self-Existent One. Refers particularly to God's covenant relationship with His people and His redemptive work (Ex. 3:14; 34:6).

I praise You, Oh Lord. You are the everlasting God. You are God almighty. You are God the Most High. You are Jehovah!

SCRIPTURE READING: Psalm 93

KEY VERSE: Exodus 15:11

Who is like You, O LORD, among the gods?
Who is like You, glorious in holiness,
Fearful in praises, doing wonders?

Another aid to the worship of God is meditation on His divine attributes. An attribute is a special quality of a person. God's attributes are the inherent features that express His distinct personality.

God is immutable. God never changes in His character or in His dealings with humankind. He can always be counted on to act consistently with His unchanging personhood, giving you great stability (Mal. 3:6; James 1:17).

God is sovereign. God is in complete control of both good and evil. Nothing can come into your life that can thwart His plan for you. This gives you incredible confidence for the present and future. God uses even your mistakes and the mistakes of others for His purposes (Rom. 8:28).

God is faithful. God always acts for your good and His glory. He can always be counted on to be true to His revealed character. This gives you security as you face uncertain problems (Ps. 89:2).

God is loving. God always moves in history and toward humankind according to His benevolence and grace. Even His wrath and judgment can be used for His loving purposes. This gives you great comfort as you face rejection and frustration (Ps. 86:5).

O Lord, I pause today to reflect on Your attributes. You are immutable.
You are sovereign. You are faithful. You are loving.

SCRIPTURE READING: Psalm 37:3–8
KEY VERSE: Psalm 30:5

His anger is but for a moment,
His favor is for life;
Weeping may endure for a night,
But joy comes in the morning.

A heart of true praise never uses the word *if*.

"If God heals my son, I will thank Him."

"If God takes care of my financial need, I will praise Him."

Rather, the fountain of genuine worship flows through all the peaks and valleys of *nevertheless*.

"If my son is not healed, nevertheless I will praise Him."

"If my bills are not paid, nevertheless I will extol Him."

Pure praise for our great and awesome God is never diminished by circumstance. Unfettered worship comes from the hearts of ones who understand that God owes us nothing, but has given us everything.

All that accompanies life is a gift from God, given because of His immeasurable love. We could not earn physical life—God gave it. We cannot merit our salvation—God bestows it through His Son, Jesus Christ, as we believe. True praise focuses on the astounding attributes and character of God. It rejoices in His goodness.

Are you delighting yourself in knowing God? Is your relationship with Him exciting and rewarding? Learn the secret of *nevertheless*. Praise God for who He is, and your song of celebration will light your path and gladden all about you.

God, You owe me nothing, but You have given me everything. Teach
me the secret of nevertheless so that I can move into a new, supernat-
ural realm of praise and worship.

SCRIPTURE READING: Philippians 2:5–11
KEY VERSE: Psalm 66:1

Make a joyful shout to God, all the earth!

There have been many courageous warriors through the ages—Charlemagne, Napoleon, Grant, Lee, Patton.

Many brilliant minds have made significant contributions—Galileo, Pasteur, Bell, Einstein, Salk.

Dozens of inspiring leaders have influenced world events—Washington, Lincoln, Churchill.

Yet all the brightest minds through the ages, all the mighty men of the centuries, and all the notable accomplishments of good men everywhere can never invoke the praise and admiration of the God-man, Jesus Christ. Think on His names.

He is the God of the whole earth; Immanuel, God with us; the Creator of all things; the Upholder of all things; the everlasting Father; the Beginning and the Ending; the Rock of my strength; the Chief Cornerstone; the Redeemer; the Great High Priest; the Amen; the Holy One of God; the Firstborn from the dead; the Lord of lords; the King of kings; the Righteous Judge.

These titles represent only a few of the attributes of our Savior. Meditate on the wonder of His person; you cannot help ascribing to Him supreme, unsurpassed, consummate worth.

Jesus is worthy of all your praise. No mortal can compare with Him.

Jesus, I praise Your name! You are Immanuel, Creator, Upholder of all things, everlasting Father, Beginning and the Ending; my Rock, Cornerstone, Redeemer, and Great High Priest. You are Lord of lords, King of kings, and my Righteous Judge.

SCRIPTURE READING: Psalm 86:6–13
KEY VERSE: Psalm 86:10

You are great, and do wondrous things;
You alone are God.

The book of Revelation reveals the priority of worship. Both angels and people, prostrate before the brilliant throne of grace, unceasingly praise the Lamb and the Father. Yet the clear teaching of the Bible is that resounding, reverberant praise should be the priority of the believer during the earthly pilgrimage also.

How much time do you engage in the exercise of worship? Perhaps more tellingly, what does worship mean to you? Do you have a strong reverence for God that is obvious in your lifestyle and witness?

The role of worship in your life can be dramatically elevated when you think correct thoughts about God. Martin Luther once said to his contemporary Erasmus, who had adopted a humanistic theology, "Your thoughts of God are too human."

You may unintentionally reduce the divine splendor of God. You may lose sight of the majesty of God, reducing Him to your very finite definitions.

The less highly you think of God, the less you will worship Him. The more exalted your thoughts of God, the more you will bow humbly before Him, acknowledging His supernatural attributes.

Father, sometimes I limit You by human reasoning. Sometimes I am
irreverent in my conduct. Set me free from these limitations so that I
can truly worship You.

SCRIPTURE READING: Psalm 84

KEY VERSES: 1 Peter 2:9–10

You are a chosen generation, a royal priesthood, a holy nation, His own special people, that you may proclaim the praises of Him who called you out of darkness into His marvelous light; who once were not a people but are now the people of God, who had not obtained mercy but now have obtained mercy.

Thinking great thoughts about God is the impetus for cultivating a life of meaningful worship. But the spiritual momentum that worship engenders will sputter if you do not understand your worth in God's eyes. Thus, worship is not only thinking correctly about God but also thinking correctly about yourself.

Too many people fail to enjoy the delight of worship because they feel guilty about their past or present sins. Once they are saved, they live in the constant light of God's unconditional love, their guilt completely atoned for through Christ's sacrificial death. They are not under condemnation any longer, even when they sin.

God declares you are of inestimable worth to Him. His Son's blood was shed for you; His heaven waits for you; His Spirit indwells you. You are precious, beloved, and honored in His sight, for you are made in His image and are His child through faith in Christ.

Reject the false accusations of the devil and the false guilt associated with his deceit. Turn away from unnecessary anxieties. God is for you, and you can worship Him with unfettered simplicity and confidence.

Father, I reject every false accusation of the devil! I am of inestimable worth to You. I am precious, beloved, and honored in Your sight. I am created in Your image, and I am Your child through faith in Jesus Christ.

SCRIPTURE READING: John 4
KEY VERSE: Psalm 66:1

Make a joyful shout to God, all the earth!

In his book *Worship: The Missing Jewel of the Evangelical Church*, A. W. Tozer wrote of the urgency for God's people to grasp the importance of devoted, passionate praise of our Savior:

> We have almost everything, but there's one thing that the churches do not have: that is the ability to worship. It's the one, shining gem that is lost to the modern church. . . .
>
> Now what are the factors that you will find present in worship? First there is boundless confidence. You cannot worship a being you cannot trust. . . . Worship rises or falls in any church altogether depending upon the attitude we take toward God, whether we see God big or whether we see Him little. Most of us see God too small; our God is too little.
>
> David said: "O magnify the Lord with me," and *magnify* doesn't mean to make God big. You can't make God big. But you can see Him big.
>
> Then there is admiration, that is appreciation of the excellency of God. . . . This admiration for God grows and grows. The God of the modern evangelical rarely astonishes anybody. . . . But when the Holy Ghost shows us God as He is, we admire Him to the point of wonder and delight.

I magnify You, Lord. You are great. You are unlimited; there is nothing too difficult for You. You are excellent. You are my God!

SCRIPTURE READING: Psalm 107:1–16
KEY VERSE: Psalm 107:1

Oh, give thanks to the LORD, for He is good!
For His mercy endures forever.

Many of us do not engage in worship when difficulty arises because we work hard at being self-reliant. We want to work it out in our wisdom, our strength, and our way. Involving ourselves in worship is tantamount to admitting defeat.

But we will all face some things that cannot be humanly resolved. There will be times when we come to the end of ourselves. Praising God in times of trouble sharpens our humility. We realize our helplessness, admitting His matchless superiority and supremacy.

As you humble yourself before God, He will exalt you at the right time. There are many promises in the Bible for you to claim, and humility is the one condition for receiving them.

Admitting your inadequacy strips away human pride, preparing your heart for the display of God's awesome power. Pride stunts worship; worship repels pride. In your trouble, readily confess your inadequacy. You can do some things, but you cannot do what God can.

Praising Him in trouble releases His power to work on your behalf. Rely on Him, not yourself.

Father, I am inadequate. There are things I am facing that cannot be humanly resolved. Strip away my pride, and prepare me for the display of Your awesome power in the midst of my circumstances.

SCRIPTURE READING: Psalm 95

KEY VERSES: Psalm 95:1–2

Oh come, let us sing to the LORD!
Let us shout joyfully to the Rock of our salvation.
Let us come before His presence with thanksgiving;
Let us shout joyfully to Him with psalms.

The Word of God gives you the basis for knowing and worshiping God, clearing away the obstacles of ignorance, apathy, and error. But when you take what you have learned about God in the Scriptures and pour your heart out through prayer, worship is fully realized on this terrestrial ball.

When you pray with your lips and your heart, you magnify God. Worship is not a subject for a textbook but the outpouring of your dependence on and love for Jesus Christ. Do not let prayer become a list. Do not let prayer drift into repetition. Do not let prayer be just a discipline.

Allow your prayer life to be a living channel of worship, telling God how much you think of Him. He wants the glory that is due His name, and your prayerful worship ascribes His worth. Prayer intimately enters the throne room of God, allowing you to exalt and glorify your Savior. Prayer links heaven and earth. When you pray, always begin with "Hallowed be Your name," and all else will fit into place. Worship is first in heaven and on earth, and communion with God is its highest expression.

Dear Lord, Your name is hallowed! Intimate communion with You is
my goal. Transform my prayer life into a living channel of worship.

SCRIPTURE READING: Psalm 138
KEY VERSE: Psalm 138:1

I will praise You with my whole heart;
Before the gods I will sing praises to You.

A. W. Tozer once stated,

> For millions of Christians . . . God is no more real than He is to the non-Christian. They go through life trying to love an ideal and be loyal to a mere principle. Over against all this cloudy vagueness stands the clear scriptural doctrine that God can be known in personal experience. A loving Personality dominates the Bible, walking among the trees of the garden and breathing fragrance over every scene.

Intimacy with God occurs on the most personal level. It is not one-way communication, but two-way—between you and the Savior. It includes a relationship that is sensitive to needs and desires.

God enjoys your fellowship. He knows your needs and longs to fulfill each one as you bring them to Him in prayer. When you grow in your desire to know Him, you become concerned about His desires and seek to please Him out of love.

Intimacy doesn't just happen. Jesus didn't just choose Peter, James, and John and immediately take them to the Mount of Transfiguration. Time weathered their relationship. Their view of Christ deepened, and their desire for His fellowship expanded. They were no longer satisfied with a casual knowledge of the Savior. Intimacy had overtaken them and changed the way they would live forever.

Has love for God overtaken you yet?

Father, overtake me with Your love. I truly want to fellowship with
You. Foster an intimacy that will change the way I live—forever.

SCRIPTURE READING: Matthew 19:16–22
KEY VERSES: Matthew 22:37–38

Jesus said to him, "'You shall love the LORD your God with all your heart, with all your soul, and with all your mind.' This is the first and great commandment."

To experience genuine intimacy with Christ, you must be willing to lay down your love for the things of this world. This doesn't mean giving up peanut butter and jelly sandwiches. But it does mean your desire for God and His fellowship exceeds your friendship with the world. God wants to bless you, yet blessings must never become what you seek above the Blesser.

A. W. Tozer commented on the quest for intimacy:

There can be no doubt that this possessive clinging to things is one of the most harmful habits in the Christian life. Because it is so natural, it is rarely recognized for the evil that it is. But its outworkings are tragic.

We are often hindered from giving up our treasures to the Lord out of fear for their safety. This is especially true when those treasures are loved relatives and friends. But we need to have no such fears. Our Lord came not to destroy but to save. Everything is safe which is so committed.

The rich young ruler found in Jesus what he had been looking for all his life (Matt. 19:16–22). However, in his heart his material possessions outweighed the need to follow Christ.

You may have given yourself to the Lord, but have you laid aside your love and desire for the world's riches? The greatest obstacle to knowing God is self-love. Make sure you don't fall prey to it.

O Lord, purge me of desire for riches of this world. I know You are able to keep all I commit into Your hands. In You, I have found the greatest treasure.

SCRIPTURE READING: Matthew 8:1–4

KEY VERSE: Psalm 142:3

When my spirit was overwhelmed within me,

Then You knew my path.

In the way in which I walk

They have secretly set a snare for me.

Consider this scene depicted in Matthew 8: "And when He had come down from the mountain, great multitudes followed Him. And behold, a leper came to Him, and bowed down to Him, saying, 'Lord, if You are willing, You can make me clean.' And He stretched out His hand and touched him, saying, 'I am willing; be cleansed.' And immediately his leprosy was cleansed" (vv. 1–3 NASB).

Jesus wants us to see Him as our only Source of help in every situation. And though the multitudes pressed in on Him, compassion rose up from within Him at the sight of the approaching man with leprosy, who was deeply despised by others.

Leprosy was a curse. All who associated with people with leprosy were considered ceremonially unclean as well. Yet the man dared to venture into the city in hopes of talking to Jesus. When Christ came near, the man immediately knelt before Him, demonstrating his adoration.

Next he told Jesus: "If You are willing, You can make me clean." Those words of tremendous faith were spoken by a man who did not doubt God's ability but feared that somehow he might be overlooked.

Perhaps you have suffered a long time. Jesus can heal your infirmity. He may choose to do so completely, or He may change the circumstances so that you can find peace and rest in your suffering. Don't let the Savior pass by. Step forward in worship, and allow Him to work in your life.

Blessed Savior, don't pass me by! By faith, I step forward right now to worship You and allow You to work in my life according to Your will.

O LORD, our Lord,
How excellent is Your name in all the earth,
Who have set Your glory above the heavens!

Psalm 19:1–4 painted this picture:

The heavens declare the glory of God;
the skies proclaim the work of his hands.
Day after day they pour forth speech;
night after night they display knowledge.
There is no speech or language
where their voice is not heard.
Their voice goes out into all the earth,
their words to the ends of the world. (NIV)

Our Maker designed all creation to be to the praise of His glory. The tiniest pebble and the tallest mountain bear testimony to God's power and love. Warbling birds, chirping crickets, and croaking frogs lend their special voices to the chorus.

Have you ever been outdoors on a clear night in an open space, where there are no artificial lights to get in the way? You cannot count the thousands of stars in the sky. In that moment outside, your feelings of awe may well up so strongly inside that you are unable to speak.

Psalm 8:1 is a wonderful prayer: "O LORD, our Lord, / How majestic is Thy name in all the earth, / Who hast displayed Thy splendor above the heavens!" (NASB).

O Lord, my Lord, how majestic is Your name in all the earth. You have
displayed Your splendor above the heavens.

SCRIPTURE READING: 1 Peter 2:1–10
KEY VERSE: Psalm 27:6

And now my head shall be lifted up above my enemies all around me;
Therefore I will offer sacrifices of joy in His tabernacle;
I will sing, yes, I will sing praises to the LORD.

Praise seems to be a natural part of what we want to do when things are going our way. But on the days when the dishwasher breaks or the children are sick or the mechanic gives us bad news about the car, it is much more difficult to be effusive with thanksgiving.

God understands how your emotions are built; He made them. He also knows the cure for a heart weighed down by concerns and irritations—praise.

Praise focuses your attention on God. When you take a long and deliberate look at the character and ways of the Lord who loved you enough to die for you, your eyes are naturally shifted away from the difficulty and onto His ability to care for you.

Praise increases your faith. Telling God what you love about Him always involves reciting His past actions of might and power on your behalf. You can look back at the times He sent special provision at just the right moment and thank Him for them. This process results in a heart that expands with joy and security in Him.

Praise gives you a sense of identity. When you praise God, you are acting as one who belongs to Him. First Peter 2:9 says that you are a member of "a people for God's own possession, that you may proclaim the excellencies of Him who has called you out of darkness into His marvelous light" (NASB). That is reason enough to praise Him forever.

Heavenly Father, when irritations and concerns come my way today,
help me praise You. Enable me to look at Your provision in the past
and rejoice at what You will do in the future.

SCRIPTURE READING: Psalm 16
KEY VERSE: Isaiah 6:3

One cried to another and said:
"Holy, holy, holy is the LORD of hosts;
The whole earth is full of His glory!"

Isaiah was overcome with awe at the wonders he beheld in his vision. He saw the Lord, sitting on a throne with a train that filled the entire temple and surrounded by seraphim with six majestic wings. It was a sight he never forgot, and it is a picture of the awe we experience when we get a glimpse of our holy, righteous, loving God.

Carole Mayball in her book *When God Whispers* takes a look at how this awe translates into everyday living:

What makes a person old at twenty and keeps another young at eighty? I think it is that sense of wonder—the insatiable curiosity and delight concerning God, the world, and people. Solomon, for all his wisdom, was jaded. When I read the book of Ecclesiastes, I see that he had too much of everything. . . .

For the wisest man on earth, Solomon was kind of dumb! He knew great truth. . . . But apparently knowing that and experiencing it were two different things for Solomon. . . . We Christ-ones know the keys to having a glad heart. They are spelled out for us clearly. . . .

Enjoy what we have (enabled by God) as we accept our "lot"— which means accepting whatever "portion and cup" (Psalm 16:5) God has given. If we do that we won't feel guilty if we "have" or cheated if we "have not."

. . . Live in the present with each moment being lived "to the hilt" and let God keep us occupied with gladness of heart.

Lord, make me thankful for what I have. Make me accepting of my lot
in life. Let me live each moment and savor it with gladness of heart.

SCRIPTURE READING: John 12:1–8
KEY VERSE: Psalm 81:1

Sing aloud to God our strength;
Make a joyful shout to the God of Jacob.

The scene was familiar. Jesus was at Lazarus's house in Bethany, reclining at the table with His friends. How He loved spending time there! However, the dynamics of their relationship had changed dramatically. Only six days before, Jesus had raised Lazarus from the dead in a miracle that drew many to faith.

Mary's relationship with the Lord had changed as well. She knew His death was at hand. Warren Wiersbe commented on her actions: "It was an act of pure love on her part, for she knew her Lord was about to endure suffering and death. . . . In a sense, Mary was showing her devotion to Jesus before it was too late. . . . Her act of love and worship was public, spontaneous, sacrificial, lavish, personal, and unembarrassed."

Quietly she knelt next to Jesus at the table, and without a word, she delicately poured out every ounce of perfume onto His feet. Then she wiped the costly rivulets away with her hair until the entire house was filled with the aroma of the spikenard and with the even sweeter fragrance of her sacrifice.

Praise doesn't have a single, narrow definition. Praise can be Mary's gentle, silent gift that expressed the longing of her heart to worship. Praising is singing songs and saying private prayers. As you grow in the Lord, your praise will assume many forms, and all are worthy when given out of love for God.

O God, teach me to praise You. To sing. To meditate. To rejoice.
Expand my definition of what it means to truly worship You.

SCRIPTURE READING: 1 Thessalonians 5:16–18
KEY VERSE: Ephesians 5:20

Giving thanks always for all things to God the Father in the name of our Lord Jesus Christ.

Cultivating and maintaining a grateful heart that continues to pulsate with thanksgiving, even in trials, present a challenge.

Your circumstances today may be bright. If so, remember that God is your Source, and give Him the praise that He deserves. However, if your situation is bleak, God still desires your sincere thanksgiving because He knows the alternatives are passivity, self-pity, depression, and possibly withdrawal from intimate fellowship with the Savior.

Giving thanks in everything (that does not leave you with many exceptions, does it?) is possible when you understand that every situation, good or evil, is used by your loving Father to further your dependence on Him and make you more like Him.

We all like control; we dislike anything or anyone that disturbs our sense of security. But God is not interested in your ease or comfort. He is determined to conform you to the image of Christ through the inevitable afflictions that accompany life.

Thanking God in the trials may be difficult, but when you do, His purposes and presence will illuminate your path and carry you through.

Lord, enable me to praise You in the bad times as well as the good. In every situation, let me learn to give thanks.

SCRIPTURE READING: Psalm 143

KEY VERSE: 1 Thessalonians 5:18

In everything give thanks; for this is the will of God in Christ Jesus for you.

Like a flashlight, praise is the most illuminating in your hour of darkness. The problem is that when trouble strikes, the last thing you feel like doing is giving thanks to God. But if you can regain your worship composure for a moment, you can become the turning point for deliverance, renewed trust, and confident hope.

Praising God in times of trouble focuses your attention on God, not the problem. When you worship, His presence, although always near, becomes even closer. Just as what happens when you wipe away the morning mist from the windshield, worship clears your vision and helps you see God in the midst of your affliction.

When you praise God in times of trouble, your sense of anticipation is intensified. God is all-powerful, all-loving, all-wise; and He is able to work in your circumstances for your good and His glory.

When you praise Him, you realize that you are not at the mercy of whim or fate, but your times are in His capable hands. Are you praising God in your trouble? Do so; and although your problem may not dissolve, God's ability to handle your problem will pervade your heart and mind.

> *Lord, as I worship You today, clear my vision and help me see You in*
> *the midst of my circumstances. I am not the victim of circumstances.*
> *My destiny is in Your hands.*

SCRIPTURE READING: 1 Timothy 6:6–12
KEY VERSE: 1 Timothy 4:15

Meditate on these things; give yourself entirely to them, that your progress may be evident to all.

The apostle Paul realized what Timothy was facing. He established the church in Ephesus, and he knew firsthand what it was like to be in a pagan environment.

We often complain because of the violence and impurity that plague our world. Timothy was in an even narrower place of service. Just as we do, he probably felt at times like putting his desk in order and walking away.

In a letter to his young prodigy, Paul encouraged him to hold on and not give up. One of Satan's greatest temptations is to get us to take our eyes off God's work or plan and put them onto our circumstances. He tells us there are greener pastures someplace far from where we are right now. This is when we become frustrated and begin looking for a way out.

Nothing can beat being in the will of God. Happiness is a feeling; joy is a fact. You can be happy for a season, but joy comes from obeying God over the long haul. There is nothing wrong with feeling happy as long as you realize it can come and go. However, joy is eternal.

Timothy's life was a testimony of encouragement. Don't be sidelined by the pursuit of happiness alone. Seek God above everything else, and He will bless your life with an overflowing sense of joy.

Precious Father, I don't want to be detoured by the pursuit of happiness. Keep my focus on You and Your purposes. That is where I will find true and lasting joy.

SCRIPTURE READING: Revelation 4
KEY VERSE: Psalm 89:5

The heavens will praise Your wonders, O LORD;
Your faithfulness also in the assembly of the saints.

It is wonderful to read of the tidal waves of worship that unceasingly sweep over heaven's celestial shores. But what good does that do you as you wake up to a rainy morning, a car with a dead battery, an angry boss, or a sick child? How can you worship with such sheer, constant joy in the face of a world that has only tribulations?

Well, you know this: God wants you to experience the pleasure of worship now as well as in heaven, so He must have a way.

And He does. Each time you open the Word of God, you encounter God, revealed accurately and divinely to you during your earthly journey. As you sink your mind and heart into studying and meditating on His Word, you will learn more and more about God and His ways.

As you do, a sense of growing reverence and awe should spring up within. Worship of God should adorn your days. He has given you His Word so that you might know and praise Him as often as you like.

Are you taking advantage of the opportunity now? If so, heaven will simply be a continuum of adoration.

Mighty God, teach me to worship You now so that I will be prepared
for eternity. Let me learn to lift heavenly praise while still here on
earth.

December

THEME: The Miphkad Gate (*Miphkad* means "to review")

REPRESENTING: Self-examination, judgment, and finishing well

KEY VERSE: 2 Corinthians 13:5

Examine yourselves as to whether you are in the faith. Test yourselves. Do you not know yourselves, that Jesus Christ is in you?—unless indeed you are disqualified.

SCRIPTURE READING: 1 Samuel 15:13–23
KEY VERSE: 1 Samuel 15:29

The Strength of Israel will not lie nor relent. For He is not a man, that He should relent.

The race of life that God has placed us in requires daily, deliberate exercise as well as a good start if we are to finish well and strong. Many of us know Christians who started with great promise but ended in tragedy and despair.

Initially Saul loved God and did His will. God even changed his heart for good, and before long, Saul had captured the hearts of his countrymen and countrywomen. However, this great man's life was spent in bitterness, hatred, and depression.

Saul offered a sacrifice when he became impatient for Samuel to arrive. It didn't seem that much at the time, but it grew into increased rationalization. He began to blame others—"the people took some of the spoil" (1 Sam. 15:21 NASB)—until Saul no longer took responsibility for his sin, and his self-will loomed larger than God's will for him.

The process hasn't changed. We flirt with a particular sin, we rationalize it—and before long we are captive to it. Our hearts are hardened to God's loving conviction, and we pursue our own destruction.

Are you rationalizing a sin today? Is there a known area of disobedience in your life? If so, go to God and confess and repent of it. God will restore you.

Lord, I want to end well. Reveal any disobedience so that I can deal with each issue. Restore me so that I can finish strong.

SCRIPTURE READING: Genesis 31:1–42

KEY VERSE: Psalm 119:105

Your word is a lamp to my feet
And a light to my path.

You may lose your spiritual bearings when circumstances seemingly navigate you farther into the blackness of despair, deepening your sense of helplessness and heightening your fears and anxieties.

You gradually may become disoriented, losing your sense of God's care and love, even wondering if He exists. God understands your frailty in these times and provides you with sure and certain guides to uphold you.

You can cling to God's Word. David, who knew soul-darkness as well as any writer of Scripture, said, "Your word is a lamp to my feet / And a light to my path" (Ps. 119:105). Each word of Scripture is a light and life giver. Elisabeth Elliot wrote in *Discipline: The Glad Surrender* that "the Bible does not explain everything necessary for our intellectual satisfaction, but it explains everything necessary for our obedience."

You can count on God's character and presence. God is ineffably kind, good, merciful, and just, despite appearances to the contrary. He is never against you, but is heartily for you and ever with you.

What He began in your life, He will complete, using even times of darkness to strengthen your trust and love for Him.

> *You are for me. Thank You, God! What You began in my life, You will complete. I rejoice that even in times of darkness, You are strengthening me.*

SCRIPTURE READING: 2 Timothy 4:8–18
KEY VERSE: 2 Timothy 4:6

I am already being poured out as a drink offering, and the time of my departure is at hand.

If anyone had occasion to quit the course God had planned for him, it was Paul. Persecutions, trials, misunderstanding, and emotional and physical distress plagued the apostle for most of his adult life. How did he arrive at the terminus of his life with such a winning spirit? How can you?

Paul didn't focus on the past. His actions before he was saved were atrocious. They would have been an albatross had he fixated on them. Christ forgives your foolish acts of the past. Don't carry around a mental ballast of guilt that will only weigh you down and steal your joy. Receive God's forgiveness and forgive yourself.

Paul didn't nurse grudges. Perhaps you have an emotional greenhouse to nourish past hurts. It's pain you can live without. Paul was betrayed and reviled at almost every stop, but his spirit remained free of bitterness or self-pity.

Paul majored on grace and embraced weakness. He was the apostle of grace, ever cognizant that his sense of worth and value was entwined in his relationship with Christ, not his performance or behavior.

Don't give up when your spirit is faint. Count on the sufficiency of God's grace, the adequacy of His help.

Father, help me finish. Keep my focus on You instead of the past. Keep me from holding grudges. Let me embrace my weakness and not give up when my spirit seems faint.

SCRIPTURE READING: Genesis 13:5–13
KEY VERSE: Proverbs 14:12

There is a way that seems right to a man,
But its end is the way of death.

The turning point came on one dark night when, after too many drinks, he slammed his speeding car into a group of teenagers, killing several and injuring others. For a moment of alcohol-induced pleasure, he is now reaping a bitter harvest of tears and regrets.

He is not alone. Countless others, lured by the appeal of the moment, have sacrificed future success and happiness. It might have been the sexual enticement to immorality or the unethical pursuit of an "attractive" business deal. Now, years later, the price is still being paid.

That is the essence of temptation. The tempter, Satan, deceives us by playing with our instincts, emotions, and attitudes. He disguises the poison hidden within the temptation, knowing that we will seldom succumb to an obviously devilish proposition.

Is there anything you are considering at the moment that you know will bring pain and distress if you yield? Is there a pot of Jacob's stew that you are willing to taste to satisfy a lustful urge rather than wait on God?

Stop now before it is too late. Today's pleasure may look and taste sweet, but if it is outside the love and will of God, it will leave you with a bitter aftertaste.

Lord, I don't want to sacrifice my future for the pleasures of sin for a
season. Help me remain within the parameters of Your will. Don't let
me stray from the straight and narrow way.

SCRIPTURE READING: Romans 7:15–25
KEY VERSE: Philippians 1:6

Being confident of this very thing, that He who has begun a good work in you will complete it until the day of Jesus Christ.

"If at first you don't succeed, try again." That Puritan work ethic is solidly ingrained in the minds of many Americans. When you become a Christian, you naturally tend to integrate this attitude into your walk with Christ.

If you fail to conquer certain habits, you keep trying. If you fall short in obeying key Scripture verses, you buckle down and try again.

Although perseverance is necessary, mere grit and determination alone will not cure your problems. Without a proper understanding of spiritual growth, pursuit of this work ethic can lead you into the proverbial brick wall.

Admission of failure in the spiritual realm is a step toward a truly abundant life. Repeated failure from your efforts is often the prerequisite for coming to the end of yourself, acknowledging that you can do nothing apart from Christ.

Failure can be the catalyst that leads you from mere trying to trusting. The difference is startling, and understanding the spiritual dynamic can be the key to a consistently satisfying Christian walk.

Dear Lord, I want to make the transition from trying to trusting. Apart from You, I can do nothing.

SCRIPTURE READING: Luke 22:31–34
KEY VERSE: Galatians 3:3

Are you so foolish? Having begun in the Spirit, are you now being made perfect by the flesh?

If you had taken a poll of Christ's apostles before His arrest and crucifixion, no doubt Peter would have been voted "most loyal." Of all Jesus' followers, Peter seemingly possessed all of the right qualities for unquestioned leadership. He was honest, unafraid of challenge, and eager to learn. When Jesus took His inner circle along on special occasions, Peter was always included.

But when the darkness of Gethsemane and Calvary drew near, Peter failed, denying his Lord and retreating into the sorrow of regret. Peter, as most of us would have done, had relied on his superior talents and commanding personality during his apprenticeship with Christ. When the crisis of Calvary appeared, however, the fault line of human frailty appeared and Peter's confidence fell to pieces.

It is still so with all of us who draw near to the Cross. We must end reliance on our own resources—education, appearance, personality, and abilities. Then we can move into the life and power that our indwelling Christ longs to impart.

Christ is the Victor over sin and death. He is your victory over dominating traits and particular affections. When you fail in your strength, you are ready to trust in the One who will never fail you.

Take it all, Lord—my reliance on education, appearance, personality, and abilities. Replace it all with dependence on the indwelling power of Christ.

SCRIPTURE READING: 1 Timothy 1:18–20
KEY VERSE: 1 Timothy 1:19

Having faith and a good conscience, which some having rejected, concerning the faith have suffered shipwreck.

Not long ago, the Titanic was discovered where it sank in the North Atlantic in 1912. The encrusted remains bore little resemblance to its former acclaim as the world's most luxurious ocean liner.

There are Christians who likewise demonstrate little of the vibrant faith they once possessed, having gone aground on the shoals of lukewarmness and compromise. Joy is passing; growth is stagnant; peace is transient.

Worst of all, they seldom express love for the person of the Lord Jesus Christ, and they rarely experience His love. What happened?

The apostle Paul wrote that a shipwrecked faith can occur when people reject a solid faith and a good conscience (1 Tim. 1:19). The teachings of God's Word are slowly and subtly replaced with counterfeit philosophies, such as humanism, materialism, and/or secularism. The authority of the Scriptures is rejected regarding personal behavior. Obedience is subjective and conditional. The quiet voice of the Holy Spirit is ignored repeatedly as they allow their conduct to be guided by reason or instinct, not God.

Is your personal faith in Christ at a low ebb? Has the adventure of faith turned sour? If you are willing, restoration is but a heartbeat away.

Father, even as Your servant Paul, I don't want to preach to others and become a castaway—a shipwrecked saint. Make me increasingly sensitive to Your Spirit, Lord.

SCRIPTURE READING: Revelation 2:1–5
KEY VERSE: Psalm 89:33

Nevertheless My lovingkindness I will not utterly take from him,
Nor allow My faithfulness to fail.

Some of the great battleships of World War II were retired to mothballs following the end of the conflict. However, in the 1990s some were retooled, refitted, and refurbished for new duty on the high seas.

Similarly God delights in restoring to full service those whose faith has been idle for years. Restoration begins with genuine repentance.

Whatever the reason for your spiritual decline—a bad church experience, a negative encounter with another believer, a serious moral mistake—God is waiting for you to assume personal responsibility and repent. You cannot blame others. Repentance realizes you have grieved God with your behavior and missed out on God's best through your rebellion and negligence.

When your repentance is genuine and complete, the next step is a rekindling of your love for Christ. Christianity is not church or Bible study or good deeds (though it includes them), but an individual relationship with Jesus.

The rekindling occurs when you return your focus to what Christ has done for you and who He is within you. You rediscover the greatness, love, mercy, and goodness of God. The love affair begins again.

Heavenly Father, please restore my faith. Rekindle my love. Ignite my
passion. Let me begin again.

Take heart, men, for I believe God that it will be just as it was told me.

For runners, the most discouraging moments are about halfway through the race. They are tired and drained, and the prospect of growing even wearier is sometimes enough to cause them to quit.

All of us face those times in our Christian experience. We start joyfully at salvation and run with eagerness as we learn new biblical principles. Then we come to a point where the feelings fade, the blessings seem to dwindle, and our commitment level fluctuates.

It is at this point that determination and endurance are developed. We read the Scriptures because we know the value of their priority, not because we always gain obvious, immediate benefits.

The determination to continue comes from the knowledge that God has set the course for you. Yesterday's troubles, today's problems, and tomorrow's circumstances are all a part of the pilgrimage. Together, they form the course God has chosen. In addition, you run because God will reward you in the end. There is a finish line. Your exhaustion and perplexity will be over. You will be in the Lord's presence forever.

Before giving up, remember that the Lord Jesus Christ is cultivating your spiritual endurance.

Almighty God, foster endurance in me—the kind it takes to finish the race. When feelings fade, blessings dwindle, and my commitment level fluctuates, give me the determination to persevere.

SCRIPTURE READING: 2 Peter 3:14–18

KEY VERSE: 2 Peter 3:18

Grow in the grace and knowledge of our Lord and Savior Jesus Christ. To Him be the glory both now and forever. Amen.

Are you a growing Christian?

That can be a difficult question to answer, for we all experience seasons of stagnation. But the essence of Christian growth is this: Are you experiencing and exhibiting the reality of Christ in a progressive manner?

The Bible says that God wants you to mature as a believer. As your walk with Christ matures, the fruit of your relationship with Him should be increasingly evident. Your knowledge of God, not intellectual but hearty devotion to Him and His ways, should be on the upswing (Col. 1:10). That entails clearer understanding of His will and ways.

Your awareness of the reality of the spiritual world should also be developing; you realize that the root cause of many problems lies in the spiritual arena. For example, people may spend too much money because they are not content. The issue is not money but personal fulfillment and peace, which ultimately are satisfied by Christ alone.

You grow not through mere self-effort, but through the abiding life, drinking in the fullness of Christ through the indwelling work of the Holy Spirit. It is growing in grace.

Lord, I want to grow. I want to mature. Increase my knowledge of You, Father. Begin the process today.

SCRIPTURE READING: 2 Peter 1:1–9

KEY VERSES: Psalm 139:23–24

Search me, O God, and know my heart;
Try me, and know my anxieties;
And see if there is any wicked way in me,
And lead me in the way everlasting.

All growth requires measurement of some means—profit or stature—but defining spiritual growth is not as standardized. However, there are some questions that you can ask yourself, allowing the Holy Spirit to reveal both your progress and your need. Here are a few considerations:

- Do I want to spend more or less time in God's Word?
- Is my prayer life more meaningful and honest, or less?
- Do I exhibit the same Christlikeness in the privacy of my home as I do in public settings?
- Is regular church attendance a consistent part of my life?
- Do I pray for others, not just myself?
- Does the person of Jesus Christ continue to be my first love; is my obedience motivated by a desire to please Him above all else?
- Do I persevere or give up when spiritual droughts hit?
- Am I concerned about the spiritual plight of my unsaved coworkers or friends?
- Do I seek the Holy Spirit's help on a daily basis or lean solely on my personal strengths and talents?

Where you fall short, ask for God's help. Where you respond positively, thank Jesus for His grace, and continue to obey.

Dear Lord, I praise You for the ways I've grown in grace and knowl-
edge. Help me to grow in those areas where I have fallen short.

SCRIPTURE READING: Hebrews 12:1–3
KEY VERSE: Hebrews 12:3

Consider Him who endured such hostility from sinners against Himself, lest you become weary and discouraged in your souls.

The writer of Hebrews noted that because we have "so great a cloud of witnesses surrounding us" (12:1 NASB), we should not grow weary in the race of life, but have hope and not lose heart. Many godly witnesses are among us today as well. You can probably think of people who struggled against all odds and yet, though they suffered horrendous trials, remained faithful to Christ. What a witness and testimony to God!

Never forget that Jesus endured the pain and embarrassment of the Cross so that you might gain the victor's crown. You don't have to be supernatural to be a winner, but you must contain a supernatural faith in Christ to wear the crown of life.

The book of Hebrews provides three insights into gaining a winning lifestyle:

First, lay aside every encumbrance. That includes sin and anything else that holds you back from being all God wants you to be.

Second, run with endurance. Don't give up. At times you may wonder whether you will ever see the finish line, but you will. God has promised it, so be faithful!

Third, fix your eyes on Jesus. Many, like Peter, take their eyes off Christ and focus on the shifting winds and swelling waves of life. But if you will keep your eyes firmly locked on Jesus, you will receive the conqueror's garland.

Jesus, You endured the Cross so that I might wear the victor's crown. Help me lay aside every weight, run with endurance, and keep my eyes fixed on You.

SCRIPTURE READING: Romans 6:15–23

KEY VERSE: Romans 6:23

For the wages of sin is death, but the gift of God is eternal life in Christ Jesus our Lord.

Taking the small, inflatable raft, he went out just beyond the wave break where he could relax and enjoy the coolness of the ocean water. He had left his glasses with his wife on the beach. Though his vision was blurry, he kept telling himself, "I can still see the shore." Soon, the sound of the lifeguard's horn and shouts of onlookers signaled that he had drifted out into dangerous water, never feeling the silent pull of the ocean's undertow.

Sin often operates this way in the lives of believers. Satan begins by tempting us to deviate only slightly from God's principles. Then he watches for our reaction. Do we find sin palatable or nauseating?

Spiritual drifting begins with the words, "I know I probably shouldn't do this, but I don't see any harm in doing it just once." Before you drift into harm's way and away from the fellowship of God, ask Him to surface any area of sin you may be harboring.

Very few of us successfully resist rationalized sin the second time around. The man who eats a hot fudge sundae and concludes that it doesn't make him fat is deceived. Make the wise choice to obey, and avoid the danger of drifting.

Heavenly Father, I don't want to drift. Surface any disobedience or compromise in my life, and keep me from the deadly spiritual undertow of sin.

SCRIPTURE READING: Ephesians 2:1–7
KEY VERSE: Ephesians 2:1

And you He made alive, who were dead in trespasses and sins.

In his biographical sketch of Abraham Lincoln, Willard Davis presents this information:

> Lincoln had been elected president though not even appearing on the ballot in ten states!
>
> Even before arriving in Washington, every mail delivery brought more death threats and ominous warnings. Close friends advised that he resign before taking the oath of office! A plot to assassinate the president-elect had been uncovered forcing the last leg of his trip to Washington to be in the dead of night, without family, under heavy guard, and incognito!

Lincoln refused to stop short of God's plan. He wrote, "When I went to Gettysburg, and saw the graves of thousands of our soldiers, I then and there consecrated myself to Christ."

Don't stop short of God's plan for your life. When temptation to quit comes, run to Him in prayer. Ask Him to encourage you as only He can. Then trust Him to lead you victoriously through the difficult times.

Precious Lord, I don't want to stop short of Your plan for my life. Lead me victoriously through the difficult times.

SCRIPTURE READING: 1 Corinthians 15:35–50
KEY VERSE: 1 Corinthians 15:49

*As we have borne the image of the man of dust, we shall also bear the image
of the heavenly Man.*

Working diligently with a small cross-stitch design, the woman leaned
over to her friend and proudly displayed her finished product. Her friend
reached out to touch it. But the woman pulled back and said, "Please
don't look at the back."

Turning the needlework over revealed an abundance of knots and
strings. It was the sure sign of a beginner's work. But a smile brightened
on her friend's face as she said, "Don't be silly. The only thing that truly
matters is the front, and it looks perfect!"

God has a design for your life. There are times when you fail to follow
His plan, and several knots are sewn into your life. From the back side,
your life may look disastrous. However, turn your life design over, and see
it from God's perspective. Yes, there were times of failure; but there also
were times of yieldedness and victory. From God's viewpoint, the knots
represent times of instruction.

He knew from the beginning that you would face times of discouragement and defeat. Yet He also knew there would be times when you
would refuse to yield to Satan's deception.

You are God's workmanship. From His viewpoint, your life is being
woven into a design that bears a remarkable resemblance to the life of His
Son.

*Dear God, I am Your work in progress. Continue to weave the threads
of my life into a design that reflects the life of Your Son, Jesus Christ.*

SCRIPTURE READING: Luke 1:68–79

KEY VERSE: 1 Corinthians 6:20

You were bought at a price; therefore glorify God in your body and in your spirit, which are God's.

Throughout the Old Testament, there were constant foreshadowings of a divine Redeemer who would deliver people from bondage and captivity. Perhaps the most interesting facet of Old Testament redemption was the kinsman-redeemer, which allowed a close family member to rescue a relative through payment of his or her debts.

The New Testament carryover is clear. Jesus is our Kinsman. He became flesh and blood so that He might share in our humanity, becoming the Son of man as well as the Son of God. By becoming human, He identified with humankind, being tempted in all things as we are, yet remaining without sin.

However, the deity of Christ provided the only acceptable price for deliverance from sin—the shedding of Christ's blood at Calvary. No one except Christ could pay the enormous, adequate price. No one except Christ could deliver us from sin's grip.

The Redeemer has come as your Kinsman, made like you so that He could pay the price as your Deliverer. He alone could purchase you from the marketplace of sin and bring you into the kingdom of God. Your Redeemer came. Your Redeemer lives.

Jesus, You became flesh and blood and shared in my humanity. You identified with me, being tempted as I am, yet without sin. You died in my place. Thank You for coming.

SCRIPTURE READING: Matthew 1:18–25
KEY VERSE: Isaiah 9:2

The people who walked in darkness
Have seen a great light;
Those who dwelt in the land of the shadow of death,
Upon them a light has shined.

The Christmas story is not just the story of Bethlehem—Christ in the cradle. It is the story of the Incarnation, God in the flesh, revealing the Father to us: "'Behold, the virgin shall be with child, and shall bear a Son, and they shall call His name Immanuel,' which translated means, 'God with us'" (Matt. 1:23 NASB).

When you look at the Lord Jesus Christ's life on earth, you have an exact portrait of the character and ways of the heavenly Father. Jesus said, "I and the Father are one" (John 10:30 NASB). The Lord's kindness, love, and holiness help you grasp the nature of the Father in heaven.

Christ also came in the flesh that He might give you a godly example. Jesus is your pattern for Christian living: "I have been crucified with Christ; and it is no longer I who live, but Christ lives in me; and the life which I now live in the flesh I live by faith in the Son of God, who loved me, and delivered Himself up for me" (Gal. 2:20 NASB).

You should treat others as Christ did. You can resist temptation; you can endure suffering. You "can do all things through [Christ] who strengthens [you]" (Phil. 4:13 NASB).

Heavenly Father, pattern my life after that of Your Son. Help me resist
temptation and endure suffering. Let Christ live in me.

SCRIPTURE READING: Hebrews 4:14–16
KEY VERSE: Psalm 103:14

He knows our frame;
He remembers that we are dust.

The Son of God became the Son of man, Immanuel—"God with us" (Matt. 1:23)—for very crucial reasons. Until Christ became the Son of man, He could not die in our place for our sins. God does not die; flesh and blood die. Christ became flesh and blood and maintained His perfect divinity so that He could pay the penalty of sin, which is death:

God demonstrates His own love toward us, in that while we were still sinners, Christ died for us. (Rom. 5:8)

This is My blood of the covenant, which is poured out for many for forgiveness of sins. (Matt. 26:28 NASB)

Until Christ became the Son of man, He could not represent us as our sympathetic and faithful High Priest. Christ understands how we feel in our frail humanity. He was weary (John 4:6), hungry (Matt. 4:2), rejected (Luke 4:28–30), and abused (Mark 15:16–20).

His earthly ministry means that Christ can identify with your hurts, pains, and heartaches. He is touched by them:

When the Lord saw her, He felt compassion for her, and said to her, "Do not weep." (Luke 7:13 NASB)

Jesus wept. (John 11:35)

You were weary. You were hungry. You were rejected and abused. You wept. Thank You, Lord, that You can identify with my needs today.

SCRIPTURE READING: John 1:1–18

KEY VERSE: Isaiah 9:6

For unto us a Child is born,

Unto us a Son is given;

And the government will be upon His shoulder.

And His name will be called

Wonderful, Counselor, Mighty God,

Everlasting Father, Prince of Peace.

The heavenly host, who appeared to the shepherds at Christ's birth, announced peace on earth. Christ's incarnation was the inaugural step for establishing reconciliation between a holy God and sinful humanity.

Humankind, though loved by God, was an enemy of God due to a rebellious nature. People also engaged in unending conflict with other people. Self continually sought preeminence. But at the coming of Christ, God's offer of peace through the sacrifice of His Son transformed the hopeless fight: "But now in Christ Jesus you who formerly were far off have been brought near by the blood of Christ" (Eph. 2:13 NASB).

By faith in Christ, you and God can be reconciled; you can become a friend of God: "Although you were formerly alienated and hostile in mind, engaged in evil deeds, yet He has now reconciled you in His fleshly body through death, in order to present you before Him holy and blameless and beyond reproach" (Col. 1:21–22 NASB).

The Prince of Peace also can revolutionize your dealings with others. True peace can come through Christ's indwelling reign in your heart: "For He Himself is our peace" (Eph. 2:14 NASB).

Jesus, thank You for bringing peace. Let Your peace rule and reign in my heart, breaking down every barrier of opposition. You are my peace.

SCRIPTURE READING: Romans 5:1–5

KEY VERSE: John 14:27

Peace I leave with you, My peace I give to you; not as the world gives do I give to you. Let not your heart be troubled, neither let it be afraid.

The peace of God is twofold—positional and experiential.

When you trust Christ for salvation, you enter into peace with God. The Lord justifies you, declares you no longer guilty of your sin, and gives you a righteous standing. This is positional peace. The Judge of all people has rendered a favorable verdict for those who place their faith in Christ's work on the cross. You can now have access to the presence of God, for you are His child, born again by His Spirit and known intimately by Him.

But there is more. You also receive the peace of God as you face life's battles and uncertainties. Through His indwelling Holy Spirit, God's indescribable peace settles your fears, calms your anxieties, and anchors your mind. "Be anxious for nothing, but in everything by prayer and supplication with thanksgiving let your requests be made known to God. And the peace of God, which surpasses all comprehension, shall guard your hearts and your minds in Christ Jesus" (Phil. 4:6–7 NASB).

You are not alone anymore. God is with you. "The Lord is near" (Phil. 4:5 NASB); "I will never desert you, nor will I ever forsake you" (Heb. 13:5 NASB).

O God, thank You for Your peace. I am not alone anymore. You are with me. You will never leave me or forsake me.

SCRIPTURE READING: Philippians 4:6–7
KEY VERSE: John 14:27

Peace I leave with you, My peace I give to you; not as the world gives do I give to you. Let not your heart be troubled, neither let it be afraid.

Peace initiatives by various parties and factions capture the attention of the news media almost daily. The terminology of these endeavors has so occupied our front pages, TV screens, and political agendas that we have defined *peace* as "the absence of conflict."

Even those of us who toil in the office, farm, or home tend to describe peace in the same manner. Peace is the removal of tension between husband and wife, parents and children, employers and employees.

We know, however, that peace can be elusive, even when such ideal conditions exist. This kind of harmony does not remove the ache, anger, and turmoil that boil within because of frustrated dreams, unreached potential, and disillusioning circumstances.

True peace is not external, not dependent upon the environment. It is internal, springing from your innermost being. This peace comes only through the inner presence of the Prince of Peace, Jesus Christ. He can settle your spirit and mind, regardless of external disarray.

If you have been restless and anxious, look to Christ for stability. His initiative at Calvary has brought you peace with God and the peace of God. This peace can never be disturbed.

O Lord, please settle my spirit and mind in the midst of the busyness of this season. Remove the anger and turmoil. Give me true peace.

SCRIPTURE READING: Philippians 2:5–11

KEY VERSE: Luke 2:11

There is born to you this day in the city of David a Savior, who is Christ the Lord.

Some people just cannot seem to get excited about Jesus Christ. Perhaps they have lost sight of who He was and what He did for us. Perhaps they have never known.

Jesus is the Son of God—our reigning Lord. He was that before time began, and He will be that at time's ending. He was in the Garden with Adam. His heart received sin's first blow.

Throughout time He watched His people struggle. He led them through the desert and longed for them to worship only Him. When Israel was blocked in on every side, He made a way through the wilderness. Still, they forgot Him and worshiped other gods.

Year after year, Jesus watched and prayed from heaven's doorway. When the longing to save and redeem His people grew to an overwhelming portion, He came to us.

However, the people of His day wanted a military leader—someone who would exalt the Jewish nation. They could not accept that Jesus was the Messiah. They plotted His death. His life was purchased for the price of a slave. He died a criminal's death, but God raised Him up as Lord.

May you know the power of His reigning love today.

Lord, over every circumstance of my life, You reign! Thank You that You made a way through the wilderness of this world to Your promised land of peace.

SCRIPTURE READING: Matthew 2:1–12

KEY VERSE: 1 Thessalonians 4:16

The Lord Himself will descend from heaven with a shout, with the voice of an archangel, and with the trumpet of God. And the dead in Christ will rise first.

Jesus came as a man, a person, much like any one of us. He willingly chose to lay aside His royal robe of glory to take on the tattered robe of humanity.

Though sinless, He knew what it felt like to cry, to laugh, and to suffer disappointment. He felt the encroachment of rejection and the sting of loneliness. He knew there would be times when we felt unloved and unwanted.

He could have chosen any number of avenues, but He chose to come as a baby. All power was His to command. Angels stood waiting to meet His every request. Yet He became a servant so that we might grasp the hope of God.

And except for a chorus of angels singing to a band of misfit shepherds, His first coming almost went unnoticed. It was not much of a birth announcement for the King of kings and the Lord of lords. He slipped into the pool of humanity with barely a ripple in the clamor of Bethlehem.

However, when He returns, He will come as the returning Lord and ruling King. His first coming opened the way to salvation. His second coming will be to establish His kingdom.

Do you know Him as Savior and Lord? If not, take this moment to ask Him to come into your heart. Ask as a child. He will not refuse you.

O God—my King—thank You for laying aside Your royal robe and taking the tattered robe of humanity. I give my life to You.

SCRIPTURE READING: Galatians 4:4–7

KEY VERSE: Galatians 4:4

When the fullness of the time had come, God sent forth His Son, born of a woman, born under the law.

Do you have a nativity scene that you put out every year in a special place? Maybe it's the mantel or hearth, or perhaps you place it in the kitchen or a main hallway. You do it to celebrate Christ's birth with a visual image of what that night in Bethlehem must have been like, the event that all history looked forward to and that the passing of years is measured from.

It was no cosmic accident that Jesus came when He did. God's timing is never random. Galatians 4:4 says that Jesus was born in the "fulness of the time" (NASB), the exact, perfect moment in history for the accomplishment of God's purposes. The Lord had the Incarnation in mind since the beginning of time, and even before creation, when in His sovereignty only God existed.

If all of these overwhelming facts seem a bit lofty, that's because the truths of His mighty plan are wrapped in an infinite mystery that we in our finite condition cannot fully comprehend. Yet it is also true that the great wonder of salvation is as simple as a tiny, gurgling baby in a manger, for all to come and worship.

Isn't it marvelous that God does not require you to understand every detail to come to Him? The redemptive process will continue to unfold, and the cries of the baby Jesus on that still and holy night echo through eternity.

Dear Lord, tonight marks the night of all nights—the night You came to earth. You knew me from the foundation of the world and worked this plan in my behalf. Thank You for Your redemptive process, which continues to unfold in my life.

SCRIPTURE READING: Luke 2

KEY VERSES: Luke 2:30–31

My eyes have seen Your salvation
Which You have prepared before the face of all peoples.

Usually when you think of a lord or a great ruler, you envision a person of formidable power, with commanding presence and dignified bearing. He lives in magnificent wealth and runs his vast household and business affairs with unquestioned authority. Everyone gives him glory and reveres the very ground he walks on.

That wasn't the case with the Lord Jesus. In fact, the very opposite was true. Jesus gave up the grandeur of heaven, veiling His glory in the flesh of a human being, in order to live with us for a time on earth.

Born in a lowly cattle stall, Jesus did not live the soft life. He learned carpentry and earned a working man's wage, never knowing the comforts of the contemporary Roman rulers. And though many acknowledged Him as Savior, Jesus certainly never enjoyed the popularity and honor that were His due.

Finally He hung naked and bleeding on a crude cross like a common criminal. Was that a picture of a reigning, sovereign Lord?

Absolutely. Appearances were certainly deceiving. Three days later, He rose again. Someday everyone will see the true picture and worship Him as almighty God. Every knee will bow, and every tongue will pronounce Him the King of kings.

Lord, I bow today in humble gratitude that You came to earth to rescue me. Thank You for Your death and resurrection. You are the King of kings.

SCRIPTURE READING: 2 Timothy 3:1–7
KEY VERSE: 2 Timothy 3:14

You must continue in the things which you have learned and been assured of, knowing from whom you have learned them.

During the last few months of Paul's life, he wrote some of his most stirring exhortations to two of his fellow workers: Timothy, who was in Ephesus, a city at the heart of paganism; and Titus, who was on the island of Crete, which had plenty of problems of its own. Both men struggled with discouragement. Timothy fought feelings of insecurity, and Titus became frustrated with the opposition from church members.

Paul gave his last words to Timothy as encouragement with the hope that when times got rough, he would not give up. When you feel like giving in, don't: "Continue in the things you have learned and become convinced of" (2 Tim. 3:14 NASB). Within every problem and trial is an opportunity for God to teach you more about His faithfulness.

Timothy and Titus learned a great deal from Paul, but it was through their trust in Jesus Christ that they were successful for the kingdom of God. Before you go to bed tonight, tell Him how much you need Him and ask Him to warm your heart with His love.

Holidays are especially difficult times for those who have recently lost a friend or loved one. If this is your situation, know that God is aware of your sorrow. He knows your loneliness and isolation. Let His presence strengthen you through the Holy Spirit and the power of His Word.

Father, when I am discouraged and feel like giving up, help me continue in the things I have learned and am convinced of. Warm my heart with Your love. Strengthen me through the Holy Spirit and the power of Your Word.

SCRIPTURE READING: 2 Timothy 3:10–14
KEY VERSE: 1 Corinthians 4:20

The kingdom of God is not in word but in power.

Paul's description of the society that is hostile toward God is chillingly current. People without Christ, he said, become increasingly belligerent, greedy, arrogant, and demanding.

You don't need a Gallup Poll to inform you these conditions have bulged into the cultural mainstream. But social opposition should never dissuade you from practicing your faith.

Christianity has been against the moral grain of every age. Instead of focusing on the spiritual bog of godlessness (a debilitating tactic), your concentration should be on God's power and His Word.

Christ is a mighty warrior in your midst, able to accomplish awesome deeds on your behalf. Have you embraced the kingdom of God that comes in power and not word only (1 Cor. 4:20)?

You can experience Christ's strength primarily through the truth of His Word. Paul exhorted Timothy—and you—to "continue in the things you have learned and become convinced of" (2 Tim. 3:14 NASB), alluding to the body of Scripture. Knowing what God says in the Bible distills truth from error.

Perspective to face trials, wisdom to make decisions, and faith to endure—all you need to face the new year—are rooted in familiarity with God's Word.

> *Establish me in Your Word, O God. Give me the perspective to face trials, the wisdom to make decisions in the days ahead, and the faith to endure.*

SCRIPTURE READING: Acts 2:23–28

KEY VERSE: Matthew 3:3

This is he who was spoken of by the prophet Isaiah, saying:
"The voice of one crying in the wilderness:
'Prepare the way of the LORD;
Make His paths straight.'"

When the Son of God came in the flesh in a rustic Bethlehem stable around 4 B.C., His birth took place only after faithful, deliberate preparation by God: "This Man, delivered up by the predetermined plan and foreknowledge of God, you nailed to a cross by the hands of godless men and put Him to death. And God raised Him up again, putting an end to the agony of death, since it was impossible for Him to be held in its power" (Acts 2:23–24 NASB).

God had dealt with nations, preserving His people, the Israelites, through the centuries, despite persecution and captivity. He had dealt with kings and empires, allowing the advanced Roman civilization to standardize transportation and communication throughout most of Europe and Asia. God came to earth at exactly the point in time, like a ripe field of wheat ready for harvest, when His sovereign, perfect mind had planned since the foundation of the earth (Eph. 3:8–12).

Christ's timing in your life is just as precise. He is preparing you today for His purposes tomorrow.

Your timing is perfect, O Lord. Prepare me today to accomplish Your purposes tomorrow.

SCRIPTURE READING: Galatians 1:11–24

KEY VERSE: Job 42:2

I know that You can do everything,

And that no purpose of Yours can be withheld from You.

Before a house is repainted, long, tedious hours of scraping and sanding are required. Before the seed is sown, dusty days of tilling and plowing are necessary. But if the paint is to adhere and last and the seed is to sprout and mature, preparation is essential.

So it was as God prepared to send Christ the Savior to earth. The Lord endured the rebellion and idolatry of people and nations. He saw His prophets ridiculed, His priests despised, and His laws rejected.

Your time of preparation for usefulness in the kingdom will not be instantaneous. But it is a requirement in order for Christ's fullness to lodge deep in your life, readying you for fruitfulness that you otherwise may never experience.

Paul noted in Galatians 1:11–24 how the Lord taught him and prepared him for three years after he was saved. Then Christ accomplished through Paul what He wanted: "Every branch in Me that does not bear fruit, He takes away; and every branch that bears fruit, He prunes it, that it may bear more fruit. . . . Abide in Me, and I in you. As the branch cannot bear fruit of itself, unless it abides in the vine, so neither can you, unless you abide in Me" (John 15:2, 4 NASB).

O Master, prune my spiritual branches so that I can be more productive during the coming year. Prepare me for fruitfulness.

SCRIPTURE READING: James 4:13–17
KEY VERSE: Proverbs 21:5

The plans of the diligent lead surely to plenty,
But those of everyone who is hasty, surely to poverty.

Many people will look back over the past year with a sense of accomplishment and hope. Others may have regrets and wish they had tackled life differently. Learning to set goals for your life is an excellent way to build encouragement into your daily routine, especially when you set reasonable goals that you can achieve without fear of failure.

Always begin the goal-setting process with prayer. Ask the Lord to show you specific areas in your life that will benefit from this type of organization. Making a list of potential growth spots will help you see the overall context of your life. Ask yourself, What would I like to accomplish in this certain area during the next year?

Make a promise to yourself that you will be open to the will of God. Allow Him to alter your goals when necessary.

Remember, He is perfectly in tune with your life and knows your strengths and weaknesses. Avoid becoming overzealous in the goal-setting process. Many who do often end up discouraged when goals are unreached. Set goals that stretch your faith but are also attainable in nature.

God is a natural goal setter. Throughout Scripture, He encouraged men and women to achieve the goals He placed before them. God wants you to achieve His best in life; allow Him to guide you as you set goals for the future.

> *Heavenly Father, thank You for all You have accomplished in and through me during the past year. As I look ahead to the future, reveal Your goals and objectives for my life. I want to fulfill Your plan.*

SCRIPTURE READING: Romans 8:28–30

KEY VERSE: 2 Timothy 4:7

I have fought the good fight, I have finished the race, I have kept the faith.

You have probably heard someone say, "Please be patient—God isn't finished with me yet." That lighthearted saying is absolutely true. When you trust Jesus as your Savior, you begin a growing process that lasts a lifetime.

In his book *Lifetime Guarantee,* Bill Gillham explains it this way: "Once a person is born from above, his nature is already Christlike, but it's infantile in maturity. He is like an oak sapling that can mature into a fully grown oak tree. . . . And by faith and obedience, as he begins to act consistently with his new nature, he will look more and more like Jesus."

The Lord engineers all the circumstances of your life to conform you to Christ's image (Rom. 8:28). God works in everything that He sends and allows in your life.

"But what about sin and failure?" you may ask. Jesus took care of your sin problem on the cross. When you trust in Him, you are forgiven.

Yes, God may discipline you and let you experience some painful consequences of wrong actions, but His plan hasn't changed. Someday you will stand in the presence of almighty God, radiant and complete, fully transformed. It's a goal worth the wait.

> *Precious Lord, I praise You for Your loving care throughout the past year. Above all, thank You that You are working in me—and You are not finished with me yet!*

Eternal Security

Dr. Stanley offers the powerful, reassuring message that believers can be certain of eternal salvation and know peace and intimacy with Christ as a result.

The Gift of Forgiveness

Dr. Stanley shows readers how to give and receive forgiveness and experience the healing and freedom forgiveness brings.

The Glorious Journey

Dr. Stanley provides crucial answers to contemporary questions and concerns along with a thoroughly biblical understanding of the foundational issues of the faith.

How to Handle Adversity

Dr. Stanley presents reassuring, Bible-based advice on how to understand and handle adversity in ways that glorify God and demonstrate His faithfulness.

How to Keep Your Kids on Your Team

Brimming with wisdom and practical advice, this book is a must for all Christian parents who want to ensure that their children grow to be loving and loyal.

How to Listen to God

Dr. Stanley's most popular book provides direction for Christians who are struggling to hear God's voice and to understand His will for their lives.

In Touch with God

This unique gift book is filled with inspirational Scriptures as well as thoughts and prayers from Dr. Stanley. It will help you know God's heart on a variety of topics, including forgiveness, relationships, Spirit-filled living, Christian character, and God's plan for your life.

The In Touch Study Series

A unique series of study guides that invite readers to study the Scriptures in light of their past experience, current emotional response, possible future application, and Spirit-prompted conviction.

Advancing Through Adversity

Learn to grow through difficult times and rediscover God's faithfulness.

Becoming Emotionally Whole

Overcome negative emotions and become happier and healthier.

Experiencing Forgiveness

Enjoy the peace that comes from giving and receiving forgiveness.

Listening to God

Experience a deeper relationship with God by learning to hear His voice.

Overcoming the Enemy

Discover God's plan for winning spiritual battles.

Relying on the Holy Spirit

Experience the joy-filled walk with God under the anointing of the Holy Spirit.

Talking with God

Discover new insights to deepen your prayer life.

Understanding Financial Stewardship

Learn what God has to say about managing your money.

The Power of the Cross

Using inspirational Scriptures as well as personal insights and heartfelt prayers, Charles Stanley encourages you to see the transforming power of the Resurrection for salvation, victory over temptation, healing of emotional pain, and restoration with the heavenly Father.

The Reason for My Hope

Dr. Stanley reveals the promises and resources God provides His children, identifying nine key reasons for all believers to have unshakable hope.

The Source of My Strength

Sharing his journey through emotional pain, Dr. Stanley encourages readers to face the hurts of the past and receive God's healing and freedom.

Winning the War Within

Dr. Stanley sets forth a reasoned, scriptural approach to triumphing over temptation and coping with trials and inner struggles.

The Wonderful Spirit-Filled Life

Dr. Stanley gives believers the keys to living an abundant life, deepening their personal relationship with Christ, and applying biblical truths.

About the Author

Dr. Charles Stanley is pastor of the 14,000-member First Baptist Church in Atlanta, Georgia. He is well-known through his *In Touch* radio and television ministry to thousands internationally and is the author of many books, including *The Source of My Strength, The Reason for My Hope, The Glorious Journey,* and the In Touch® Study Series.

Dr. Stanley received his bachelor of arts degree from the University of Richmond, his bachelor of divinity degree from Southwestern Theological Seminary, and his master's and doctor's degrees from Luther Rice Seminary. He has twice been elected president of the Southern Baptist Convention.

OTHER BESTSELLING BOOKS BY CHARLES STANLEY

The Reason for My Hope

Charles Stanley shares his personal struggles to remain focused on Christ and keep hope alive in the middle of difficult circumstances. In his insightful and familiar style, Stanley leads you along the path to hope, identifying the promises and resources God provides to help you reach your own hope-filled destination.

0-8407-7765-5 • Hardcover • 256 pages • Christian Living

The Power of the Cross

Dr. Stanley combines inspirational Scripture, heartfelt prayers, and personal insight to help you know, love, and appreciate the wonder-working power of the Cross.

0-7852-7065-5 • Printed Hardcover • 208 pages • Gift/Devotional

In Touch With God

In this special gift book, Dr. Stanley offers inspirational insights along with related Scriptures to help you keep in touch with God on a variety of topics, including forgiveness, relationships, spiritual warfare, adversity, and conscience.

0-7852-7117-1 • Printed Hardcover • 208 pages • Gift/Devotional